Innovations in Investment Management

Innovations in Investment Management

Cutting-Edge Research from the Exclusive JOIM Conference Series

EDITED BY
H. Gifford Fong

FOREWORD BY Martin L. Leibowitz, PhD

Viva Books

New Delhi | Mumbai | Chennai | Kolkata | Bangalore | Hyderabad | Kochi | Guwahati

First Indian Edition 2009

VIVA BOOKS PRIVATE LIMITED

- 4737/23 Ansari Road, Daryaganj, New Delhi 110 002
  E-mail: vivadelhi@vivagroupindia.net, Tel. 42242200
- 76, Service Industries, Shirvane, Sector 1, Nerul, Navi Mumbai 400 706
  E-mail: vivamumbai@vivagroupindia.net, Tel. 27721273, 27721274
- Jamals Fazal Chambers, 26 Greams Road, Chennai 600 006
  E-mail: vivachennai@vivagroupindia.net, Tel. 28290304, 28294241
- B-103, Jindal Towers, 21/1A/3 Darga Road, Kolkata 700 017
  E-mail: vivakolkata@vivagroupindia.net, Tel. 22836381, 22816713
- 7, Sovereign Park Apartments, 56-58, K. R. Road, Basavanagudi, Bangalore 560 004
  E-mail: vivabangalore@vivagroupindia.net, Tel. 26607409, 26607410
- 101-102 Mughal Marc Apartments, 3-4-637 to 641, Narayanguda, Hyderabad 500 029
  E-mail: vivahyderabad@vivagroupindia.net, Tel. 27564481, 27564482
- First Floor, Beevi Towers, SRM Road, Kaloor, Kochi 682 018, Kerala
  E-mail: vivakochi@vivagroupindia.net, Tel: 0484-2403055, 2403056
- H. No. 12, P. B. Road, Rehabari, Near Arya Hospital, Guwahati 781 008
  E-mail: vivaguwahati@vivagroupindia.net, Tel: 0361-2735624

www.vivagroupindia.com

Published by arrangement with

Bloomberg Press
731 Lexington Avenue
New York, NY 10022

ISBN-10: 81-309-1172-8
ISBN-13: 978-81-309-1172-4

Published by Vinod Vasishtha for Viva Books Private Limited, 4737/23, Ansari Road, Daryaganj, New Delhi - 110 002.

Printed and bound by Raj Press, R-3, Inderpuri, New Delhi - 110 012.

CONTENTS

LIST OF ILLUSTRATIONS

FOREWORD

MARTIN L. LEIBOWITZ, PhD

GIFFORD FONG HAS BEEN deeply involved in many facets of the financial markets for a number of years. He founded and is managing a successful firm specializing in fixed-income analytics, and is a highly respected global expert in this field. Several major sovereign wealth funds have called upon his expertise over a span of years. He and his associates have published numerous groundbreaking papers relating to the fixed-income markets. Several of these studies form the foundation for the basic yield curve and credit models that are used throughout the bond market.

Feeling the need to "give back" to the financial profession that has been so bountiful to him and his family, Fong served as chair of the program committee at the Institute for Quantitative Research in Finance (the Q-Group) for over twelve years. In this capacity, he reached out to leading-edge academics and practitioners and provided outstanding semiannual seminars. With an enviable energy level, he also accepted the (sometimes arduous) role of editor-in-chief for the *Financial Analysts Journal*—the most widely read journal in this field.

Naturally, as might be expected with such activities, Gifford acquired a stellar network of academics, managers, analysts, asset owners, chief investment officers, and even a few actuaries. It is a tribute to Gifford's genial style that all these individuals also count him as their good friend. This feat is even more remarkable since Gifford's role as an impresario so often called for corralling, nudging, and even that most treacherous of all relationships—acting as their editor!

Gifford's goal has been to bridge the gap between market practitioners and the best academic thinking, whether that of literal academics or of theoretically oriented practitioners. With the increasing complexity of real-world problems, he believes that there is a special need for a more rigorous distribution of these findings. To that end, Gifford went one step beyond and founded the *Journal Of Investment Management* (JOIM), and subsequently launched the JOIM Conference Series. To the surprise of none who know Gifford and his almost magical convening powers,

JOIM immediately attracted a board of advisers that included no fewer than five Nobel laureates. Each issue of the JOIM journal has included "must-read" papers for participants in various market segments.

The semiannual JOIM seminar series has consistently offered presentations of novel research by some of the most respected names in the field. Drawing upon the high regard for himself and the JOIM concept, Gifford has attracted a unique spectrum of speakers, including such leading lights as Paul Samuelson, William F. Sharpe, Myron Scholes, and Robert Engle, to name a few.

The present volume, *Innovations in Investment Management*, is a selection of highlights from recent JOIM conferences. The topics address several of the most pressing problems of the day—pension funding, the complex relationship between equity and debt, transaction costs, the search for alpha, and the almost eerily topical subject of hedge funds and systemic risks.

The authors are all well known in their fields, and these papers are right in the center of their expertise.

In addition to writing a number of highly readable textbooks, Zvi Bodie has created innovative ways of looking at long-term asset returns, pension finance, liability risk, and option theory. In the paper in this volume, he presents—in simple, basic terms—the key principles that should guide all investors, whether institutional or individual. And with his penetrating analysis, he explores several of the traditional rules that are commonly espoused.

Sanjiv Das is a well-recognized expert on security valuation. His chapter presents a new model for pricing securities with a debt-equity linkage. This model is "simple" in the sense of enabling a range of complex instruments to be valued based upon a small number of measurable variables. The paper is somewhat more intensely analytical than most of the chapters. However, it addresses an issue—correlated default risk—that has become one of broad concern in recent months. These concerns affect a wider swath of the securities markets than ever before, and their potential impact on the financial system as a whole has been vividly demonstrated by recent history.

Barclays Global Investors (BGI) is one of the largest single investment managers in the world, and it is known for devoting major resources to groundbreaking research on all facets of institutional investing. The investment profession owes a particular debt to the BGI scholars for developing a formal theoretical framework for active investing within a risk-controlled context. The containment of transaction costs is an integral component of successful active investment. There is no student who has studied the trading costs problem in as much depth as Ananth

Madhavan, who heads the Global Trading Research Group at BGI. In his chapter, Madhavan develops a transaction cost model that can be integrated into the portfolio optimization process, and demonstrates how incorporating transaction cost forecasting can improve net active return.

Robert C. Merton is a professor at Harvard Business School and a 1997 Nobel laureate. Merton played a key role in the development of option theory and its applications, but his work spans the entire field of finance. His study of option theory and its generalization in "continuous-time finance" are monumental achievements. Unfortunately, given its reach into the heights of stochastic calculus, some of this work tends to be out of the reach of many practitioners. However, Merton is a deep thinker and a very clear expositor of the broad mega trends within the financial world. This chapter falls into the latter category, with Merton exploring the progression of retirement plans from the defined-benefit (DB) to the defined-contribution (DC) format—and beyond. Without a single equation or graph, Merton provides a highly readable exploration of the problems and possible solutions to the challenge of providing decent retirements in today's world.

One of the most confounding questions in finance has to do with the relationships between equities and interest rates. The interaction of interest rates and bond returns forms the baseline for evaluating all risk premia. Within asset/liability frameworks, equities and bonds are broadly equivalent sources of risk, so their comovements can have dramatic impact on a fund's surplus status. Unfortunately, most past efforts to characterize the bond-equity relationship have come to naught. The current thinking is that this relationship is highly dependent on specific market regimes. In his chapter, Terry Marsh provides an exceptionally comprehensive review of this classic problem, and puts forward a conditional factor model that relates equity and interest rate movements on a daily basis.

Any discussion of pension issues would be severely flawed without considering the work of Barton Waring, founder and leader of BGI's Client Advisory Group from 1996 until his retirement in 2006. During this period, Waring and his associates delved deeply into all aspects of pension investment. Their studies went beyond the narrow economics of the funds themselves to encompass both the regulatory and accounting contexts as well as the broader questions relating to total corporate risk. In this paper, Waring provides as lucid a summary of the overall pension problem as one is likely to find anywhere. He pulls no punches in presenting his conclusions, many of which are quite dramatic, including his description of the dangers inherent in the seemingly inevitable trend of conversions from DB pension plans to DC plans. After reading Waring's work, one will have a far deeper appreciation of the fundamental issues involved in assuring adequate retirements for corporate and public employees.

Liquidity problems are often the source of market debacles. Consequently, any realistic risk assessment must incorporate liquidity risk as a key component. Such analyses can be difficult even in intensively traded markets, but they become far more problematic in markets where actual trades are sparser. The increasing institutional diversification into less-tradable asset classes has exacerbated the need for ways of estimating both the implicit liquidity risk and the associated return premiums (if any). By studying a database of U.S. corporate bond transactions and holdings, George Chacko has developed a new measure of liquidity that does not depend on trading.

The last paper in this book deals with one of the most important questions in today's financial markets: the enormous growth of hedge funds and their potential for creating systemic problems. In a series of studies, Andy Lo and his associates have probed virtually all facets of the hedge fund market. In an area where many academic analyses tend to be treated with light regard (at best), Lo's public lectures always draw overflow crowds from the hedge fund community itself. He is well known for showing how certain facets of hedge fund return can be systematically replicated as well as for identifying the many facets that appear to be true alpha sources. His paper in this book proposes several new risk measures that are based on an analysis of hedge funds' illiquidity and the time-varying correlations of their returns. His conclusions are sobering, to say the least, suggesting that "the hedge fund industry may be heading into a challenging period . . ." With the high regard that Lo commands both in academia and within the hedge fund world, these findings deserve to be taken most seriously.

From this brief overview, one can see that the chapters in this book focus on topics of great current importance—and they represent the latest thinking of the highest echelon of acknowledged experts in their respective fields. We should all be grateful to Gifford Fong and the JOIM Conference Series for bringing this compendium together in this timely volume.

EDITOR'S NOTE AND ACKNOWLEDGMENTS

The foundations of modern investment management are based upon a theoretical framework that has been developed over many years. The framework is subject to constant refinement, testing, and evolution, with rigorous research at the core of this activity.

The mission of both the *Journal Of Investment Management* (JOIM) and the JOIM Conference Series is to bridge the theory and the practice of investment management. The JOIM Conference Series provides a platform for timely presentations of important and high-quality research; the JOIM is the forum for written work. Showcasing the highest quality research with practical significance and serving both professional investors and academia are central to mission of the JOIM and the conference series.

In the spring of 2003, the first issue of the JOIM was published. At this writing, the subscription base of the JOIM is approximately 15,000, which includes many of the leading libraries around the world. Encouraged by the success of the JOIM, in 2006 I launched the JOIM Conference Series, which is membership-based and held twice a year. High-quality research is presented over a two-day period, with ample opportunity for interaction between presenters and attendees. Open discussion as well as a designated discussant provide a stimulating forum for the research presented.

I selected the articles in this book from the two JOIM conferences held in 2006. They represent the hard work and dedication of a group of presenters faithful to the discipline of rigorous research and the objective of contributing to the practice of investment management.

My thanks to all of those who have participated in this collection.

For their unfailing perseverance to excellence, I extend my gratitude to the staff of the JOIM and the JOIM conference, including Christine Proctor, Tim Fong, and Harriet Fong. Also, a special thanks to Sophia Efthimiatou of Bloomberg Press for her encouragement and her commitment to this book.

CHAPTER 1

A New Generation of Pension Fund Management

ROBERT C. MERTON

Who—Robert C. Merton received the 1997 Nobel Prize in Economics for a new method for pricing derivative securities. He is the John and Natty McArthur University Professor at the Harvard Business School, past president of the American Finance Association, and a member of the National Academy of Sciences. In 1993, he received the inaugural Financial Engineer of the Year award from the International Association of Financial Engineers. Formerly a senior adviser to Salomon Inc. and JPMorgan and cofounder and principal of Long-Term Capital Management, Merton is currently chief science officer of Trinsum Group, Inc., which offers SmartNest, a pension-solution system. Merton has a BS in engineering mathematics from Columbia University, an MS in applied mathematics from the California Institute of Technology, and a PhD in economics from the Massachusetts Institute of Technology.

New Thinking—The legacy of the defined-benefit (DB) plan might be the defined-contribution (DC) plan, but the legacy of the DC plan will replace both the DB and the DC plans. Although still in the early stages of implementation, this "next-generation" plan will be able to provide the solution of predictable cash flow for life, without credit risk, offering the cash flow profile of a DB plan, but through a model derived from the subscriber's DC assets.

Introduction

In talking about pension plans at this point in American economic and corporate history, we need to discuss three linked issues: the DB corporate plans that worked for our parents; the DC plans we're getting today, because corporations no longer want to bear the expense and risk of the DB plan; and how we can reshape the DC plan into something that feels more like a DB plan in the near future. Although this chapter focuses on a U.S. context and corporate pension plans, retirement and asset-management issues are a global challenge, and, indeed, while the details vary across geopolitical borders, the fundamentals are shared by employers and employees across the globe. What's happening with the DB plan, why is it happening, and what are the implications for asset markets and asset management?

I. The Defined-Benefit Plan

In 1990, DB plans were approximately 22 percent of the retirement market in the United States. The DC percentage was pretty close, but a little bit smaller. By 2004, however, DB plans represented only 14 percent, and DC plans were almost double that. In the year from April 2005 to April 2006, of the 627 Fortune 1000 companies intending to freeze or terminate their DB plans, 113 had already essentially either ended or frozen them, and the announcements of DB plan terminations were up 60 percent from a year earlier.

The watershed event occurred in January of 2006, when IBM, long known for being employee-centric, highly rated, and overfunded, decided to end its DB plan—even for existing employees. There have been several other major defections since, the most recent being DuPont. What's happening here?

Well, it's safe to say that companies are *not* discontinuing their plans because their employees marched on their HR departments to say, "We hate defined-benefit plans." On the contrary, employees loved the plans. The problem was the plans were too costly, both to fund and to carry the risk on the balance sheet. But this awareness of the cost factor was not entirely unanticipated. Some academics and financial practitioners were well aware of it long ago, and they even published analyses explaining why the existing accounting treatment would lead to the underestimation of plan costs.

How Did the DB Plans End Up Being So Costly?

Pension accounting was almost surely the key reason that the costs of DB plans were systematically underestimated. Under the accounting rules, the plan sponsor's projected future contributions to support benefits were determined by assuming that future expected returns on the pension fund assets would be realized, without making any adjustment or provision for the risk of those assets. Pension advisers thus saw that pension funds, by holding higher-risk assets with higher expected returns, would lower the calculated future contributions by the plan sponsor. Since future contributions are the cost of the plan, the advisers concluded that, by investing more heavily in risky assets, principally equities, the cost of the plan could be reduced.[1] This practice, which makes no adjustment for risk, in effect treats the expected returns on the portfolio and projected future contributions as "sure things."[2] This pension accounting treatment is equivalent to applying an above-market, risk-free discount rate to compute the present value of future pension benefits, which will understate the cost estimate for plan liabilities.

If, for example, the risk-free rate is 5 percent and the expected return on the portfolio is 9 percent, there's a 400-basis-point spread. If you are calculating pension liabilities with an effective duration of ten years and you used 9 percent instead of 5 percent, you'd get two-thirds of the cost. In other words, if you discounted at 9 percent over ten years instead of 5 percent, you'd end up with two-thirds of the true present value of the costs. Now try flipping that over: If you used the 9 percent discount rate and forecasted your needed contributions based on that, in effect you'd be treating the liabilities—or the cost of servicing those liabilities—as if they were two-thirds of the actual cost. What you thought was a dollar's worth of benefits was really costing you a dollar and a half.[3]

It wasn't that the unions or the employees were any smarter than the corporations were in understanding that the benefits were really worth more than they appeared to be. It's just that, generally, when someone offers you a choice of two things, and one of them is considerably more costly to produce, you usually perceive the value and choose the costlier one, even if you don't explicitly know its price. If my company was giving away company cars and I offered you a choice of a Toyota Camry or a Bentley, and you had no clue as to their prices and could never sell them, I'd still bet that you, along with most people, would choose the Bentley—just because a $200,000 car is likely to be more attractive and have better features than a $30,000 car.

The second reason that the DB plans ended up being so costly was that when the volatility of the pension assets' earnings and contributions was smoothed, the results were both a higher projected rate of return and an unrealistically lower reported volatility rate, which led to an inadequate provision or projected contribution reserve for the risk of the assets. But all of this was already understood, at least by academics.

When, in the 1990s, the markets in the U.S. and the U.K. were going up, it wasn't a problem that caught plan sponsors' attention. Between 2000 and 2002, however, a convergence of circumstances led to a substantial drop in global stock markets and falling interest rates, which resulted in falling pension assets and rising pension liabilities, that weakened company balance sheets and caused large companies in already troubled industries to go bankrupt. All of this surely *did* capture plan sponsors' attention. This is what really killed the DB plans, and this is why they're not coming back. They cost a lot more than plan sponsors *thought* they cost.

Then, at the same time that the inhospitable economic climate was putting corporations under financial stress, something else was happening: Changes were proposed to accounting standards[4] to make them more accurately reflect valuations and volatilities. The eventual implementation of those standards will have a material impact on companies' balance sheets and on earnings volatility—because the companies are holding equities in the pension funds—that will extend far beyond the economic cycle.

All of that said, there is still more than $2 trillion in pension assets left in corporate DB plans in the U.S. alone, which are going to be there for a long time. Also worth noting is that as pension accounting changes to reflect economics and risk more realistically, it is likely to create an investment trend within the DB area: I predict that existing DB plans will move in the direction of matching the duration of the liabilities with the duration of the assets—plus alpha. I'm not predicting total immunization, but, rather, *moving toward* matching the duration—plus alpha.

The Cost of Holding Passive Risk

Market risk, systematic, indexed risk—not alpha, not superior performance—is clearly a passive risk. Anybody can get that, and it's a zero net present value (NPV) investment. A firm can't buy a million dollars' worth of the Standard & Poor's 500 and expect the market to value it at more than a million dollars. Is there a problem with corporations holding passive investment like that in their pension plans?

Well, yes, there is a definite cost to corporations for holding passive risk:

- ***Risk identity.*** The balance sheet of the firm[5] (not just the accounting identity, but also the value identity that assumes that the value of the left side has to equal the value of the right side) also has a *risk* identity. That risk identity holds that the total volatility of the left side has to be borne by the right side—by debt and equity. If you accept that, then, once you determine a desired credit rating, which specifies the amount of risk that the debt will bear, there is no flexibility regarding the amount of equity you need. Given the riskiness of the assets, the amount of equity you need is completely determined by the amount of debt you have and its desired credit rating. That's the risk identity, and in any consideration of total risk, volatility of assets drives the amount of equity you need.
- ***The frictional costs of volatility.*** Even if you hold a passive asset like the S&P 500, it still creates volatility in the asset base of the

> firm, and thus some amount of equity has to be held to cushion that asset's volatility. Since equity has significant frictional costs, and that asset has a zero NPV, holding a passive asset is a losing proposition. Even if the asset is fairly valued, to hold it you have to have additional equity to cushion its volatility, and since equity has frictional costs, it is a net-negative deal. As a practical matter, it can be very hard to strip out some of those passive risks at an acceptable price, except in the area of pension funds, where it is relatively easy to eliminate one type of risk: systematic market risk.[6]

The frictional risks of holding passive investments in the firm are the tax disadvantage of equity versus debt financing (debt interest payments are tax-deductible and equity dividends are not) and the discount in public equity prices from the inherent conflict of interests between owners and managers of the firm, which we'll call "agency cost." We don't *have* a precise number to assign to agency cost, but we know it's significant.

If you concede that there are frictional costs to holding passive assets in the firm, then you have to concede that it's a losing proposition, and, if it's a losing proposition, then you have to consider that the risk profiles of the pension funds affect more than the pension plan beneficiaries. Rating agencies and investors are coming to recognize that pension plans need to be integrated into corporate risk assessments and that risk mismatches between plan assets and liabilities are large. The agencies have already been looking at the deficits and surpluses, but now they're also starting to think about risk mismatch between assets and liabilities. In addition, the FASB changes previously mentioned, when they become effective, will make more transparent these risk mismatches through greater reported earnings volatility. These are the reasons why you'll see corporations moving toward not taking systemic risks.

Alpha risks can be justified, and alpha-generating investments will continue to be included, because, if you have a positive alpha after fees are deducted, that's equivalent to a positive net-present-value project, and then the scale of the project is determined by the trade-off between the value increment from the project and the added frictional cost of equity to support its risk.

If my prediction were to prove correct, that existing DB plans will move in the direction of matching the durations of liabilities and assets, what would be the implications for the capital markets? What if all the pension funds sold off all their passive equities exposures and bought debt (while, of course, retaining any alpha generators)? What would that do to the markets? Would it crush the equity markets and cause debt prices to rise and interest-rate spreads to tighten?

It's not likely to, at least in any sustained sense. Just imagine, for example, if General Electric Co. (GE) and its pension plan sold IBM stock and bought IBM bonds, and IBM sold GE stock and bought GE bonds. Imagine that all the pension funds sold their stock and bought bonds. What would happen then is that, because the risk of the left side of the balance sheet was going down—because the pension funds would be getting out of equities and into debt—firms wouldn't need as much equity to maintain the same credit rating. They would be permitted by the market to recapitalize their capital structure as a consequence of lowering their asset risk; they would issue more debt and buy back their own equity. They wouldn't need as much equity as a cushion, because they would have gotten rid of passive risks. If you follow that line of thinking, it would turn out that, when GE was selling IBM stock, IBM would want to buy its stock back and issue bonds. That would mean that the bond spread that you thought was going to tighten from greater fund demand wouldn't necessarily tighten at all, because bonds would be being issued to provide extra supply.

And then guess what IBM would be doing: IBM would be selling its GE stock, and GE would be buying its stock back and issuing bonds to finance the purchases. So there would be no sustained disequilibrium; the whole process would not, after all, destroy the equity market.

What you would observe after this is that debt-to-equity ratios would go up. If you examine U.S. pension plans, you'd see that they look very much like Japanese cross-holdings: GE is holding IBM stock in its portfolio, and IBM is holding GE stock in its portfolios, and there's an awful lot of stock there that's going nowhere.

II. The Changing Asset-Management Process

Taking It Apart: The Bifurcation into Alpha and Beta

What are the trends we're seeing now in asset management, and what do those trends imply for the future? The biggest one is something you could call "barbell investing."[7]

There has been huge growth in asset management businesses offering pure exposures to beta, such as index funds, exchanged-traded funds (ETFs), and derivatives, which are very efficient, low in cost, and the most scalable.

The other area where we've seen tremendous growth, clearly, is in "pure" alpha generation, from hedge funds, private equity, and direct real estate funds. The growth has been at the two ends, pure beta and more-or-less pure alpha generation.

The cost of the barbell growth has been to the middle, the traditional style of asset management, which mixes the two together and is essentially a long-only style. (Many of the star managers in the middle, in fact, have left to start their own hedge funds.) What are the implications of this barbell investing?

One implication is that institutions will move into alternatives, which we're seeing, whether outsourced or captive. Now think about the way this will work, beginning with a status quo equilibrium analysis. Even if institutions end up with holdings identical to what they had before this change in institutional structure, it should still *appear* that they are going into alternatives. Why is that?

The answer is bifurcation. What used to be all in the middle is now bifurcated. Institutional investors must move to new places to re-create what they had before—perhaps more efficiently, perhaps not. Thus, the trend toward alternatives is almost going to have to happen just because of the change in the asset-management-business structure, whether or not there are any extra returns to be generated from it.

The second implication of barbell investing regards the transparency of strategies and the source of value added. You pay one fee rate for alpha and quite a lower one for beta. When the two were plugged together, that wasn't very transparent. But this new structure is going to be much more transparent, and the composition of each component of the whole will be much more easily measured. The very existence of the bifurcation, the separation of alpha and beta, is providing a transparency that is making pension funds much more sensitive and fund managers more aware of what they're doing. This, in turn, will have the effect of accelerating the dynamic: Alphas will become betas as new exposure becomes systematized and resulting fees go down for a given strategy. After all, what do alpha and beta mean? If an investor is doing the best he or she can, and the investor's manager can improve the investor's risk-return frontier, that manager has created an alpha for that investor, however he's done it. It might not be an alpha for a smarter investor who has already incorporated it, but everything is relative.

To illustrate what I mean when I say alphas are becoming betas, consider the small-stock-versus-large-stock risk premium, or consider the value-versus-growth risk premium. If your investor client hasn't been using either of those strategies before, or if his benchmark had been simply the broad market undifferentiated, then you could create an alpha for that investor simply by tilting into small stocks or tilting into value stocks. You would be creating value for your investor because you would be doing better for him or her than he was doing before. Once the source of added return is recognized, however, then very efficient means arise for creating those differentiated exposures, and, so, from a fee point of view, the strategy would be taken out of the alpha class and put into the beta class.

You would see similar effects from momentum (if it exists) or from any other strategy that, once recognized and systematized, could be provided at low cost. Once that happens, why would anyone pay a premium fee for the asset management? That's what I mean when I say that by bifurcating the industry the dynamic process of alpha generating strategies transforming into beta strategies will accelerate—for better or for worse.

Putting It Together Again: The Assembler Function

So, now that we've separated the alpha and the beta, what's next is putting them back together again—assembling them into the institutional portfolio, but in a totally different way from the preset, blended style we had before. Institutions are going to be looking for skilled assemblers who can take the two ends of the barbell, the alpha and the beta, and assemble them in a much richer, more sophisticated way.

The function of the assembler could be to take pure alphas and mix them with pure betas, or perhaps create some sort of transparent prepackaged mix of specific beta exposures plus alpha, like the S&P 500 plus alpha, or the Morgan Stanley Capital International funds (MSCI) plus alpha, or whatever beta index you like plus alpha.

I believe there are already investment firms doing this—not offering pure alpha, but offering a combination: having the pension-fund investment committee choose the index to combine with the alpha. Institutions will need to decide on the mix of indexes to use as well as the mix of alpha providers. The assemblers to perform this role can be inside the institution or outsourced. The need for people in the assembler function is going to grow tremendously and have a significant impact on the industry.

What skills will an assembler have to have? He'll have to develop new, integrated, and consistent methods of measuring risk for alternative and traditional asset classes. Whether you're talking about hedge funds, private equity, or real estate, if you're going to be assembling alphas and betas in pension-fund portfolios that include them, you will need to have consistent risk measures to be able to combine them with traditional asset classes of stocks and bonds.

Let me give you an example: When you're dealing with alternatives that don't have much of a secondary market, such as private equity or direct real estate investment or structured products such as collateralized debt obligations (CDOs), you're going to have to take into account the effect of stale pricing. That's a problem we've always had to deal with, and it principally affects the correlations between returns in measuring the contribution to portfolio risk. But let me tell you about an experiment that I ran that illustrates the impact of stale pricing.

I created a firm, a hypothetical private-equity fund, called "S&P 500 Private." Now, just between us (don't tell anybody), the only asset of that portfolio was the S&P 500. My hypothetical portfolio provided its investors with a weekly, not a monthly, NAV.[8] Although the NAV was reported each week, the portfolio was priced only every two weeks. I knew the true price of my portfolio, the S&P 500 Private, today, because I had just priced it in the market, but I knew that next week I wasn't going to reprice it. The reported price next week thus would be a stale price and identical to the reported price this week. Then, the following week, I'd take into account whatever happened for the two-week interval and reprice the portfolio to market.

Now you have a picture of the portfolio's reported performance: Since it was being repriced to market every other week, it had a very systematic pattern. It would look as if there had been no price change for almost two weeks; then it would move either up or down; then no price change for almost two weeks; then up or down. The price dynamics were very transparent, with stale prices reported every other week.

Now let's assume that we wanted to measure the performance of S&P 500 Private, relative to our benchmark, the S&P 500. What did we know was the true alpha and beta of S&P 500 Private? Its beta was 1.00 and its alpha was 0.00, because the benchmark and the portfolio were identical.[9] What if I had run the weekly reported NAV against the benchmark? The average return, or average excess return, would, of course, have been unaffected, because the average return of any portfolio depends only on the beginning and ending points of the sample period, whether you sample once a week or once every two weeks.

But how would the estimate of the beta be affected by stale pricing? We know the true beta is 1.0, and we know the beta equals the ratio of the standard deviations of the fund's and the benchmark's returns multiplied by their correlation.[10]

What got hammered by this systematic stale pricing, however, was the estimate of correlation between the portfolio's and benchmark's returns. In reality, the actual correlation was perfect; the true portfolio value and the benchmark moved exactly in tandem. But, because we were using stale prices half the time—regardless of how the S&P 500 benchmark was actually performing—the reported NAV didn't move in half of the weeks. This produced a measured correlation with the benchmark a little under 0.5. Estimated beta, therefore, instead of being 1.0, was 0.5. We had understated the systematic beta risk of the fund.

Now consider the estimate of alpha, which equals the average excess return of the funds, less the beta, times the benchmark's excess return.

Since the average returns didn't change, and the estimated beta was understated by half, the alpha, by definition, has to be equal to half the realized excess return on the benchmark—in this case, the S&P 500. Guess what: When I ran this for the five-year period from 1995 to 2000, the annual estimated alpha came out to be 1,000 basis points!

It sounds like a joke, but that's how it works. Granted, 1995 to 2000 was a pretty hot period, with the excess return on the S&P 500 roughly 20 percent, and because the estimated beta was understated by half, the estimated alpha was roughly half of 20 percent, or 1,000 basis points.

This is a fast pass on the effects of stale pricing on performance measurement, but you can see intuitively—the point of this transparent exercise—that it's an overestimate of alpha caused by a very simple temporal misalignment of returns. The point is that these errors in the estimate of alpha can be very, very large, and, therefore, if you don't correct for stale pricing, it's not just a round-off error; it can have a huge impact on estimated performance of a fund.

With an actual private-equity portfolio, the stale-pricing problem is far more severe than in the hypothesized example: It doesn't get marked to market every other week; it gets marked only when there's a new round of financing, or an initial public offering (IPO), or another exit, or, occasionally, a write-off. So it could be a rainy Thursday night when one of those events occurs. Now you have some idea of what that does to the estimated correlation. This is not to say that private equity as an asset class has not earned superior excess returns. It does say that, in the world we're in, when you get into this assembly process, this integration of the pension-fund portfolio components, it's going to be very, very important to take all of this into account. Tools for doing so exist, but the way we measure performance will have to be very different from what it was in the past.

Sustainable Returns for Alternative Investments

Let's talk about sustainable returns for alternatives, in particular, for hedge funds. The question is, What are the sources of sustainable returns for hedge funds? Let me offer three:

1. Market exposure. Even managers of hedge funds that try not to, can, in very subtle ways, have systematic stock-market exposure from their trading strategies, such as in convertible-bond arbitrage. They may think they have stock-market risk hedged out if they short the underlying stock against a long position in the convertible, but, if they don't hedge out the volatility exposure of the convertible, and they're exposed to changes in volatility, then they have implicitly taken risk in the stock market even without intending to, because stock returns and changes in volatility are negatively correlated.

2. Liquidity-event risk. What I mean by *liquidity-event* risk is not bid-/ask- spread liquidity, but the kind of liquidity event that shocks the market, causing market transactions to shut down. In such a market, until market players can figure out what's going on, it will stay that way, and there's a flight to quality.

My colleague George Chacko studied returns on the CSFB/Tremont Hedge Fund Indexes for all styles of hedge funds from 1994 to 2004. What he found was that, by using a single factor from the equity market for liquidity—even though hedge funds of different styles take positions across all the markets—much of the residual alpha performance for all styles became insignificant.

Consider corporate bonds in terms of liquidity exposure. For exchange-listed equities, the median time between trades is perhaps a couple of minutes, depending on the float. For corporate bonds, however, the median time between trades is six months, because most corporate bonds don't trade at all. There's a tremendous difference in liquidity between corporate bonds and equities.

Again, consider convertible-bond arbitrage. You go long the (illiquid) corporate bond, and you short the (liquid) equity. So you do have liquidity exposure, whether you want to or not. Or look at long-short equity arbitrage. Typically, the short equity position is in the larger-cap stocks that are more liquid, easier to borrow to short sell, and less likely to get squeezed out of the short position,[11] and the long position is typically in smaller, less-liquid stocks.

There are many sophisticated strategies being used, and there are delays and lags, but it appears—at least from the data we see—that hedge funds are systematically taking on liquidity-event risk. There's nothing wrong with that, but investors in hedge funds should be aware of it.

3. Institutional rigidities. From a financial-system perspective, I think this risk is the most interesting, and it's one I've believed in for a very long time. What is it that all hedge funds have in common? Certainly not strategies; they undertake all different strategies. The one essential characteristic that makes a hedge fund a hedge fund, the commonality that binds them all together, is that they're minimally regulated institutions, certainly relative to mutual funds, banks, insurance companies, or even pension funds, or any other kind of funds.

Institutional rigidities can occur from many different factors—accounting rules, regulatory agencies, taxes, asset classes, geography, transaction times, or methodologies, to name a few. What I mean by the impact of rigidity is the situation that occurs when an investment manager would *like* to take a position, or get rid of a position, *but is prevented from doing so by some controlling factor outside the trading strategy*. There are many such rigidities, and the changes that come with globalization mean that the web of rigidities is becoming ever more complex, because of regional differences in regulations and standards.

The markets that are perhaps most affected by institutional rigidities are the credit markets, especially in the area of accounting. In the equity markets, almost everyone's accounting is already performed on a mark-to-market basis. In the credit markets, however, while some players are mark to market, a vast number of them are not. That accounting difference gives rise to different tactics and accommodations, such as the creation of huge structured-investment vehicles (SIVs). Some transactions are for entities held at their historical basis or book value for a price that would never hold water with any trader. These situations are all examples of pure accounting rigidity.

Another institutional rigidity involving credit ratings relates to certain restrictions placed on institutions that invest in bonds. Sometimes a restriction specifies that a fund may hold only investment-grade bonds. If you're an investment manager holding General Motors Corp. (GM) or Ford bonds, and if those bonds drop below investment grade, you might love holding them or even want to buy more of them. But if you are not allowed to hold bonds rated below investment grade, you don't have any choice: Not only can you not buy any more; you have to start liquidating what you have. That's a rigid rule you are bound by.

Institutional rigidities exist and have to be considered, but hedge funds, because they're not regulated, face far fewer institutional rigidities than other institutions such as banks, insurance companies, pension funds, and mutual funds and thus are the natural counterparties to intermediate the constraints these rigidities create for these other institutions. We normally think of banks as intermediaries that work face-to-face with their customers for their services. Hedge funds can also perform the intermediation function but do so anomalously through the financial markets instead of face-to-face with the entities that are receiving their intermediation services.

I have a test, at least a mental test, for identifying when the hedge fund transactions are providing intermediation services to entities restricted by institutional rigidity: If the hedge fund says to the entity with the institutional rigidity, "I'm going to tell you how we can make money from you in this trade," and even tells the entity how much money it will make, but the entity nevertheless still makes the trade, then it's not that the entity was a less-well-informed counterpart to a transaction. It's simply that the hedge fund was providing a service for the entity by loosening or eliminating a costly rigidity, and it was willing to pay for the hedge fund to do that. I believe that, because of the profits they have been making, hedge funds have been acting as intermediaries and providing an intermediation service.[12]

III. What the Future Will Look Like for Retirement Plans

We've followed the evolution of pension plans, from the defined benefit,[13] to the bifurcation of alpha and beta, to the reassembling of alpha and beta. Now I'd like to look at that reassembling and consider what opportunities it will give us for the future.

The functionality of employers' providing pension plans for employees is not going to cease. Indeed, our focus-group studies tell us that, in terms of financial services advice, employees place great trust in their employers—more than in any financial services institution. So it looks as if employers should continue to be in the business of providing life-cycle and retirement services to their employees. How are employers handling that part of their business?

By default, plan sponsors are going into DC plans, because they're all getting out of DB plans. But I don't believe that's the end of the story, because I don't believe that the DC plan is a long-term solution as it's typically constituted now. Converting to DC plans does address the concerns of the plans' sponsors; it gets rid of the sponsors' balance-sheet risk and enables them to better contain and calculate their costs as a percentage of wages, which is what they were looking for. But the problem of allocating savings and planning investment portfolios imposes more risk on individuals. It calls on them to make complex and important choices that they didn't have to make in the past, that they're not equipped to make now, and that I doubt that they could be educated to make in the future.

Whether someone is a brain surgeon, a professor, or an auto–assembly-line worker, he or she is now expected to solve a very complex, intertemporal financial optimization problem. What was that DB promise again? *That the retiree would have enough income in retirement to maintain the standard of living he enjoyed in the latter part of his work life.* That's a short explanation that's not a bad approximation of what you might say to twenty-five-, thirty-five-, forty-five-, or fifty-five-year-olds as a likely expectation of what they will want when they do retire. You notice that the statement doesn't mention projected rates of return, and it doesn't address the skill sets needed for understanding risk-return frontiers. The promise is only to solve the problem, and this is what most people will want, a pension solution.

What we're doing for people with DC plans now is giving them a little advice, but basically we're telling them—whether they're brain surgeons, professors, or assembly-line workers—that they are primarily responsible for solving an intertemporal problem like the one in the following box:

The Problem the Employee Has, but Doesn't Want to Deal With

- ❑ You're going to be making/receiving contributions or making contributions proportional to your wages for the next twenty-two years.
- ❑ You're going to have to invest those monies in something.
- ❑ At the end of twenty-two years, you'll have *some* amount of money, but, by the way, it's not the *amount* of money that matters; it's that you want a certain standard of living in retirement, and so you want a *flow* of inflation-protected income that will enable you to maintain that standard of living.

They will have to deal with the problem of not knowing whether their retirement money will be enough or not—even if they know how much money they will have at the end of twenty-two years—because that's going to depend on what the real interest rates are. We've all seen TIPS[14] at 4 percent and then 2 percent; there's a big difference between investing money at 4 percent and at 2 percent. The amount needed to provide income for life will also depend on mortality/longevity tables at the time of their retirement.

So people will have all of those needs and all of those risks, and we're expecting them to solve the problem of optimal accumulation and execute the prescription of that solution. I just don't think that expectation is reasonable as a long-term solution. It's a little bit like going in for surgery, and, as you're being wheeled in to the operating room, having the surgeon look down at you and ask, "Sir [or Madam], would you rather have seven sutures or sixteen?" That seems the sort of thing that the surgeon might be better prepared to answer than the patient. But that's analogous to what's happening with DC plans in the current environment.

People really liked the patterned simplicity of the DB, and they just want to maintain their standard of living. Now we are in danger of repeating the mistake employers made: treating expected returns as risk free over long horizons and undervaluing the cost of DB plans, because we figured on a 9 percent return when we should have figured on 5 percent. With DC plans, particularly for the longer time horizons, financial advisers too often treat the equity returns very much as if they're darned near risk free. If we don't correct that, we risk having some of the same problems with the DC plans that we had with the DB plans. But this time the consequences of overly optimistic return assumptions and underestimation of the risks to get them will fall directly on individuals and not on corporations, who can at least attempt, even if painfully, to make up the legacy costs.

What do I think is the next-generation solution? I think the next-generation solution is to recognize first that there is a problem that cannot be solved by simply assuming higher returns with the same risk. You can't build an entire retirement system with an essential pillar for success being the creation of alpha. There's a limited amount of alpha out there, and a viable pension solution must be scalable to millions of participants investing trillions of dollars. No matter how talented you are, you can't prudently assume you can continue to create significant alpha—even if you're doing it today—for the next thirty years. That's too aggressive a statement to build a system around.

What are the alternatives? Individuals will have to choose among the following:

- Reducing their consumption during their working years to support the benefits they want postretirement
- Reducing the term of their retirement and working longer
- Lowering the benefits they will receive in retirement

That's it. Those are the choices, and those choices must be part of the process of managing these funds, and there's nothing magical about it. Remember my earlier analogy? When you have Bentleys and you are giving them away at $30,000 apiece, it's great. But once you recognize that the Bentley is a $200,000 vehicle, you're going to have to come up with $200,000 if you still want to buy a Bentley. I don't know what you think, but I think that a lot of people who were quite happy to get the Bentleys at $30,000 will be willing to reconcile themselves to Toyotas, if the price tag on the Bentley is $200,000.

Our job as pension-solution providers and asset managers is to find a mechanism for getting people to be engaged in this part of the process, to reconcile themselves to the realities, and to adjust their positions to arrive at an optimum solution.

We have to improve efficiency in extracting value fully from every asset. Housing, for example, the single biggest asset for most American baby boomer households, has to be utilized much better than it is now. Essentially, the house is a very special asset at retirement, because it serves two functions: First, it provides prepaid consumption, just like an annuity. If the house is the one the person wants to retire in, ownership is the best hedge for the housing part of his consumption. Using an "average" housing index to calculate your retirement needs won't work if you want to live in Cambridge, or Boston, or New York City. You have to use the housing index for the region you want to live in; that's why ownership of the house is a very good hedge.

In addition to that, however, the house has embedded in it additional value, which, with maintenance, it will have. The trick is to strip out of the house that part of its value that is not prepaid consumption and to utilize that in an efficient way either to add to retirement benefits or, if the goal is to leave money to family or charity, to allow more efficient bequests.

The point is that it's not just housing that has to be added in; *all* of a person's assets have to be accounted for and used efficiently. We are no longer in a position in which we can waste assets; we cannot afford *not* to take into account everything that the individual has, in order to design the best retirement plan. That's a key element.

So, back to my question, What will the future look like for retirement plans? I think that what we will see is that this next generation of plans will be the best of the DB and the DC. From the DB side, we will have the simplicity and the focused target on standard of living. From the DC side, we'll have portability, meaningful customization, minimal credit risk to the beneficiaries, and the absence of residual liability or uncertainty to the corporation. This is a major challenge, but it's also a great opportunity. In the U.S. alone, there are 76 million baby boomers about to retire, and the payout-versus-accumulation solution must be addressed. A daunting challenge indeed. But we also have wonderful, modern financial technology with which to execute a solution, and we have the science of finance as we know it and more than three decades of experience in effectively putting the science of finance into practice.

I believe we have some really exciting and rewarding times ahead for financial services. Providing pension benefits is the challenge, but I think we can meet it. It's an engineering problem, not a basic science problem. Every time you have a major new generational change like this one, there are huge opportunities for creating franchises and adding value. How good is it to be able to come home from work and say, "Hey, we really accomplished something for a lot of people: We're giving them a better, more-efficient retirement"?

Chapter Notes

1. It is perhaps no surprise that corporate pension funds typically allocated 60–70 percent of assets to high-expected-return equities.

2. Some advisers believed that because the time horizon of the pension plan was long, the expected return on the portfolio was risk free, at least over the long run.

3. If that cost is calculated for an 18-year duration, that number doubles to $2 real cost per $1 of perceived cost.

4. By the FASB (the Financial Accounting Standards Board).

5. From the pension fund manager's perspective, the firm's assets, debt, and equity.

6. The direction that we're going in today is to strip out more and more risk, not only from pension fund assets, but also from other parts of the firm's balance sheet, to manage financial risk.

7. A descriptive term, not a technical one.

8. Net asset value.

9. I've assumed away any transaction cost.

10. For technical reasons, even if you use true prices only every other week, the estimated standard deviation comes out about the same as using them every week, because the variance estimate treats the two-week move as if it took place in one week. And so it overstates the true volatility by a factor of two for half the weeks and understates it to be zero for the other half, resulting in an approximately correct estimate for the overall sample period.

11. By demands for short covering.

12. Before you think about regulating hedge funds or any other entities, you need to have an understanding of what functions they're performing. If you regulate hedge funds that are functioning as intermediaries and make them just like mutual funds or banks, they won't be able to perform their intermediary function anymore: Once regulated, they would have the same institutional rigidities as the very entities they're working for.

13. I actually saw it written once as "divine benefit," which wasn't too far from the truth.

14. Treasury inflation-protected securities.

CHAPTER 2

Teaching Financial Literacy

What the Retail Investor Needs to Know

ZVI BODIE

Who—Zvi Bodie is the Norman and Adele Barron Professor of Finance and Economics at Boston University School of Management. He holds a PhD from the Massachusetts Institute of Technology and has served on the finance faculty at the Harvard Business School and at the MIT Sloan School of Management. His textbook *Investments*, coauthored by Alex Kane and Alan Marcus, has been translated into ten languages and is the market leader at business schools around the world. It is also used in the certification programs of the Chartered Financial Analyst (CFA) Institute, the Society of Actuaries, and several other professional associations. With Michael J. Clowes, Bodie wrote *Worry-Free Investing: A Safe Approach to Achieving Your Lifetime Financial Goals* (2003), which is geared toward the general public. In September 2007, the Retirement Income Industry Association honored Bodie with the award for Lifetime Achievement in Applied Retirement Research.

New Thinking—Bodie is critical of how popular financial education websites present the basics of investing to beginners. He suggests ways to improve that content. In this chapter, he focuses on some fundamental questions:

- ❑ What is the difference between saving and investing?
- ❑ Which investments are safest in the long run?
- ❑ Should everyone hold a diversified investment portfolio?
- ❑ What is the correct way to take account of inflation?

Introduction

As this chapter is being edited, in December 2007, many Americans, especially the "boomers," are very worried about how to pay for the college education of their children, their own retirement, and many other rising costs they will face in the future as government spending on entitlement programs declines. What sort of financial education, or, to be more specific, *investment* education, ought financial professionals provide to their retail-client customers—not to the institutions, but to the individuals who are the end users—to help them cope with their life-cycle needs? Those needs have never been greater than now, as pension plans change from defined benefit (DB) to defined contribution (DC), and employees have to make their own saving and investment decisions.[1]

Unfortunately, the financial advice and explanations you find on the Internet when you google "How should I invest for retirement?" is promotional rather than educational. It is written to induce people to buy certain products—usually equity funds—rather than to help them frame their decisions in a rational way. Even the investor education provided by government agencies such as the Securities and Exchange Commission, which a consumer might think is impartial, presents many of the same misleading marketing pitches as the industry sources do, rather than advice based on sound economic reasoning. I would like to extend an invitation to all my readers from universities and professional associations to join me in a challenging but extremely worthwhile endeavor. I believe we have a mission: to design, produce, and disseminate objective, genuinely trustworthy financial education based on the fundamental principles of economics. In this brief chapter, I try to demonstrate what I have in mind.

Inertia, Misinformation and Slogans: How the Retail Investor Came to Be So Unprepared

In the early days of 401(k) plans, most people, when asked to choose among investment options, stuck with the default option. Unfortunately, the default option was usually a money market fund, and the choice turned out to be a bad one. The default option *should* have been an inflation-indexed DB plan. When it became apparent that so many people, through inertia, were "choosing" the default option, there was general agreement that, if people were more educated, they would learn to diversify out of money market funds. That thinking is what gave birth to the kind of slogans (in italics) that are causing problems today:

"*You can't afford not to take risk.*" This simply flies in the face of common sense. The fact is that the less you can afford to lose, the less you can afford to take risk.

"*Investing in safe assets is not safe for the long run, because you need the growth of equities to keep up with inflation.*" What people didn't realize about this particular slogan, which was reinforced by the Ibbotson charts about the long-term performance of stocks, was that it took for granted that people who already had defined-benefit plans—and *also* had 401(k)s—would invest their 401(k) money in mutual funds. That made perfect sense when the defined benefit was the base and the mutual fund investments only an add-on; with the safe allocation in their defined-benefit plan, people could afford to take on some risk in an incremental allocation. What we're looking at now, however, is a completely different situation, because now in most cases the 401(k) plan is *replacing* the defined-benefit plan—and if some politicians have their way, the 401(k) will replace even Social Security.

"*Our economy has been growing for the last two hundred years—a diversified portfolio of stocks gives the investor a way to participate in that growth.*" Perhaps, for 90 percent of the people who are targeted by this kind of investment advice, the correct solution is to hold whatever it is that the mutual fund companies are trying to sell. I'm not arguing that there's no risk premium on equities. I am simply saying that equities are not safe, no matter how long your time horizon is.

Marketing Versus Education: Getting Real About Financial Risk

One of the problems with the way such investing slogans are accepted is the result of the way they are presented. There is a difference between marketing and education. Providers have a responsibility to indicate which is which.

Some people hear that they get a premium for taking a risk, and, without understanding the whole picture, they want to go for the premium. Some of them can afford to risk a certain portion of their assets, but there is another 10 percent who cannot afford to take any risk at all, who should not under any circumstances be investing in equities. Some people with low incomes are in jobs that have a very high correlation with the stock market; these people are *already* overexposed to equities. Should they be putting their retirement money into equities as well? What's more, many in this same group of people, who cannot afford any risk whatsoever, are using their 401(k) plans for severance, or unemployment, insurance, instead of using them for retirement.

In the category, not of slogans, but of misinformation is an unsafe investment approach that was outlined in a book put out by a leading discount broker on the subject of retirement planning. The heuristic for the average investor—and maybe it was a good one—was that the percentage of a portfolio that should be in equities was 100 minus your age. That would mean that, if you were fifty, you would have exactly half your portfolio in equities. The book, however, was proposing that the equities proportion stay at 50 percent even at ages sixty, seventy, and beyond.

The problem is that, although the principle of diversification works across securities and asset classes, it does *not* work over time. Even a highly diversified portfolio of stocks does not become safe in the long run. Yet here is the kind of thing customers are told on a typical website: Invest in stocks, either individually or in mutual funds, for long-term growth. While in any given year stocks can be more volatile than other investments, over time, they have typically outperformed all other types of investments while staying ahead of inflation. Stocks should be the core of a long-term investing strategy.

If stocks are so great for the long run, then why don't the same firms offering this advice offer a performance guarantee to pay at least what a customer contributes to a diversified equity portfolio adjusted for inflation? After all, the firm managing the fund is in a much better position to evaluate and manage the risk than the customer is. If the firm believes what it is saying, it ought to offer a free guarantee for its product. That's what other industries do. Of course, option-pricing theory shows that such a guarantee is far from free. A European-style put option that guarantees against a shortfall relative to the U.S. Treasury rate costs more the longer its time horizon. Its price *increases* with the square root of T, where T is the time horizon.[2] So, even though the probability of a shortfall falls as the time horizon gets longer, the cost of insuring against a shortfall increases. That is the simplest argument I can use to explain to people why they need to be concerned about the downside risk of equities in the long run. After all, we all pay to insure against events that have a very low probability of occurring because of their severity. What could be more severe than reaching retirement age and being broke?

Teaching the Basic Concepts of Financial Literacy

Now that we've established what misinformation retail investors are exposed to, let's talk about how to fix the problem: How do we teach the basic concepts of financial literacy?

Finance is an applied branch of the science of economics, in the same way that medicine is an applied branch of the science of biology. In teaching the basics of finance, we should remain true to the basic concepts and principles of economics, not contradict them, as do many of the popular investment-education websites. Among the most basic concepts of economics that play a role in financial decision-making are saving, investing, matching, and diversifying. Here is what students are taught in a course on the principles of economics:

Saving

Saving is income minus consumption. Saving can be used either to reduce debt or to increase assets.[3]

Investing

Investing focuses on the types of assets that people put their savings into. The spectrum of asset choices goes from short run to long run and from safe to risky. A basic tenet in economics states that saving equals investment. Therefore, anyone who is a saver is also, by definition, an investor.

Matching

Matching is the safest investment strategy for achieving a specific goal. To eliminate the risk of falling short of an investment goal at a specific future date, the investor needs to match the maturity of his investment to the date of his goal, with target-dated, inflation-protected investments, such as Series I savings bonds or Treasury inflation-protected securities (TIPS).

Diversifying

Diversifying means reducing your exposure to risk by not "putting all your eggs in one basket." Instead of investing in the stock of a single company, investors need to allocate diversified investment funds among the stocks of different companies in different industries. Because some of the gains will cancel some of the losses, the risk of the portfolio of stocks will be lower than the risk of an investment of equal size in a single stock.

Principles of Rational Financial Decision-Making

As with other applied sciences, like medicine or engineering, best practices in finance evolve as knowledge advances—but some core principles of rational financial decision-making remain constant. These principles should be taught in a way that is completely consistent with the basic concepts and definitions of economics—as simply as possible, but not more simply.

In addition, the misleading financial advertising of "popular literature" needs to be exposed for what it is by the regulatory authorities charged with consumer protection.

I think the following qualify as basic principles of rational financial decision-making:

Principle 1

Financial choices should be framed in terms of objectives and constraints. Rational choice is about maximizing your welfare subject to resource constraints. To make a rational retirement plan, people should save in their working years to provide roughly the same standard of living *after* retirement as before.

Principle 2

Take account of inflation in a consistent way. Among the most basic ideas in economics is the distinction between nominal and real—that is, inflation adjusted—units of account. For example, in measuring the level of aggregate economic activity in a given year, economists distinguish between *nominal* gross domestic product (GDP), measured in prices actually charged for goods and services in that year, and *real* GDP, measured in prices of a common base year. This distinction between nominal and real also applies to interest rates and to projected benefits in retirement planning. Adjust for inflation in all calculations. This means using real—constant-dollar—forecasts of cash flows and real rates of return rather than nominal ones. It is common for people to mistakenly compute projected retirement income based on an observed market rate of interest *without* subtracting the expected rate of inflation. When they add the resulting income figure to projected Social Security benefits, they get an unrealistically high projected retirement income. The higher the expected rate of inflation, the worse this upward bias becomes. Real rates of interest can be low or even negative.[4]

Principle 3

A security's price is generally a good estimate of its fair market value.[5] Prices of publicly traded securities reflect assessments of informed investors. It takes only two competing bidders who are well informed for prices to reflect available information accurately. If a deal looks too good to be true, it probably is not as good as it looks. Sometimes an asset seems like a bargain to you only because you are unaware of some risk that better-informed investors know about.

Principle 4

Seek advice only from a trustworthy source, and make sure you understand the scientific evidence for that advice. Many professional advisers are paid commissions by financial firms, which thus creates an incentive for them to steer you toward products that might not be in your best interest. [If you're not sure which advisers you can trust, check an organization of fee-only financial planners, such as the National Association of Personal Financial Advisors (NAPFA).] When you're comparing and evaluating investment managers, beware of "survivorship bias." Investment companies that have existed for a long time will appear to have funds with superior performance, because the funds that performed badly no longer exist. A firm's track record can be misleading if no adjustment is made for the funds that did not survive.

Financial Literacy FAQs

QUESTION: *Can you trust the advice you get from your employer? If you are an employee, you are inclined to trust your employer's benefits department as a source of financial advice when you are trying to choose the default option in retirement and health plans. Is your trust justified?*

ANSWER: Maybe. You need to ask some questions: Are your employer's interests aligned with your own? Employers must obey the law, but do the "safe harbor" rules set by regulators correspond to your needs and preferences? Get answers to these questions from the benefits department itself. If you are told to seek advice from a professional financial planner, be sure that the planner's advice is not self-serving.

QUESTION: *So whom can you trust?*

ANSWER: Your best protection is knowledge of the basics. Ask your adviser what she thinks of safe financial products that are free of sales commissions, such as I Bonds and other investments at TreasuryDirect. If the adviser is either unaware of them or tries to talk you out of them, seek advice elsewhere. Look at the list at the end of this chapter of helpful websites that offer impartial advice and assistance.

QUESTION: *If people restrict themselves only to "safe investing" and don't take a certain amount of risk, isn't it likely that a lot* *of them will never reach their investment goals by the time they reach sixty-five?*

ANSWER: That's right; they won't. In the past, with the establishment of Social Security and private DB pensions, a certain cohort of people was able to retire at sixty-five. That won't be true in the future. Even those retiring this year cannot collect their full Social Security until they are almost sixty-six. People born in 1970 won't be able to collect full Social Security until they reach sixty-seven. The date is continually being pushed back. With a life expectancy of eighty-five or so, we are being unrealistic if we expect the system will provide enough income for everyone to retire at age sixty-five. It just won't work, and information that says it *will* work can't be trusted.

Helpful Websites

For basic information:

www.napfa.org—National Association of Personal Financial Advisors

For fee-free services:

www.annualcreditreport.com—Free personal credit report

www.TreasuryDirect.gov—Commission-free investment in Treasuries, including TIPS and I Bonds

www.choosetosave.org/ballpark—A ballpark estimate of how much to save for retirement

For information on targeted tuition plans:

www.collegesavings.com/program.html

www.independent529plan.org

The following sites are government or regulatory agencies that get their "educational material" from biased industry sources. Exercise caution in using them:

www.sec.gov—SEC (Securities and Exchange Commission)

www.nasaa.org—NASAA (North America Securities Administrators Association)

www.finra.org/index.htm—FINRA (Financial Industry Regulatory Authority)

Chapter Notes

1. In a DB plan, the sponsor of the plan assumes the risk of a shortfall at retirement, but, in a DC plan, the individual participants bear that risk themselves.

2. See Zvi Bodie, "On the Risk of Stocks in the Long Run." *Financial Analysts Journal* 51 (May/June 1995): 18–22.

3. It's not always clear whether a particular outlay should be considered as consumption or as saving. For example, if you spend money on acquiring more education to increase your earning power in the future, you ought to consider it saving, but education expense is usually treated as consumption.

4. College Savings Bank CDs, for example, offer a guaranteed interest rate that is negative measured in units of tuition. See www.collegesavings.com/program.html.

5. The law of one price is that, in a competitive market, identical goods must sell for the same price after adjusting for transaction costs and shipping costs. This law is enforced by the force of arbitrage: that is, traders buying at the low price and simultaneously selling at the higher price and thereby eliminating price discrepancies that are larger than the transaction costs.

CHAPTER 3

Managing Pension Funding Risks Using Modern Portfolio Theory

BARTON WARING

Who—Barton Waring, Managing Director and Chief Investment Officer for Investment Policy and Strategy, *Emeritus*, Barclays Global Investors (BGI), started BGI's client advisory group in 1996 and led it until his retirement in 2006. His research and published articles have focused on helping today's investors control their risks and enhance their returns, in both beta and alpha dimensions. He is continuing to research and write on these topics in his emeritus role. While most of his client work has been for BGI's "strategic" clients, the largest of the world's institutional investors (defined benefit retirement plans, foundations, endowments, social security systems, and central banks), his research has also often been directed at the investment strategy needs of individuals. He has published over two dozen articles on surplus asset allocation, manager structure optimization and risk budgeting, and on defined contribution/individual investor investment strategy. Five of these articles have won outstanding article awards from their respective journals, and these and many others are widely cited as setting today's standards of practice. He serves on editorial advisory boards for the *Journal of Portfolio Management*, the *Financial Analysts Journal*, and the *Journal of Investing*.

His background prior to BGI also dealt intensively with classical investment strategy and policy issues. He was the manager of the specialist

---

This chapter is adapted from a talk given by the author at the *Journal Of Investment Management* annual conference on March 29, 2006, in San Francisco. Portions of the material used here were extracted from Waring (2004a) and (2004b) with the permission of Institutional Investor Journals; all rights reserved.

investment strategy consulting firm Ibbotson Associates, Inc., coleader of Towers Perrin's asset-liability practice and the head of two of its regional asset consulting practices, and he started and led Morgan Stanley Asset Management's original defined contribution business in 1992, implementing the lifestyle fund concepts that he pioneered in 1989 and that he has also written about frequently. Waring received his BS degree in economics from the University of Oregon, his JD degree from Lewis and Clark College, with honors, and his master's degree in finance from Yale University.

New Thinking—Waring's chapter discusses the many useful implications that come from replacing the accounting and actuarial view of the pension liability with an economist's market value view of the liability. The insights include opportunities to more completely control pension costs through better benefit policy decisions, and to more fully understand the limitations of contribution policy decisions once a benefit policy has been set. Here he discusses the implications for investment policy. The insights for investment policy are that all sponsors should first be fully hedged to the market-related (beta) risks of the liability, essentially a mix of long-term TIPS and longer-term bonds. Then and only then should they consider equities and other risky-asset classes, and perhaps also active management. In effect, he demonstrates a "four fund theorem" for investment policy in the presence of a liability, but the two key funds are the liability-matching portfolio and the risky-asset portfolio.

He punctures many prevalent myths, including the common one that sponsors "must" invest in equities "in order to pay for the plan"; they might help pay for the plan, but they also might make it more expensive. He demonstrates useful new tools for making investment policy risk/return decisions.

The bottom line is that sponsors should not be afraid of mark-to-market, or economic accounting. It doesn't increase risk and costs but allows the sponsors to control and decrease risks and costs by supporting better benefit, contribution, and investment policies.

Where Are the Problems, and Where Are the Opportunities?

For a number of reasons, I have been interested in understanding defined benefit (DB) pension plans and improving their management for many, many years; I have devoted a lot of research to learning how pensions really work and figuring out the consequences of managing them using both traditional and newer techniques. I believe there is a lot to be gained by looking at pension management more closely than has been the habit in prior practice, and through the lens of modern portfolio theory, which has not been done to any great degree.

My approach is to look for the basic "finance facts" in the problem and to try to use as many conventional, generally accepted tools as I can to solve the investment-policy problem (and other pension-policy problems), avoiding the temptation to use complex analytical processes that don't tie to modern portfolio theory as has so often been done in the past.

But first, let's look at our current situation and provide some context for my underlying contention that managing these plans better is of critical societal importance.

Pension Funding Risk and the Trend Toward Defined Contribution Plans

Why is better integration of pension-funding liability into pension policy decisions so critical? Our failure to have done so, so far, has resulted in a much more volatile risk experience for plan sponsors than would have occurred if we had been more properly integrating the liability for all these years. This volatile risk experience—volatile funding ratios, volatile contribution levels, and volatile pension expense levels—is having a widespread and significant undesirable social impact: As a result of experiencing the downside of these risks, many sponsors are shutting down or threatening to shut down their DB plans.

In fact, defined benefit plans are in danger of extinction. A very large majority of the remaining active corporate plan sponsors are threatening to terminate their pension plans if we go to a mark-to-market accounting system. Of course, for better or for worse, mark-to-market accounting, properly done, is a synonym for economic accounting of the pension plan, and corporate sponsors fear that it will create too much additional risk and too much additional cost in the pension plan—risk and cost that they already feel to be too high. So in reaction to this perceived threat of further volatility, there is a trend forming, of sponsors excluding new employees from their DB plans, and maybe even excluding existing employees from further accruals. And in some cases sponsors are converting the plans entirely to defined contribution (DC) plans. That has already happened in the United Kingdom, where very few corporate plans and only some public plans remain. Of course, public employee DB plans normally lag corporate plans, but the danger is there for public plans also. And it is real.

Now to some a conversion to DC plans doesn't sound like a bad thing. But the fact is that defined contribution plans just don't meet most people's retirement needs, at least in the manner in which they are customarily operated today. There's really no better tool than a defined benefit pension plan for creating a fund that will be successful in spreading a portion of one's working life income over one's retirement years in sufficient dollar size to provide a meaningful standard of living beyond the time that it makes sense to keep working.

Defined contribution retirement plans aren't nearly so successful at this task. Dallas Salisbury, president and CEO of the Employee Benefit Research Institute (EBRI), has said that account balances for defined contribution plans today average only about $150,000 at time of retirement, and that the median—half above and half below—is around $50,000. Yes, only $50,000. And this isn't a data error; the highest comparable figure I've been able to find after looking at several sources is only about $66,000. That's not a fabulous retirement nest egg, if you'll allow the understatement.

There's only one practical[1] way to make sure that enough money is going to be available to provide a meaningful retirement benefit, to take advantage of things like the insurance principle and the value of life annuities, to spread out life span risk: That is with a defined benefit (DB) plan.

But today, only 22 percent or so of the people in the U.S. workforce are covered by defined benefit plans. That percentage is down substantially from ten or twenty years ago. And there's news every week, it seems, that some major plan—IBM's or another company's—is terminating some portion of its employees' future accruals under defined benefit plans.

But plan sponsors are getting bad advice. Mark-to-market will not really add risk, as the argument claims; it merely gets rid of some cosmetic accounting-smoothing opportunities that spread real risk over time so it can't be seen as clearly as it happens. So the very premise of the argument that supports shutting down DB plans is simply wrong. The risk there is the risk that is there already.

In fact, quite the opposite is true: Mark-to-market, or an economic view of the pension-fund liability, combined with surplus optimization to develop the pension investment policy, provide the tools through which these sponsors can control the risk in their plans, to levels well below that which they have been experiencing using historic risk control procedures. Ironically, mark-to-market is the path to a lower risk and cost DB plan future, not to a higher risk and cost future.

The misconception runs deep that the smoothing opportunities in the current accounting system control risk. Nothing is further from the truth. Risk comes from the interaction of the markets with the liability, which in turn comes from the plan's benefit policy (plus some other more minor forecasting risks), and it merely shows up in the accounting system—it isn't created, enhanced, reduced, or in any way controlled by the accounting system. Accounting systems record what happens; they don't change it. Even the "best" smoothing methods merely shift the period of reporting in the hope that future good experience will cover up recent bad experience.

A case in point is what happened in 2001 and 2002, when interest rates went down significantly. As a result, the pension liability went up in value much more than did the pension plans' asset portfolios—given that their exposure to bonds was (and still is today) quite small. And at the same time the equity markets had a very bad spell, driving total asset values down—and without a corresponding effect on the liability. While the accounting system "smoothed" some of this risk experience by spreading it over several periods, it didn't make it go away, and the result was that most U.S. plan sponsors, both private and public, went from very well-funded positions to underfunded or marginally funded positions, feeling the pinch severely.

This particular risk was there in 2002 because of the investment policies that were in place: small allocations to very-short-duration bond portfolios, and a large allocation to equities. This is very much unlike what we might call the liability portfolio, which has very long duration and very few equity-like characteristics. The liability is very much like a large all-bond portfolio. There is a great deal of mismatch between these two holdings, the liability and the assets, and this is the source of the unnecessary risk that made the 2002 experience so painful.

Clearly the interest-rate hedge between a long-duration liability and a small-dollar allocation to short-duration bonds, as is typical of today's pension-investment policies, is nearly nonexistent. Such a policy leaves the plan exposed to tremendous losses when rates decline. And under the conventional approaches to developing pension plan investment policies, plans have been driving equity percentages persistently upward over the last couple decades so that the average equity (and other risky asset) allocation is now approaching 75 percent—far higher than any equity-like component in the liability—and the total interest-rate exposure needed to match the liability has gone down to only 25 percent or so, and that is in bonds of quite short duration. While the higher equity allocation isn't unambiguously wrong (the reduced bond allocation is!), I doubt that many plan sponsors have a clear understanding of what this exposure means to their plan during periods when the markets are performing badly.

So what happened in 2001 and 2002 is perfectly foreseeable: Pension plans were unhedged to interest-rate risk; in addition, they were taking huge amounts of equity risk not related to anything in the liability. That's a lot of opportunity for the liability to go up dramatically while the assets go down dramatically, as happened. The plans' accounting systems, with all their smoothing tools, could not absorb the losses comfortably, even when spread over multiple accounting periods.

But regardless of the accounting, the risk was always there from the moment this investment policy was put in place. The accounting system didn't create the risk, and mark-to-market wouldn't have changed it. The investment policy created it by virtue of being so unlinked from the liability—that is, from being disconnected from the benefit policy.

The fairly safe conclusion is that the technology of the past—the traditional asset/liability study consisting of asset-only optimization followed by a stochastic Monte Carlo process—is a completely failed technology. It never did control risk, and we have a dramatic and recent, but far from unique, demonstration of its failure in 2001 and 2002.

Cost is at issue here as well as risk. Investment policy is the primary and best vehicle for controlling pension funding risk, for a given benefit policy. But the economic view of the liability will give management and labor excellent information about the true cost of each benefit feature being negotiated, insuring that the benefit policy chosen is one that the sponsor can and will be able to afford, thus controlling the total cost of the plan. How do benefit levels, and changes to benefit levels, affect the affordability of the plan for the sponsor and the acceptability of the plan for the employees?

And benefit design—*benefit policy*—can even have an impact on the types of risks that the sponsor takes on—which relates to my offhand reference, above, to certain forecasting errors that cannot be easily hedged in the markets. Can we design a DB plan with a liability that is more completely hedgeable with assets, by changing some of the benefit policies so that they have less opportunity for actuarial forecasting errors? For (a not necessarily popular) example, consider promising benefits based on each year's actual pay instead of on final pay, thus avoiding the risk of unforeseeable wage inflation?

Investment policy can dramatically help to reduce risk, through insightful liability hedging, and can contribute to the cost of the plan through thoughtful exposure to the premiums available for taking on market risk. At minimum the following questions should be answered by the investment policy:

- ❑ What are the hedgeable financial characteristics of the liability?
- ❑ How much do we allocate to bonds and other assets to hedge those characteristics? For what durations (establishing our "hedging beta" position)?
- ❑ How much do we allocate to equities and other risky-asset classes, beyond the minimum amount that our hedging decision requires (establishing our "surplus beta" position)?
- ❑ After the beta decisions are made, how do we incorporate active management into our investment policy? Few sponsors today seem willing to give up on their quest for alpha.

And of course, we're also concerned about *contribution policy*. Although I will argue that the expected present value of all future contributions is completely determined by benefit policy, the actual realized level, as well as the volatility, of required contributions is heavily a function of investment policy. Thus, higher allocations to equities don't reduce the present value of future contributions, but they may—if strong returns on the investment portfolio are realized over time—decrease the *actual*, as opposed to the expected, level of future contributions. And the level of benefit security enjoyed by the plan's participants is strongly affected by the sponsor's decision on how fast to make contributions. There is a fair amount of discretion—different "funding methods" have different timing, although at the end of the day they all need to fund the same benefit.

- ❑ How do specific candidates for investment policy affect contribution levels and volatility?
- ❑ Should contributions be biased to be paid earlier, or later?

My thesis is that the risks that have made plan sponsors feel like they need to shut down their DB pension plans can be brought largely under control, and in some scenarios *completely* under control, by using improved benefit policies to manage the size and the volatility characteristics of the liability, using improved approaches to investment policy to hedge the risk of the liability and to add additional return where the additional risk can be tolerated, and using improved contribution policies to make sure that the plan remains sensibly solvent at all times. Pension plan sponsorship doesn't have to be a risky proposition, nor does the cost need to be higher than planned and expected.

Defined benefit pension plans are good things, and we're better off as a society if more of our older people, rather than fewer, were to have these plans. We need to grow, not shrink, the portion of the population with defined benefit plans from its current level of only 22 percent. And we need to be "on a mission" to do so, with focus and intent, as we are already at a late point in the game.[2]

Pension Plan Management Policies

I've referred to three types of pension policy a number of times. Let's go through what I mean by each.

1. Benefit policy is the foundation: How big is the benefit? How is it determined? What is its total cost (which will be spread over the life of the plan) and the present value of all future benefit promises? Which portion of that present value is for current employees and

which portion for past employees? What about the present value of future benefits of this policy with respect to unhired future employees, and can the cost of those benefits be afforded in the future as a reasonable percentage of salaries (will a problem be developing over time)? What features of the benefits are affected by (are correlated with) market movements, and thus cause volatility to the present value of the liability that might be hedged? What sources of volatility are not hedgeable, being from forecast errors that bear no relationship (have no correlation) to the markets? The level of the present value of future benefits and the volatility and hedgeability of the liability that is based on these benefits drive much of the balance of the rest of our discussion.

2. Investment policy is about how the assets are invested. I make the case in this chapter that success for the investment policy requires first that whatever risk *can be avoided* through careful hedging of the liabilities with the assets *should be avoided.* Second, I argue that there is room for the thoughtful plan sponsor to make an effort to reduce future contribution requirements by investing the portfolio in assets that carry risk premiums (historically we've called them "equities," and even "equity-like assets") or that might earn positive alphas (active management). Overly *conservative* investment policies, without exposure to risky assets, miss out on fully taking advantage of investing the funds in something that earns more than the risk-free rate. But caution and balance is in order here, as overly *aggressive* investment policies can endanger the plan, if and when returns go badly negative.
3. Contribution policy is about the rate at which a sponsor sets aside funds to pay for promised benefits. In a very real sense there is only one question to answer regarding contribution policy: How do we spread the present value of unfunded future benefit obligations into contribution payments over time in such a way that all owed benefits are always funded? Interestingly, this is very closely tied to the question of establishing an appropriate economic measure of normal cost (that hasn't been clear in traditional actuarial approaches). Contribution policy must always tie the assets to the economic present value of the benefit policy, the liability, through some sense of accrual of benefits over time, and through a mandate to make up prior shortfalls as soon as is possible. In an ideal world, the contribution would be sufficient to make up any economic deficit relative to an economic "benefit security" measure of the liability at the end of each period (I'll define this term later). There is also an interaction between investment success and contribution levels. Under past

practice, investment success has been presumed ahead of the fact (the "expected return assumption"). Under the approach of this discussion, investment success has to be actually experienced, before it acts to reduce contributions. I'll show how this observation feeds a concern about the volatility of contributions back into the investment-policy decision (and even into the benefit policy decision).

We're going to focus most of our attention on the second element, investment policy, because the audience for this chapter is investment professionals. But it is very much worth noting that we can't avoid incorporating and addressing the other elements of pension policy—because they all interact with each other.

While "asset allocation policy" is, of course, the standard phrase to describe investment policy, I prefer the full term "pension investment policy" for its linguistic parallelism with the other two important pension policies. I'll use the terms interchangeably below.

So benefit policy, investment policy, and contribution policy are all like different sides of the same rock. To some extent we cannot talk about one without talking about the others. And the top side of the rock, the starting point for determining investment policy, has to be benefit policy, the present value of which is our pension liability, economically measured.

The Missing Factor: Benefit Policy and the Liability

Yet benefit policy and the liability that it generates has never been the starting point for determining investment policy in the past; rather it has been involved only as the "tail of the dog." Historically, asset allocation policy has been dominated by the actuarial practitioners, the professionals who calculate the valuation of the liability and determine contributions (and support the determination of pension expense). Their nearly universal practice has been to first do an asset-only optimization, from which a half dozen or so possible candidate mixes are chosen off the asset-only frontier without any influence from the liability whatsoever. It is only in a *second* stage that the candidate mixes are cranked through a very large Monte Carlo model that deals with how these candidate asset mixes might flow into and interact with the liability. This model creates accumulated benefit obligation (ABO) and projected benefit obligation (PBO) forecast ranges, contribution forecast ranges, and pension expense forecast ranges, over the next, say, ten years, for a given asset-only optimal investment policy interacting with the accounting rather than the economic version of the liability. That's what we've called an "asset-liability" study to date.

However, no matter what we called the study, the liability is obviously missing from the key first step, where the candidate mixes are determined, and it needs to be incorporated. Otherwise, how can we know that any of the candidate mixes provide any amount of hedging to the liability, much less an optimal amount of hedging? Furthermore, this liability needs to be the undistorted *economic* version of the liability, rather than the distorted accounting version. Without these changes, the second stage of the problem can only attempt to answer the question, "Which of these *particular*, but not especially well-chosen, candidate mixes is best?" But the right question to answer is, "Which mix, of all possible mixes, is best, given this liability?" Stated this way, it is clear that the right answer must involve some degree of hedging of the assets to the liability, a relationship that is completely absent using the traditional asset-liability study.

The observation that the liability needs to be incorporated, using a process known generally by the phrase "surplus optimization," goes way back to the early 1980s and even has its seeds in the 1970s with some of Jack Treynor's work (1976). Today, the buzzword is "liability-relative investing" or "liability-driven investing," as if this were some sort of a brilliant new observation. It may have in fact been brilliant when first observed, but it is not new. The elephant in the room has always been the liability, and unfortunately it's been consistently and persistently ignored. Surplus optimization is the technology of choice for incorporating it, and we'll talk about it in some detail.

The benefit of this approach over the traditional actuarial approach[3] is that integrating the liability into the determination of the proper mix is an idea at the core of investment finance theory, because the hedging that results helps to avoid taking uncompensated risks. It's not a novel idea; it's a very sensible approach to thinking about how to integrate the liability; none better have emerged that are practical.[4]

Managing the Economics—and Thus the Accounting

A helpful way to look at any pension plan is from the point of view of the student accountant's T account (see **FIGURE 3.1**). Let's discuss some aspects of a pension plan in this context. In particular, let's develop the notion of the economic liability.

The wealth of the plan is equal to the assets minus the liability; it is not just the assets. If the wealth of the plan is greatly diminished (deficits get larger or assets get smaller), the result is adverse consequences in terms of larger contributions, bigger balance sheet liability disclosures, and increased pension expense. Therefore, assets by themselves are not the portfolio of interest, but rather the portfolio of interest is the *assets minus the liabilities*, what we are calling the surplus (or deficit; the sign is unimportant to the concept). And that is what pension plan managers should focus on and optimize—through surplus optimization.

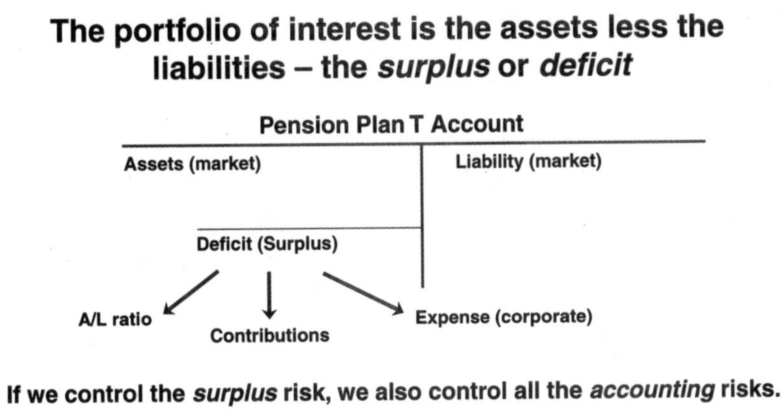

FIGURE **3.1** *An Accounting Student's T Account for the Pension Plan*

Source: Barclays Global Investors

If we think about the liability's economic characteristics just as we would do if it were an asset—its risks, its return, its correlations with items in the asset portfolio—we can determine investment policy by *optimizing* on the sum of the asset classes and the liability, the surplus (or deficit). Traditionally, managers have strived to maximize the expected return of the assets, taken alone, while controlling the risk to the assets, taken alone, before incorporating any liability inputs. For our "new" approach, surplus optimization, we can just rephrase this objective function: We maximize the growth rate of the surplus (equivalent to the shrinkage rate of the deficit), while controlling the risk to (volatility of) the growth rate of the surplus. In other words, we want the surplus growing as fast as possible (or the deficit shrinking as fast as possible), but not at a rate that requires a risk level to the surplus or deficit that we cannot tolerate. It is that simple. And all, repeat all, asset class mixes that come out of this effort will call for full liability hedging (within the limits of the availability of appropriately priced hedging instruments).

For these reasons it is important to look at the underlying true financial risk characteristics of the liability and to match them up with financial risk characteristics in the assets in a manner that supports this effort to hedge out as much risk as possible. We do this hedging *before* thinking about investing the assets more aggressively in the search for higher returns. But both the hedging decision and the risky-asset investment decision are integral parts of the surplus optimization process.

Let's discuss the economic nature of the liability some more. The liability, historically, has been viewed from an actuarial point of view rather than from a market value or economic point of view, and, of course, in actuarial practice the liability can take on many different values (some claim upwards of seventeen different values, although I cannot personally count quite that many!).

However, if we invoke the well-known principle called the "law of one price," we should quickly conclude that the liability has only one correct approach to valuation, and that it is economically grounded: In an efficient market, all identical goods will, and must, have only one price. This is a result of the fact that if there is more than one price, someone will be able to construct an arbitrage trade that will, when repeated aggressively, drive the market back to a single, common price. So it seems very unlikely that liability can really have seventeen truly different valuations![5]

Somewhere in all the valuation calculations—if we get rid of the smoothing and amortization gadgets traditionally used and discount the future benefit payments at appropriate market-determined discount rates—the liability has a *true* present value, the *economic liability*. This term, too, has been around in the literature as far back as a 1976 article by Jack Treynor, Patrick Regan, and William Priest Jr. That article came out as the Employee Retirement Income Security Act (ERISA) was being put into practice.[6] Yet in practice, even today, we tend to be focused on the actuarial versions of the liability, values that can't be compared on a level playing field to the clearly economic values of the assets themselves because of amortization rules, discount rate differences, and other differences.

The actuarial and accounting measures of the liability at best can be given credit only as "book values." Book values that vary from current market values aren't unusual and are a good place to make the point that needs making here. For example, there's nothing wrong with carrying real estate at book value, the common practice, and marking it to market only when we sell it. No one is fooled or misled; everyone making decisions about acquiring, selling, or managing the piece of property will do so by reference to its true economic value, not its book value.

A liability valuation on the books is just that: a book value. But this book value has a true market value somewhere inside it, as does the real property we just discussed; we just never in the past have stopped to look for the true value of the liability.

And the liability's true, or economic, value has true underlying volatility. It consists simply of a stream of cash flows going out into the future, and the streams of cash flows essentially constitute nothing more than a complicated long-term coupon bond—which also has volatility as interest rates change. And these liability "bonds" are not even all that complicated.

At least, they are not so complicated that they cannot be valued at market. And the liability's market risks, or volatilities; its expected return (or discount rate); and the correlations between it and other investable asset classes can all be understood in terms developable through conventional forms of financial analysis. Most of the actuarial Monte Carlo models and other big, complex models applied to this problem, however, attempt to manage and understand these interactions with simple brute force. We do not have to go that way; we can use modern portfolio theory to guide us, and in the process both simplify the solution and make it much more accurate.

There is another important observation here, relating to how we set up the assets to work closely with the liability, that is, to hedge it: *If we manage the economics of the pension plan, the accounting will surely follow.*

Just like a real estate value that stays at book for years but eventually goes on the books at market when the property is sold, the accounting always follows the economics, sooner or later. And thus sooner or later, and usually sooner, the economics of the liability do in fact flow into the accounting, no matter on what basis the accounting is actually figured. If the economics aren't managed well, and are too risky, then the accounting will be risky even through the obscuring lens of smoothing practices. If the economics are managed very well and most risks are successfully hedged, then the accounting will be very stable and predictable, with only mortality risk and a few other unhedgeable forecasting-error factors to cause volatility.

So *if we control the economic risks, we also control the actuarial and accounting risks.* Admittedly, the accounting can add a modest appearance of risk control with its smoothing gadgets, but these are cosmetic only. The real risk control happens on the economic side, through appropriate hedging of the assets with the liability, a process controlled through the surplus optimization technique.

The Level and Volatility of the Pension Surplus or Deficit Control All the Accounting Risks

Often (if not always!) lost in the pension risk control discussion is that the size and volatility of the economic deficit or surplus directly control all the accounting variables of interest, such as the funding or asset/liability ratio, contribution levels, and even pension expense levels (albeit more obliquely). This isn't apparent under conventional accounting rules, because it is obscured behind the various different measures of the liability that are used in the different accounting statements and behind the smoothing mechanisms and other artificialities of today's accounting standards. But it is nonetheless the fact.

Focusing on contributions for the moment, and to make my point, it is commonly believed that they are substantially (although not completely) independent of investment experience. But I can show that the economically required and sensible contribution is a perfect function of the economic deficit. And under the principle that the accounting follows the economics, if the economically required contribution is a function of the economic deficit, then the accounting contribution is also—sooner or later.

Let's build the simplest possible relevant example: If we know that we will owe a single payment liability in fifteen years that we could cover completely and without risk by investing in a Treasury bond worth $10 today (that is, our liability is truly worth $10; we just showed how to find the correct discount rate!), and our assets are worth only $6 today, how big should our contribution be? Any of our teenage children would know without hesitation that the answer is $4; one has to satisfy the current deficit in order to secure ultimate payment of the obligation. This is the economic, or true, required contribution for this stone-simple pension plan analog. This contribution could maintain the liability in a fully funded, totally safe manner, with no default risk if it is invested in the riskless asset (there are other investment choices, of course, but I'll not explore them now).

But if we ask the actuary the same question, we can imagine hearing him explain something very different, if he was thinking in the DB pension plan context: "Well, wait just a minute. If we assume that your investments will earn higher than risk-free rates because we choose to invest in equities, then we can discount your liability at that higher rate of return—which makes the liability worth only, let's see, $7, not $10! So we then have a deficit, and thus a contribution, of only $1!" A pause, then, "But wait, I can help you more: You don't have to pay the whole dollar now; we can amortize it over, let's say, thirty years, so your actual contribution today is only about 3.33 cents!"

That is how "minimum required" contributions have been calculated historically: The rules allow an artificially high discount rate, the expected return on assets, which most of the time operates to make the liability smaller. And if there is still a deficit even then, it is amortized over a very long period of time. This contribution amount is completely divorced from the reality of the economic contribution; thus the required contribution is in fact divorced from any real intent to fund the plan. (The IRS establishes maximum contribution rules, which add an upside boundary framing the other end of the range from this minimum contribution boundary; the good news is that many [but not all] plan sponsors take advantage of the guidance of thoughtful actuaries to provide better funding than the minimum.)

Note that this example "plan," economically speaking, is in deficit after the minimum required contribution nearly as much as it was before the contribution. The true liability is really \$10; the few pennies of contribution don't improve solvency materially.

This type of wishful calculation ignores an insight that is key to understanding pension finance and to seeing through the murk of current standard practices. Let me state it in its most blindingly obvious form as a general axiom, and then as a corollary to make it more relevant to real life:

> **Axiom:** At the time of initiation of a new plan, the economic present value of all future contributions is and must be equal to the economic present value of all future benefit payments.
>
> **Corollary:** For an existing plan, the economic present value of future contributions for benefits already economically earned (but not yet paid) is and must be equal to the economic present value of all future benefit payments, plus (minus) any current deficit (surplus) between this latter value and assets already on hand.

The axiom is a tautology and must be taken as true. The only difference in the corollary is that I introduced a sense of economic accrual of benefits into the language and incorporated ending period surpluses or deficits since there will no doubt have been prior contributions. Over time, the sum of all the annual contributions must be enough to pay for the benefits promised; no one year's contribution can be looked at in isolation.

Regardless of obviousness, these observations have not informed most contribution discussions that I have ever sat through, and I doubt that they've come up in many (or any) others. More typically, such decisions are made as if this year's contribution amount stands on its own; I've never heard an actuary make the remark (although no doubt it has happened) that a dollar of contribution avoided this year will need to be made up, with interest, in future years!

My point is that we need this type of economically informed observation in every pension-oriented discussion around each of the accounting variables of concern. For example, we learn here that if we postpone an economically required contribution by taking advantage of minimum contribution calculations, the balance of the economically required contribution doesn't go away or disappear. It patiently waits for us to pay it later—with interest. A contribution smaller than the economically required contribution—the deficit between assets and the economic liability—can be interpreted as meaning that a portion of today's cost of labor is being "borrowed." This portion is deferred to tomorrow's generations of shareholders and must be borne by tomorrow's profits if there are any—or if there aren't, defaulted pensioners will experience it as a defaulted pension promise, and the sponsor's shareholders as a loss of equity.

This is serious stuff. Unpaid prior year labor costs really can get so large that they can no longer be paid at all. Take United Airlines' history, for example: They deferred their economically required contributions year after year, and eventually the deficit got so large that even the minimum required contributions were too large to be paid from ordinary corporate cash flows. The plan, and the company, tumbled to the ground, broken. The labor force lost much of the value of the plan, and the shareholders lost most of their equity.

There is change happening on this front, moving contribution calculations closer to economic levels, at least for corporate plans. Historically, the actuarial discount rates used to determine contributions and other accounting entries were uniformly based on expected asset returns, which tended to understate the true liability substantially (consistent with my simple example, above). The correct rate from well-proven finance theory would be a risk-free rate (or more precisely a curve of risk-free rates for different liability payment horizons). Although it has caused much grumbling, the Pension Protection Act of 2006 changed the discount rate for determining the liability when making required contribution calculations to a rate similar to that used on the balance sheet, and it also shortened the amortization period. This is a change in the right direction (although the exceptions to these rules that have been authorized in certain troubled industries may cause troubling experiences in years to come).[7]

Public employee pension plans have issues here, still, not being subject to the same regulatory frameworks as corporate plans. Because all discount rates in public plans are still based on the expected return on assets rather than on the economic discount rate, the stated liabilities of public plans are still heavily *under*stated—at the extremes by more than half, not just when they calculate contributions but also when they report their liability's size and their funding adequacy. By using very high discount rates based on high-equity (and completely unhedged) investment policies, public plans are, in effect, deferring to future taxpayers a large portion of the payments needed to provide the stated benefits with security over time. Public plans are with few exceptions economically underfunded, and often are getting more so.

Again, when we control the risk to the economic surplus, we control the risk to the accounting surplus. And since the economically required contribution is directly a function of the economic deficit or surplus, if the risk to the economic surplus is controlled, then it should be self-evident that the risk to both the economic and the accounting version of the required contribution is controlled as well. *Investment policy can control contribution volatility.*

So, one of the most important things that we can do to control the various accounting risks is to control the economic risks of the surplus.

I think it is obvious enough that this controls funding ratio volatility; we've discussed in depth how it controls contribution volatility, and at another time I can show how it controls pension expense volatility.

Surplus Optimization

- *Controlling surplus beta* means controlling the net market risk exposure of the assets, relative to the liabilities:
  - First, hedge the liability (see *duration matching*, below), and then consider taking market risk over and above—that is, "surplus beta."
  - How much market risk do we want to take? Market risk is rewarded, but only in expectation—so it *is* risky!
- *Duration matching* means controlling the interest rate mismatch between the assets and the liabilities, that is, "surplus duration." It is the most important part of hedging the liability, particularly when the liability is all in a single currency. This is the hedging referred to in the "controlling surplus beta" discussion, above.
  - *Duration* is a measure of how a financial asset or liability changes in value when interest rates change.
  - Pension liabilities have at least two primary durations: one for *inflation* sensitivity, and one for *real interest-rate* sensitivity.
  - Think of the *net* surplus durations between the assets and liabilities as just factor betas—surplus beta—for explaining surplus changes with rate changes: If the factors (durations) of the assets are set up to match the factor betas (durations) of the liabilities, we have a perfect hedge, and we can proceed to considering adding surplus beta, as explained above.

Calculating Surplus Efficient Frontiers

Surplus Optimization

> The goal of asset allocation analysis should be stated in terms of surplus. The objective is to maximize the risk-adjusted future value of the surplus.
>
> —William F. Sharpe in *Asset Allocation* (1990)

William Sharpe has been one of the longstanding voices advocating surplus optimization approaches: maximizing the growth rate of the surplus (shrinking the deficit) while controlling the risk or volatility of the growth rate of the surplus (deficit). Of course, when we say "surplus," we mean it in the very general sense of the net of assets less the economic liability, regardless of whether the plan is in positive or negative surplus—to an economist a deficit is just a negative surplus—so you won't hear the term "deficit optimization"!

In the 1980s, we first started seeing references to surplus optimization in the literature. I recall Roger Ibbotson teaching it to me one afternoon in about 1987, in connection with consulting work he and I were doing for New York Life and Metropolitan Life Insurance Co. (with respect to their general account and their liabilities). Also in that time frame, Martin Leibowitz wrote several pieces that discussed surplus optimization (1987, 1988, 1991; see collected works 1992), as did Robert Arnott and Peter Bernstein (1988; my favorite!). There were other usages of the term in that time, by others. Maybe someone knows who really first invented "surplus optimization," but the concept seems to have just emerged out of the discussion of investment policy during that time, with no single apparent source. By 1990, two articles by Sharpe and Lawrence Tint and another, by Sharpe alone, advocated a new and improved way of calculating the surplus frontier, and these articles did generate some wide notice for the concept, especially because of the prominence of their primary author.

Yet, even though the concept and the methods were very well established as far back as 1990, today very few asset liability studies are conducted using surplus optimization. My belief is that this is because the conventional view of the liability—a smoothed, actuarial, and accounting view, with an artificially determined discount rate—never fit comfortably into the surplus optimization framework. And it shouldn't have, at least not in that form. The expected returns and risks of an asset are neither smoothed nor artificial, and to try to mathematically relate them to smoothed and artificial liability values didn't and doesn't make sense. Surplus optimization can only be done using an economic measure of the liability.

Conceptualizing Surplus Optimization: The Four- (or Maybe Five-!) Fund Theorem

Surplus optimization can be thought of in a two-fund theorem sort of way, or more properly in a three- (or four- or five-) fund theorem sort of a way! Recall that the classic, asset-only, two-fund theorem of Tobin (1958), and later of Sharpe's capital asset pricing model (CAPM) (1964), showed that all investment policies were simple combinations of the risk-free asset (usually taken to be cash) and the risky-asset portfolio, and that all points on the efficient frontier (if unconstrained, it is congruent with the capital market line) could be had by various long and short combinations of those two assets.

Surplus optimization has a related result, allowing any liability-relative investment policy to be expressed as the sum of a number of specific funds. The first component, or fund, is cash, Tobin's original risk-free asset. The second fund represents the horizon premium of the equivalent long-term bond fund that matches the interest-rate risks in the bond-like liability (by matching the dual dollar durations of the liability with those of the assets; additional duration and risk factors could be employed as well). Together with cash, this "liability-matching portfolio" fund is the risk-free asset wherever there is a liability. Together they also represent the minimum surplus variance portfolio, a hedging portfolio that takes the interest-rate risk out of the plan.[8]

The third portfolio, or fund, is the risky-asset portfolio, just as it is in the classic asset-only two-fund theorem. The risky-asset portfolio provides the "surplus beta," or equilibrium policy mix, for the assets of the plan.

The fourth portfolio would be the "alpha portfolio," which attempts to add value through active management.

And a fifth portfolio could be a currency portfolio, designed to convert the assets to currency exposures that hedge the currency exposures inherent in the liability (any currency "bets" beyond this policy currency exposure are more properly considered as part of the alpha portfolio). This portfolio isn't normally much of an issue in a U.S. plan, but where it is important, we might alternatively consider it as a component of the first, liability-matching portfolio rather than as the "fifth fund." One might more generally think of currencies merely as a factor exposure in the liability, which could be matched with a parallel factor exposure in the assets; I'll default to that view.

Every pension investment policy is the sum of these portfolios, but today the first one, the liability-matching portfolio, is incompletely considered. A sponsor dramatically improves the risk-return relationships driven by its investment policy when it first brings the liability fully into the process. Once the decision to hedge the liability is considered, it should thereafter be automatic and require little further discussion.[9] It costs nothing in expected return, and substantially decreases risk. And avoiding uncompensated risks should be one of the first rules of portfolio construction.

The "surplus beta," or market risk exposure, decision involved in the trade-off between the risky-asset portfolio and the risk-free-asset portfolio has to do not so much with hedging the liability but more with deciding how to gain the desired trade-off of expected return for risk. These two portfolios will trade off against each other to represent the net exposure to the risky-asset portfolio with its attendant risk premiums; the weights of the risky-asset portfolio and of cash together represent one decision, as to hold less cash (to short more cash) implies that one can hold more risky assets. This decision, once made, should reflect the sponsor's tolerance for market risk—as for any other investor, an investor with a liability really only has to answer one question, and that is a question about its tolerance for this risk.

And it is apparent enough that the active portfolio should also reflect the sponsor's aggressiveness and tolerance for *active* risk, or alpha risk.

Where Is the Money to Buy All These Funds?

We need to explore how one might accomplish holding both a hedging portfolio and a risky-asset portfolio (how to hold an alpha portfolio will immediately follow from the same logic).

There is a bit of a problem at first blush that we need to get past in order to proceed: Let's say that we have an economic liability of $1,000 and assets of $1,000. If we use the assets to acquire a hedging portfolio of physical bonds, then there are no assets left over with which to purchase a risky-asset portfolio (or a hedge fund, or . . .).

But wait, we have options. We could invest the entire portfolio in the physical liability-matching assets and then simultaneously use that portfolio as security to borrow cash and purchase physical risky-asset positions; this is just a slight step away from Tobin's and Sharpe's versions, in that they both started with a positive cash position, and this option appears to start with a zero *net* cash position.[10]

Or, we could hold the entire portfolio in cash, and obtain all of our liability-matching positions as well as our risky-asset positions using a combination of interest-rate derivatives and S&P 500 futures. Or we could mix and match.

In any event, all that is required is that one separate the cash or risk-free-asset component of returns from the horizon risk premia of the bond portfolio and the equity and equity-like risk premia of the risky-asset portfolio, which frees the mind to the use of various derivatives and allows the desired exposures to be purchased without regard to traditional physicals-only limitations. In past pension investment-policy practice we always thought of our investment policy in terms of such a physicals-only asset portfolio; but that is seldom going to be practical in a more fully engineered, surplus-optimization-based investment policy. Derivatives are going to be required somewhere in the portfolio if risky-asset positions are going to be used.

In practice, the latter approach of mixing and matching is what will work; the former was just to make a point. One needn't—and couldn't—hold the entire portfolio in cash, nor borrow all the cash for the risky-asset positions, nor hold all the exposures in derivatives. A mix of these approaches would usually be appropriate, a mix that allows the plan to hold all the exposures it needs. If derivatives will do the job, use them to preserve cash. If not, then use the cash.

We will almost certainly find ourselves holding bond and risky-asset positions that in sum are equivalent to physical positions that are much larger than the worth of the assets themselves. Is this "leverage" in some form that is inconsistent with fiduciary requirements? Of course not. Yes, more than 100 percent of the portfolio will be invested, so in some trivial sense there is in fact leverage. But the bond derivatives are being used to hedge away all or most of the interest-rate risk in the liability, and the risky-asset derivatives are simply being used to seek an intentionally chosen exposure in the hope of realizing the equity risk premium. This latter will certainly be less than 100 percent of the portfolio, and my expectation is that it will be well less than today's 70 percent average. These holdings are all for a proper, risk-controlled purpose, and are quite consistent with fiduciary purposes, rather than violative of them. When we picture this portfolio in factor space, it is only 100 percent invested, not leveraged at all.

Defining Surplus Returns Formally

FIGURE 3.2 shows a very simple development of the mathematical form for surplus return. The first line consists of a tautological equivalence: Assets at time zero (A_0) times the return of surplus during the period of interest, defined in terms of assets ($R_{S(A)}$), has to equal the beginning assets (A_0) times the return of the assets during the period (R_A) minus the beginning liabilities (L_0) times the return of the liabilities (R_L).

We can set up the following equation to track changes in surplus wealth (RHS) expressed by reference to the assets:

$$A_0 \cdot R_{S(A)} = A_0 \cdot R_A - L_0 \cdot R_L$$

This defines a *surplus return* as:

$$R_{S(A)} = R_A - \frac{L_0}{A_0} \cdot R_L$$

FIGURE 3.2 *Defining Surplus Return*

Source: Barclays Global Investors

To derive a definition of surplus return from this, we divide both sides through by A_0. The return of the surplus is the return of the assets (R_A) minus a leverage factor (L_0/A_0) times the return of the liability (R_L) (the leverage factor simply corrects for inequalities in size between the assets and the liabilities). So, surplus return, the net return of the combined assets and liabilities, correctly tracks changes in the plan's wealth. This definition and the alternatives[11] are all good general definitions of surplus return.

Modeling the Economic Liability

So, what expected return estimate do we use for the liability in this definition when conducting forward-looking surplus optimization? If we recognize that the liability is in many ways very much like a bond, the question will be, What kind of bond or bonds are needed to mimic the liability, and what would be the expected return of such a portfolio of bonds? Basically, as discussed earlier, the economic liability can be described as a laddered combination of real and nominal bonds, all risk-free to the extent that the plan is well funded on an economic basis.

Some risks in the liability are not market risks, and so are not hedgeable with market instruments. There's mortality risk, for one: The fact that people tend to live longer than their assumed expectancy tends to make the liability larger. Various other actuarial gains and losses arising from misestimation (ages of retirement, likelihood of early departure from the company, the probability that there will be a surviving spouse, the final pay at time of retirement) show up, year after year.

The fact that we can't hedge these risks is because they are uncorrelated to the markets—so they are alphas in the technical, regression sense of the term. One must be careful when proposing to assume that these liability alphas—unlike alphas derived from an attempt to manage funds actively—average to a mean of zero (in expectation). Because of some persistent biases in estimation of the factors mentioned above, these alphas probably are not mean zero, although in an ideal world they would be. For instance, because today's life expectancy tables tend to underestimate longevity increases, mortality risk turns out for many plans to mean that the liability has been persistently underestimated and as a result pension expense and contributions have been persistently higher than they would be if the tables had been fairly estimated.

We can incorporate these liability alphas into the calculation of surplus return, but we have to recognize that even if we do, we cannot do anything to hedge them; there are no investable opposing assets. The asset alphas from active management do not hedge the liability alphas, of course, as they tend almost definitionally to be uncorrelated with the liability alphas.

Modeling the Economic Liability

1. Use best estimates of all variables in estimating future benefit payments.
   - ❑ Include the present value of all foreseeable benefits, including newly awarded benefits and fairly expected COLAs.
   - ❑ No "artificial" assumptions for expected inflation, population growth rate, etc.
2. Use market-related discount rate appropriate to the liability.
   - ❑ We only care about the liability's market-related return and risk characteristics, for asset allocation purposes.
3. Select the measure of the liability you are interested in.
   - ❑ Standard practice today is to solely look at some small measure, such as the ABO.
   - ❑ My preference would be to use a measure well-oriented to protecting the security of benefits, perhaps a PBO or a similar instrument.
4. Match the dual durations of the assets to the liability, by adjusting the bond portfolio (requires coordination with surplus optimization).
5. The economic liability isn't a new idea, but it has been used so little that it often feels like one.
   - ❑ Read Treynor, Regan, and Priest (1976), Bookstaber and Gold (1988), Mulvey (1989).

Source: Barclays Global Investors

And the betas on the asset side, of course, again by definition—by construction, really—are not correlated with any alphas. So, in some sense, the liability alphas present no problem,[12] and we can ignore them. However, if we really want to see a total risk picture or a total liability growth rate picture, we should include them in our calculations. We can also make a decision about whether to include the liability alpha effects in any output charts, which can be drawn with or without them. (See **FIGURE 3.3**.)

For my own work, I use a fairly simple factor model of liability returns that includes just the factors for the correlation structure between bonds and stocks (the big ones are inflation duration and real interest rate duration; for U.S. sponsors currencies are not a factor that we have been asked to include yet). These must all be market factors; we are trying to express

$$R_L = R_F + \beta_L \mu_Q + \alpha_L$$

No real difference from assets—the liability is an asset to *someone* and can be described in a multifactor CAPM model.

Beta risks are dominated by bonds, inflation-linked bonds.

- Possibly some equities in larger definitions of liability

Alpha risks in the liability are sponsor-specific:

- Can't be hedged: "No solution, no problem"
- Examples: Mortality risk; benefit decisions not related to market decisions; fixed COLAs; fixed-crediting rate premiums on cash balance plans (bonds plus 2%); etc.
- Can be managed, but not through investment policy

Only beta risk matters to a liability-relative asset allocation solution.

Expected Return = Discount Rate = Cost of Capital

FIGURE 3.3 *Modeling Economic Liability*

Source: Barclays Global Investors

the liability in terms that can be hedged by assets. And in turn, I like to look at assets using factors that I find in the liability, trying to maximize the factors in common. Equities, for example, can be viewed using a three-factor model: that is, inflation duration, real-rate duration, and the "other equity-risk-premium" factor. Highlighting these common factors provides an insight into how equities do, and do not, hedge the portfolio. The basic focus is to control the beta risk between the assets and the liabilities; so one's preferred factor models should be built with this need in mind, finding as many common factors as are potentially useful.

Because the liability is essentially a fixed-income instrument, the explanatory power in a relationship to equities is going to be relatively low (other equity-risk-premium risk dominates a regression). So we can no doubt do better than simple two-factor and three-factor models, but the simple models do a pretty good job of satisfying the 70/30 or 80/20 rule.

Surplus Optimization

We defined the expected return of the surplus, above, in terms of asset and liability returns. As discussed, asset—and liability—expected returns can be further broken down into their components of the risk-free rate, of beta (or betas) times the risk premium, and of alpha—for both asset and liability total returns.

$$R_A = R_F + \beta_A r_Q + \alpha_A$$
$$R_L = R_F + \beta_L r_Q + \alpha_L$$

In this notation, a capital R is an expected total return, and a lower case r is an expected excess return over the risk-free rate. Subscript Q refers to portfolio Q, the world market portfolio of risky assets, so that r_Q is the equilibrium expected excess return (risk premium) of the world market portfolio of risky assets (a useful simplification, but in practice we'll break the beta factors down more finely). Subscripts A and L refer to the assets and the liabilities, respectively. I express beta here as if it were a classic single factor beta, for algebraic and presentation simplicity; in practice I express this as a vector-matrix product of holdings and factor exposures (multiple betas) across the available asset classes, although one that is macroconsistent with portfolio Q.

If these are the expected returns for assets and liabilities, then our definition of the return of the surplus, above, needs to be fleshed out in greater detail to reflect these important subcomponents of return. First, we have the general form of surplus return (from above):

$$R_{S(A)} = R_A - \frac{L_0}{A_0} R_L$$

We can fully populate this equation with our more detailed return terms:

$$R_{S(A)} = (R_F + \beta_A r_Q + \alpha_A) - \frac{L_0}{A_0}(R_F + \beta_L r_Q + \alpha_L)$$

And then, reorganizing to collect like terms, we get:

$$R_{S(A)} = \underbrace{\left(1 - \frac{L_0}{A_0}\right) R_F}_{\text{Cash}} + \underbrace{\left(\beta_A r_Q - \frac{L_0}{A_0}\beta_L r_Q\right)}_{\text{Surplus Beta(s)}} + \underbrace{\left(\alpha_A - \frac{L_0}{A_0}\alpha_L\right)}_{\text{Alphas}}$$

Fine so far. We need a utility function if we are going to set up an optimization. The general aim is to maximize the utility of the surplus (U_S):

$$Max\,(U_S) = R_S - \lambda_S \sigma_S^2$$

We want to maximize the utility of the surplus, defined as the expected total return of the surplus less the product of the total variance of the surplus times a risk aversion term, lambda, that converts this variance into a return-equivalent risk penalty. We optimize by varying the amount of exposure to the holdings of risky assets that comprise the world market portfolio until utility is maximized. This will simultaneously vary the expected total return across the assets (and thus the net return of the surplus) and the total risk of the assets (and thus the net risk of the surplus). Of course, the liability doesn't

Locating the Two Beta-Related Funds

The surplus beta term in the fully populated form of the surplus return is $\beta_{S(A)} = \beta_A - \frac{L_0}{A_0}\beta_L$. We can think of β_A as composed of the betas for the liability-hedging portfolio and for the risky-asset portfolio (of equities and other assets having a risk premium); that is, $\beta_A = \beta_{LHP} + \beta_{RAP}$. In such a case, it must be true that the hedging portfolio's beta must equal the liability's beta after adjustment for their relative valuations, $\beta_{LHP} = \frac{L_0}{A_0}\beta_L$, as the hedging portfolio by construction must offset the liability's beta or betas (in the ideal circumstance in which the right hedging instruments are available and appropriately priced). Otherwise, the optimizer will not have minimized surplus risk at each level of surplus return.

As a result, we can say that surplus beta reduces simply to the beta of the risky-asset portfolio:

$$\beta_{S(A)} = \beta_A - \frac{L_0}{A_0}\beta_L = \cancel{\beta_{LHP}} + \beta_{RAP} - \cancel{\frac{L_0}{A_0}\beta_L}$$
$$= \beta_{RAP}$$

We don't literally reduce our math to these terms, because it is common for the hedging instruments to *not* be fully available or fairly priced, and we have to be able to find the optimal solution even when it is less than perfect. So in practice we retain the granular detail.

The point is that we do in fact have two beta funds in surplus optimization, the liability-hedging portfolio, with its long-duration interest-rate factor betas, and the risky-asset portfolio with many equity-like betas.

change; it is a constant. For a given risk aversion (lambda), we will find one, and only one, optimal set of holdings of these asset classes that will maximize surplus utility; it will always include the best possible hedging portfolio.

I just showed the expansion of the term R_S that we can use to populate this utility function; I won't trouble the reader with the slightly more difficult expansion of the risk term σ_S^2. But when we do expand both and insert them into the utility function and then do some simplifying to keep the moving parts down to a relatively small handful, we get the following form of surplus utility, with each portion labeled:

$$Max\,(U_S) = \underbrace{\left(1 - \frac{L_0}{A_0}\right)R_F}_{\text{Cash}} + \underbrace{\beta_S r_Q - \lambda_\beta \beta_S^2 \sigma_Q^2}_{\text{Surplus Beta Utility}}$$

$$\underbrace{+\left(\alpha_A - \frac{L_0}{A_0}\alpha_L\right) - \lambda_\omega\left(\omega_A^2 - 2\frac{L_0}{A_0}\omega_{A,L} + \left(\frac{L_0}{A_0}\right)^2 \omega_L^2\right)}_{\text{Alpha Utility}}$$

Here, surplus beta has the logical meaning $\beta_S = \beta_A - \frac{L_0}{A_0}\beta_L$, and we further decompose surplus lambda, λ_S, into two terms, a surplus lambda for beta risk and one for omega risk, λ_ω (omega risk is the risk associated with alphas, or residuals). These might or might not have different values, but that is another discussion.

In this discussion, we're emphasizing the beta aspects at the expense, perhaps, of a full discussion of the alpha aspects. For readers interested in the most complicated piece, the long third line describing alpha utility, see Waring (2004b).

Note that there is a risk-free-rate component of utility and that it might be positive or negative, depending on whether the plan is overfunded or underfunded. This is important for underfunded plans, because the negative cash return has to be made up from contributions or other asset returns or from somewhere else, if the plan is to be kept from trending further into deficit at this negative rate. This shows that, in effect, a sponsor is always paying interest on any underfunding! You don't save on financing costs by putting off contributions, except perhaps to the extent of the default premium that one is required to pay. And I could show that you don't avoid it either; the labor force is implicitly charging the sponsor for it.

Note that the risk-free-rate component of utility does not change with asset allocation policy; it is a constant, invariant to different investment policies. This reinforces my earlier point that we can obtain any combination of the liability-matching portfolio and the risky-asset portfolio that is desired (while there are no limitations in theory, of course there are in practice).

The key to investment policy, then, is to acknowledge that the best policy will hold a liability-matching portfolio plus a risky-asset portfolio that is bigger or smaller depending on aversion to surplus risk. At one extreme, with a very large aversion to surplus risk, we know that we could simply hold asset betas that are identical to the liability's betas, the liability-hedging portfolio, with no holding of other risky assets whatsoever. This will give us a zero surplus beta risk and a zero surplus beta return. (There is no hope that the investments will help pay for the plan beyond covering the discount rate, but on the other hand they won't make it more expensive, either.) If we want to go further than this, taking on some market risk in the search for equity risk premiums, we can choose a lambda that gives us a positive surplus beta. In this case we will have an expected return with a positive surplus beta—but we will also have an appropriate amount of surplus beta risk.

Cash Flow Matching

Sometimes people do "cash flow matching" as a crude way to create what seems to be the minimum-surplus-variance portfolio or liability-matching portfolio. Because we cannot match the long-distant future cash flows (there are no 60-year bonds), the approach has its limitations; there are additional limitations when the plan is underfunded (there isn't enough cash!). In concept and in spirit, however, it is an excellent way of trying to capture that kind of portfolio.

But cash flow matching can't readily go to the next level: It has no easy means of contemplating holding equities or other risky assets along with the liability-hedging portfolio, implementing an investment policy that includes an allocation to risky assets in a theoretically consistent and appropriate form. For all three of these reasons, cash-flow matching is not a very effective tool for investment policy for pensions, at least today.

A Case Study in Surplus Asset Allocation

The facts in this case study are real, but they have been well-disguised to protect the confidentiality of the sponsor.

The Sponsor's Current Policy, in Asset-Only Space

FIGURE 3.4 shows a traditional asset-only efficient frontier for a large plan sponsor, and **FIGURE 3.5** shows the details of the current policy that came from that efficient frontier.

The then-current policy for this sponsor plots neatly, right on top of the asset-only frontier. This sponsor's work, in an asset-only context, was perfectly good. We might argue with the aggressiveness of its risk-return decision—about 75 percent equity—but it gets credit for having chosen a portfolio that is efficient in the context in which it chose to look at the problem.

But it is this context that is most troublesome: It was an asset-only process. The liability, the present value of the benefit policy, needed to be incorporated into the decision. And it was not.

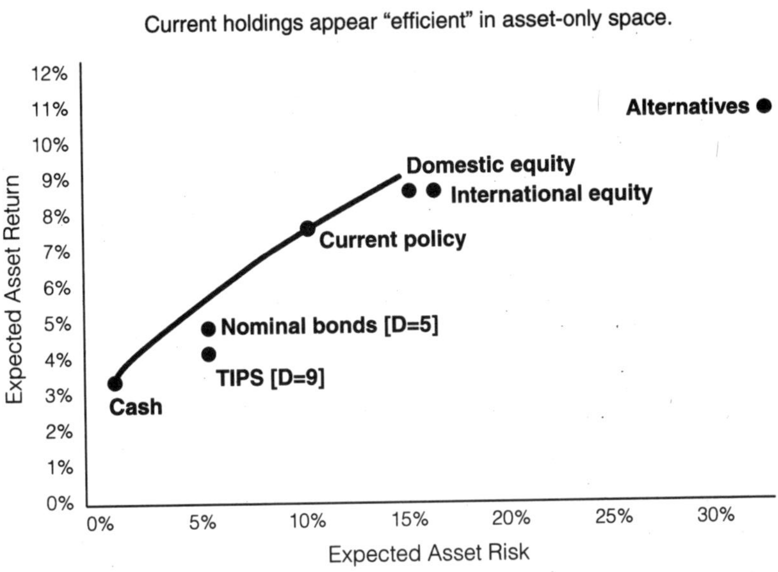

FIGURE 3.4 *Examining the Sponsor's Existing Investment Policy Through the Asset-Only Lens*

Source: Barclays Global Investors

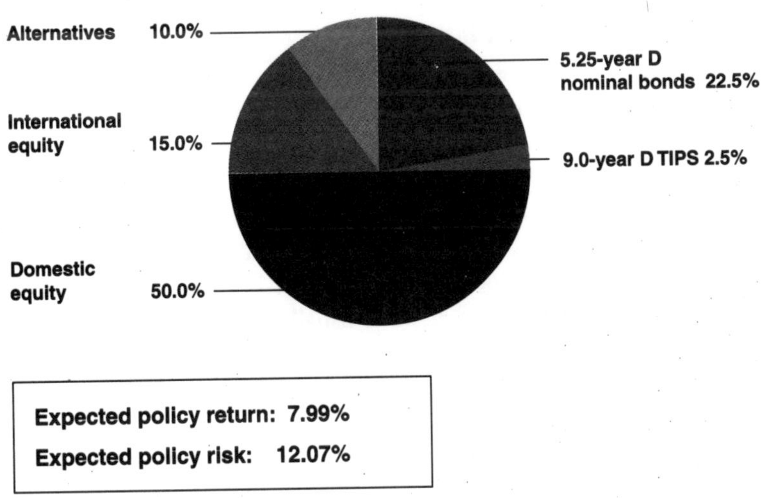

FIGURE 3.5 *Current Policy Detail*

Source: Barclays Global Investors

Modeling the Liability in Practice

To model the betas of the typical U.S. sponsor's liability, we need to use at least a two-factor model, with real interest rates and inflation components. We can imagine other factors—perhaps convexity or yield curve twist, or (especially for multinational sponsors) even currencies. But the big two are real rates and inflation.

We could use nominal rates, which combine real interest rates and inflation rates, but this would be quite imprecise. Wage inflation between today and the date a given employee will retire will have a direct impact on his or her final pay and thus on benefit levels. Since wage inflation is tightly (but not perfectly) connected to consumer price index (CPI) inflation, we can capture much of this risk by evaluating the inflation duration of the liability. Mathematically, in the numerator of the pricing equation, there is some inflation, and this numerator effect offsets some of the inflation that is always present in the discount rate in the denominator. The consequence is that inflation duration is typically lower than real-rate duration in most plans. And it can get very low if there are automatic cost of living allowances based on CPI incorporated into the post-retirement benefit payout period (as for many public employee retirement plans). The difference in sensitivity of the liability to real and inflation rate changes mandates that we decompose nominal rates into these components. (See **FIGURE 3.6.**)

Calculating Liability Durations

When asked for the duration of the liability, an actuary gives us a number like 15 or 20 and asserts that it is a nominal duration because he or she just changed the discount rate by a small percentage, recalculated the value, and looked at the percentage change in the value. However, if we dig into the math, what the actuary gave us was actually a real-rate duration: that is, the duration with respect to changes in the real rate, not the nominal rate. The duration figure does not consider the inflation effect I just described in the numerator since there is usually not any real interest-rate term in the numerator—and only the denominator was changed. The logical conclusion is that this purportedly nominal duration is in reality a real-rate duration. In fact, I can readily show that there is no proper partial derivative of the pension-liability pricing formula taken with respect to the nominal rate *wherever there is any kind of inflation in the numerator*. The conclusion is that there is no proper *nominal* duration for a pension liability; it simply doesn't exist.

But one can ask the actuary to calculate the real-rate duration specifically, and to also calculate the inflation duration specifically. I have a

The liability has two separate durations, not a single, nominal duration.[1]

- Real interest rate duration (typically long, 12 to 25 years)
- Inflation duration (typically less than 10 years; approaches zero if COLA)
- The MSV portfolio, or "hedge portfolio," is mostly bonds.

The assets should reflect a similar dual duration pair as the liability.[2]

- Including a measure for the durations of equities
  - Durations of equities are "loose," but quantifiable.
  - The good news is that equities can be included in a duration-matching solution, unlike traditional duration matching.
- The solution is a *total portfolio* duration solution.
- But it is controlled by setting the TIPS and nominal bond allocations and durations.[3]

1. Goodman and Marshall, in Arnott and Fabozzi, op. *Asset Allocation*, Probus 1998.
2. Leibowitz, "Total Portfolio Duration." *Financial Analysts Journal*, Sept–Oct 1986.
3. Waring, *Journal of Portfolio Management*, Summer 2004.

FIGURE 3.6 *Duration in the Liability: The Role of Bonds*

Source: Barclays Global Investors

preprinted instruction sheet that helps with these requests, and invariably the actuary involved is interested and enthusiastic in helping with this analysis once given the opportunity. As part of this request for assistance, one would request forecast cash flows usable for valuing the relevant measure of the economic liability (often something like an economic PBO is used to proxy the benefit security liability), using market determined discount rates, usually the government bond and Treasury inflation-protected securities (TIPS) yield curves.

The results are always revealing, especially for inflation duration. Inflation duration could approach zero in a final pay plan that also has full cost of living allowances (COLAs) in the retirement stage, and would be somewhere between 5 and 12 for typical final pay plans that do not have COLAs. Plans with modest or occasional retiree COLAs might be on the lower end of this scale, 5 or 6.

Finding the Liability-Matching Portfolio Solution

The sum of the factor (or duration) exposures on the liability side should look like the sum of the factor exposures on the asset side. This liability-matching solution can be conveniently solved in closed form, without resort to an optimizer, as is implied in **FIGURE 3.7** (see Waring 2004a). This

Perfect duration hedge:

$$A \cdot D_A \equiv L \cdot D_L$$

Same, breaking out the asset classes:

$$TIPS \cdot D_{TIPS} + Nom \cdot D_{Nom} + E \cdot D_E \equiv L \cdot D_L$$

By including two constraints in the form of this equation (one for real interest rate duration, one for inflation duration), and with appropriate bond and TIPS asset classes available to it, the optimizer will provide only fully duration-matched solutions.

FIGURE 3.7 *Dollar-Duration Matching and Surplus Optimization*

Source: Barclays Global Investors

is convenient, as we don't yet know enough about the equilibrium covariances of these interest rate factors with all of the remaining asset class factors to confidently use them in an unconstrained optimization process, the seemingly more natural alternative method. As our knowledge improves about these equilibrium correlations, unconstrained optimization may become more appropriate. But there is no loss in this closed-form procedure, as matching the liability doesn't even require optimization if suitable hedging instruments are available.

The Liability-Matching Portfolio from the Case Study

FIGURE 3.8 shows our plan sponsor's actual real interest rate durations and inflation durations. This sponsor's *liability* durations are around 17 for real interest rates and 11 for inflation; these values were computed with the assistance of the plan actuary.

This figure also shows the *asset* durations of the plan's current investment policy. To calculate these durations, we evaluated durations for all the asset class components and took the weighted average; this included the equity portfolio. These aggregate asset durations are around 7 for real interest rates and 1 for inflation.

The aggregate asset durations and the aggregate liability durations in this example are not of the same scale, which should alert us to the possibility of a severe mismatch. And of course we can calculate the degree of mismatch, the weighted net of the asset and liability durations, giving us what I call "surplus duration" as shown in **FIGURE 3.9**. It is about the same

FIGURE 3.8 *Understanding Interest-Rate Risks*

Liability durations	*Valuation Weight*	*Real duration* Duration	*Real duration* $ Dur.(m)	*Inflation duration* Duration	*Inflation duration* $ Dur.(m)
1) Retired/inactive	55.2%	12.87	$926	12.67	$912
2) Current employees	44.8%	22.89	$1,335	8.41	$490
Aggregate plan	**100%**	**17.36**	**$2,261**	**10.76**	**$1,402**

Asset class durations	*Composition*	*Real duration* Duration	*Real duration* $ Dur.(m)	*Inflation duration* Duration	*Inflation duration* $ Dur.(m)
Equity and equity-like	75.0%	8.00	$820	0.00	$0
Nominal bonds (5.25-year nominal duration)	22.5%	5.25	$161	5.25	$161
TIPS (9-year real duration)	2.5%	9.00	$31	0.00	$0
Aggregate plan assets	**100%**	**7.41**	**$1,012**	**1.18**	**$161**

Source: Barclays Global Investors

FIGURE 3.9 *How Much Net (Surplus) Interest-Rate Risk Is in the Current Policy?*

	Real duration Duration	*Real duration* $ Dur. (m)	*Inflation duration* Duration	*Inflation duration* $ Dur. (m)
Liability	17.36	$2,261	10.76	$1,402
Assets	7.41	$1,012	1.18	$161
Surplus duration	(9.58)	($1,249)	(9.52)	($1,241)

What this means for this plan sponsor: These surplus durations represent uncompensated risk

- For a 1% decrease in the real rate, surplus will go down by roughly 9.6%, or $1,249m
- For a 1% decrease in the inflation rate, surplus will go down by roughly 9.5%, or $1,241m

Summary: *This plan has large bets on both inflation rate increases and real rate increases*

Surplus calculations based on using the market-valued benefit security A/L of 105%.

Source: Barclays Global Investors

for both real rates and inflation rates, at about –9.5 (giving us a surplus duration that is almost nominal, but opposite in sign to what we usually think of for bond duration).

What does it mean for this plan to have a surplus duration of –9.5, nominal? The plan has bet that its surplus would improve (or the deficit would decrease) by 9.5 percent (scaled to the assets) for every single percentage point that interest rates go up, whether from a change in the real interest rate or the inflation rate or part of each! The opposite is also true, unfortunately: There would be an equal 9.5 percent loss if interest rates went down. This is a mighty big "bet" on the yield curve; an implicit rather than an explicit bet, but it is a bet, regardless.

This degree of mismatch is typical of the investment policies of American plan sponsors. And it is the main reason why plans experienced such an unpleasant period in 2001 and 2002 (it didn't help that equity markets also went the wrong direction, of course). They lost the bet.

Discussing This Interest Rate Bet with Affected Plan Sponsors

Is this the right bet to make for an underfunded plan? Experience tells me that many if not most sponsors are tempted to leave this bet "on," even after they have finally taken the trouble to completely understand it. There is something about the underlying low level of exposure to duration in the pension assets being the "status quo" that makes it acceptable, even though the sponsors would never allow such a large bet to be made intentionally. They, and every other sponsor they know, have the same bet, and it is hard to leave the pack. And besides, aren't interest rates going to be going up?![13]

For the sponsor who does think that rates are going up and who questions whether it makes sense to take the bet off now (using the status quo as his or her implicit benchmark), there is another way to think about the investment-policy decision. I recommend that they put in place an investment policy that calls for fully hedging the interest-rate risks in the liability as an equilibrium pension investment policy. But the active, or alpha, policy could allow for duration bets within some boundaries of size or risk based on, hopefully, valuable non-equilibrium "insights" or "views," which leaves room for specific interest rate bets. Interest rate bets are, after all, about alpha, not beta. I'll guarantee, however, that the explicit active duration bet that any given sponsor will make won't have a surplus duration of –9.5! Prudent sponsors make small, explicit bets, not large ones.

The Surplus Efficient Frontier in Practice

FIGURE 3.10 shows our case study sponsor's surplus efficient frontier, in surplus return versus surplus risk space. If a plan is fully funded, the frontier

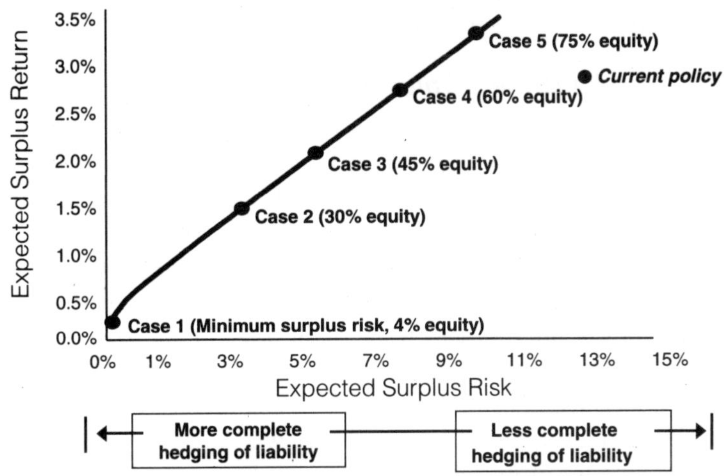

FIGURE 3.10 *Detail: The Surplus Efficient Frontier in "Surplus Graphical Space"*

Source: Barclays Global Investors

would go through the origin; at the origin the surplus return and surplus risk are both zero, meaning that the liability is perfectly hedged by the assets.

This sponsor is among the fortunate ones. While the plan was hurt badly in 2001–2002 by large adverse interest-rate and equity movements, it is still slightly more than fully funded—and we've evaluated its liability on an economic basis so that we're looking at it in its full measure. As a result, the straight-line, unconstrained version of the surplus frontier intersects the y-axis just slightly above zero. This is a good thing; refer to the funding level discussion, below.

Note that the current policy is a bit below and well to the right of its equivalent 75 percent equity position on the surplus frontier. This is entirely the result of the interest-rate mismatch. We can have a policy with 75 percent equity and still be fully hedged to interest rates and on the surplus frontier, but here we don't have the interest-rate hedging. In round numbers, there is about a 3 percent additional surplus risk—simply from taking on that duration mismatch.

In Figure 3.10 we see that if we move further to the left, we are fully hedged to the liability and hold a smaller degree of risky-asset exposures. If we move further to the right, the liability is still fully hedged, but we hold a larger proportion of risky assets. In total, we are becoming less well hedged as we move to the right, but only because we are taking on risky-asset risk, not because we are ignoring the liability.

Funding Level and the Surplus Efficient Frontier

If the plan is underfunded, the surplus frontier intersects the y-axis below the origin. This occurs commonly today, although it isn't the situation in our case study. In **FIGURE 3.11**, I show several surplus frontiers (in surplus return versus surplus risk graphical space) at different funding levels. We can focus on the straight (unconstrained) frontiers, to see more clearly what is going on "under the hood" with various funding levels. (Unlike the curved versions of the frontiers, the straight ones do not have constraints on negative holdings of cash and the like.)

In an underfunded condition, the efficient frontier starts, on the left-hand side, with a surplus return that is below zero, and only if there is a substantial amount of surplus risk taken will the expected surplus return be as high as zero. A negative surplus return means that the deficit will tend to *increase* over time, absent the helpful effect of deficit-reducing contributions. The surplus or deficit is expected to improve over time only if the surplus return is above zero.

We can see that an underfunded sponsor would have to take a tremendous amount of risk just to stay even (to have a zero expected surplus return), and more risk still to try to get ahead of the liability. And this risk

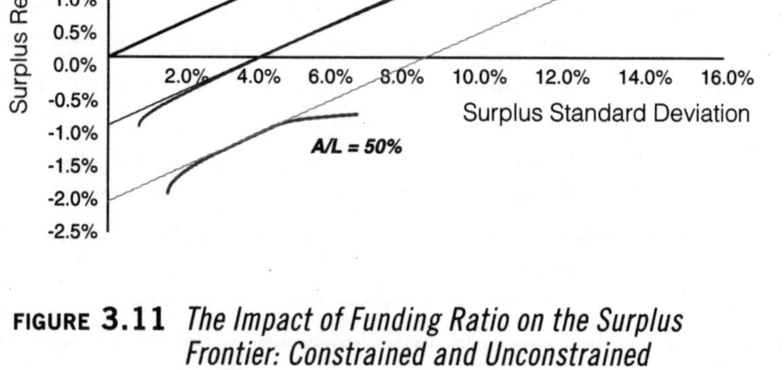

FIGURE 3.11 *The Impact of Funding Ratio on the Surplus Frontier: Constrained and Unconstrained*

Source: Barclays Global Investors

means that the deficit might stay even or get better, *but it might also get much worse as a result.* This is what risk *is*!

So there is a kind of headwind in the return space against any underfunded plan sponsor, and as the reader might expect, a tailwind for overfunded plan sponsors. We can trace this problem directly to the risk-free-rate component of surplus return, discussed above.

This is a tremendous problem, and one not previously discussed. Effectively, an underfunded sponsor borrows from itself, literally still owing with interest any economically required contributions that have not been made. We can see this now only because we are looking at the liability in an economically sensitive way.

A Surplus Optimization Output Data Table for Mixes of Interest

FIGURE 3.12 presents the output data version of the surplus frontier seen graphically in Figure 3.11. The surplus risk for the current policy portfolio, 13.25 percent, goes down to 10.5 percent with the elimination of the interest rate mismatch. So getting the hedging portfolio right has a tremendous value in surplus risk reduction.

How are we accomplishing the required leverage in this particular solution? There are several roads to Rome here, but for this specific solution, notice that the bond duration values increase a great deal relative to the current portfolio, giving nearly constant values for total "dollar durations"

FIGURE 3.12 *Optimal Mixes from the Surplus Efficient Frontier*

		Surplus optimal mixes				
Asset class:	***Current policy***	***Case 1***	***Case 2***	***Case 3***	***Case 4***	***Case 5***
Equity-like	75.0%	4.3%	30.0%	45.0%	60.0%	75.0%
Domestic equity	50.0%	3.3%	20.0%	30.0%	40.0%	50.0%
International equity	15.0%	1.0%	6.0%	9.0%	12.0%	15.0%
Alternatives	10.0%	0.0%	4.0%	6.0%	8.0%	10.0%
Bonds	25.0%	95.7%	70.0%	55.0%	40.0%	25.0%
Nominal bonds	22.5%	60.6%	50.8%	43.6%	34.9%	24.3%
Duration	*5.25*	*16.9*	*20.2*	*23.5*	*29.3*	*42.1*
TIPS	2.5%	35.2%	19.3%	11.4%	5.1%	0.7%
Duration	*9.00*	*16.9*	*20.2*	*23.5*	*29.3*	*42.1*
Expected surplus return	2.76%	0.20%	1.36%	2.02%	2.68%	3.32%
Expected surplus risk	13.24%	0.08%	3.86%	6.09%	8.32%	10.55%
Duration mismatch						
Real	-9.58	*0 (matched)*	*0 (matched)*	*0 (matched)*	*0 (matched)*	*0 (matched)*
Inflation	-9.52	*0 (matched)*	*0 (matched)*	*0 (matched)*	*0 (matched)*	*0 (matched)*
Asset-only return	7.99%	5.43%	6.59%	7.25%	7.91%	8.55%
Asset-only risk	12.07%	12.40%	12.95%	13.73%	14.78%	16.06%

The ratio of domestic equity to international equity to alternatives is constrained to be in a 50 : 15 : 10 ratio, consistent with current policy.

Source: Barclays Global Investors

from bonds, as the equity exposure increases. While equities do have some interest rate hedging characteristics, and we have taken these into account, bonds are more powerful in this dimension. So, in an all-physicals implementation, as the equity portion of the portfolio increases, we have to increase the duration of the remaining bond portfolio. The old ways of thinking about duration matching looked only at the bond portfolio in isolation, so it didn't and couldn't control the total portfolio duration so that the liability would be truly matched.

Evaluating the Risky-Asset Exposure Level

The growth-of-a-dollar charts in **FIGURE 3.13** show the growth of wealth over time, including the random variation on future wealth that results from underlying risk in the portfolios. (When I worked at Ibbotson Associates, where these charts were originally invented, we colloquially referred to these growth-of-a-dollar charts as "tulips," and their return distribution sibling charts as "trumpets.") It is instructive to compare the two charts, the one on the left having a more conservative investment policy than the one on the right. Of course, we expect to find a risk-return relationship consistent with the notion that higher expected returns and higher risks go together.

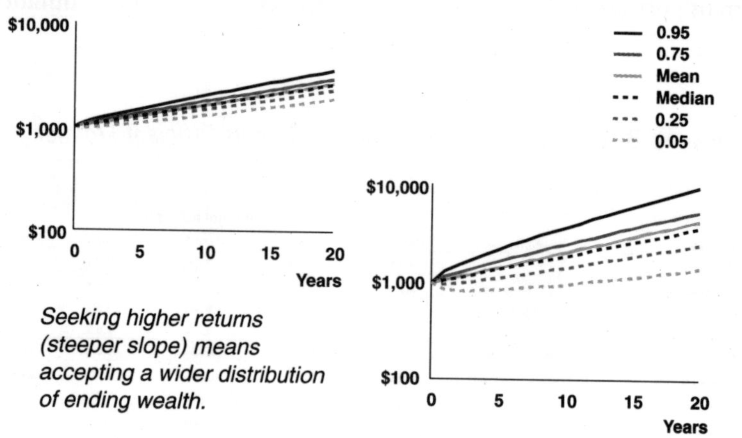

***Left:* Asset "tulip," minimum surplus variance portfolio (mostly fixed income, asset beta .405)**
***Right:* Asset "tulip," 100% equity portfolio (asset beta 1.44)**

FIGURE 3.13 *A Fair Risk-Return Trade-Off*

Note: The average return may be higher for the more aggressive policy on the right, but its worst-case possibilities are also much worse.

Source: Barclays Global Investors

And in fact, the slope of the median growth line for a conservative investment policy is going to be lower relative to a more aggressive policy (lower return), but the distribution of results around the median will be tighter than for the more aggressive policy (lower risk). So, to increase the slope, that is, to increase the expected return, we go to a more aggressive policy, but the consequence of that decision is that we will also increase the spread of possible realizations. *We might end up worse off.* That is "what risk is," at least in an asset-only context. Is there a surplus analog?

A "Surplus Tulip" Chart to Help Understand Pension Risk and Return Trade-Offs

Well, yes, there is such an analog, although it isn't easily calculated (there are some complexities in the mathematics of how two lognormal distributions of opposite sign add together). But **FIGURE 3.14** and **FIGURE 3.15** show such surplus tulips—they are "growth of a dollar of surplus" charts—worked out by my colleague Dr. Duane Whitney in support of our pension policy research efforts. As one would suppose, these charts take into account the natural growth rates of both the assets and the liabilities, and also take into account the anticipated comovement of the assets and the liabilities. That is, when interest rates go up on the asset side, they go up on the liability side by the same amount. Most importantly, these surplus

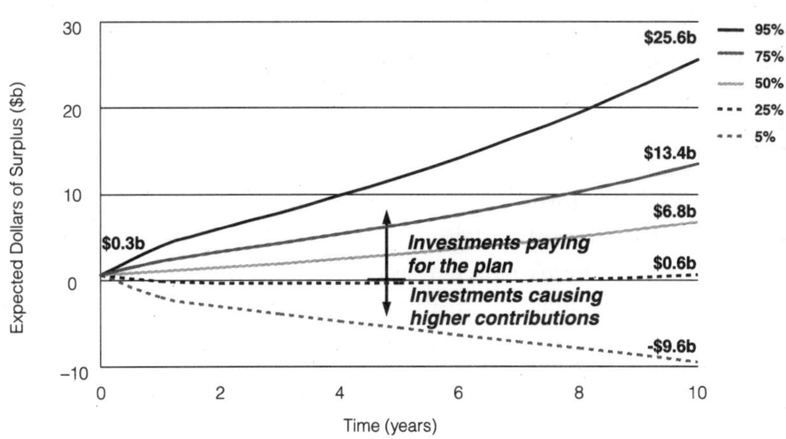

Source: Barclays Global Investors

FIGURE 3.14 *Surplus Tulip: Current Policy: 75% Equity-Like Asset Classes Shown as a Distribution of Surplus Dollars over Time*

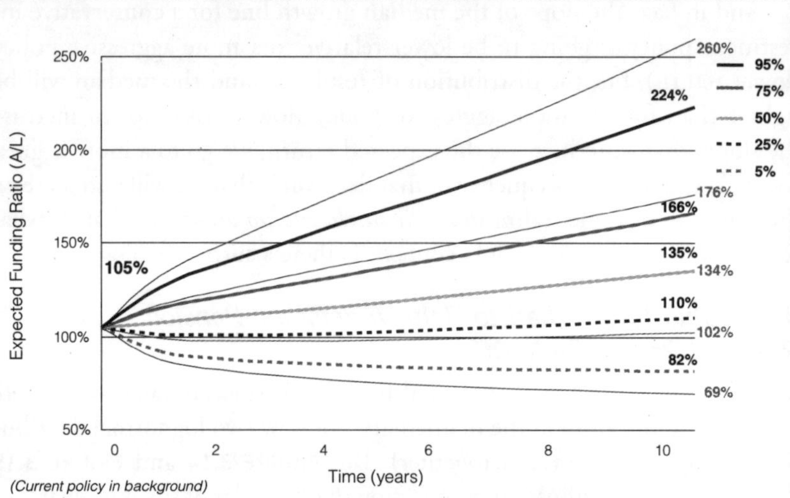

FIGURE 3.15 *Surplus Tulip: Current Policy Shown as a Distribution of Asset/Liability Ratios*

Source: Barclays Global Investors

tulips show the full range of possible outcomes associated with a given choice of investment policy today.

In fact, there are two kinds of surplus tulip charts that show about the same thing, but some people have a preference for one over the other: We can show this chart in the form just mentioned, as the distribution of dollars of surplus over time given different investment-policy decisions. Or we can show it as the distribution of the plan's asset/liability ratio over time, given the same set of different investment-policy decisions. It turns out that this latter form is relatively easier to calculate, and it conveys much the same information (although it is not exactly the same), but on the other hand it doesn't represent as good a view of true wealth changes as does the surplus dollar chart. But when it does not distort the picture too badly, we sometimes use the asset liability version rather than the surplus dollar versions, simply because it is easier to understand for many of our client audiences.

Figure 3.15 and **FIGURE 3.16** show the two forms of these surplus tulips. The asset/liability (A/L) version (Figure 3.15) actually shows two different investment policies (the "current policy," comparable to the first surplus dollar chart, is in faint, background lines, and an "improved" version of that policy, with full interest rate hedging to the liability, is in the foreground with heavier lines).

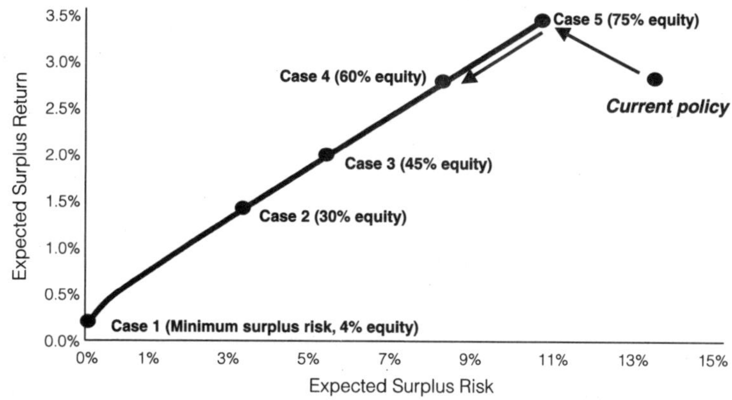

Reducing the stock-bond mix to 60/40 (from 75/25) reduces the volatility of surplus but has minimal impact on the surplus return.

- Expected surplus return = 2.68%
- Expected surplus risk = 8.32%

FIGURE 3.16 *Full Surplus Efficient Frontier Showing Suggestions of Policies to Be Considered*

Source: Barclays Global Investors

Surplus tulips, in either form, are invaluable to the investment-policy decision-making process, because they represent, in the most meaningful way possible, the real trade-off between risk and return for an investor with a liability. We can compare alternative investment policies using these tools, to show how the sponsor's expected experience may differ in terms of risk and return over time. Again if we concentrate our attention on the median and on the fifth percentile worst-case outcomes, we are using a "pretty good" means to make a lot of information manageable.[14] The reader might again expect to see a fair trade-off of risk and return. But before we do this for our case study sponsor, let's deal with a common misconception.

Does a Sponsor Have to Hold More Equities to Pay for the Plan?

Many sponsors feel that their plan *must* hold a lot of equities to get their higher expected returns, "to pay for the plan." But their advisers have forgotten to tell them that investors don't "get" *expected* returns for anything other than for risk-free instruments. What we do get is a *realized* return drawn from a distribution that is merely centered on the expected return.

With equities and other risky assets, this distribution—which on the downside represents unwelcome risk—is quite wide. If it does happen over a multiple-year period that returns do come in at expectation or above, then yes, the investment policy will have helped to pay for the plan. But if realizations are lower, then the investment policy will have made the plan more expensive! Contributions will be higher in that event, not lower. As always in investments, there is a risk-return trade-off.

These surplus tulips have a fringe benefit (Figure 3.16 and **FIGURE 3.17**): They can be interpreted to give a direct readout of the trend to be expected in future contribution levels, because contributions are a direct function of surpluses and deficits. Portions of the distributions that are in deficit regions of the graph (the lower portion of the graph, below zero) indicate directly the probability and degree that contributions will have to trend above normal costs, in order to replace losses from poor investment performance. And, symmetrically, portions of the tulip in surplus (the upper portion) represent the probability that contributions will be *lower* than normal costs—the equity investments will in these more fortunate scenarios in fact help pay for the plan. I show this with arrows on one of the figures (Figure 3.14) in the middle of the surplus dollar chart. You pay your money, and you take your choice! You can have certainty, and one level of cost, or you can take some risk and hope that the costs will be lower—but they might turn out higher.

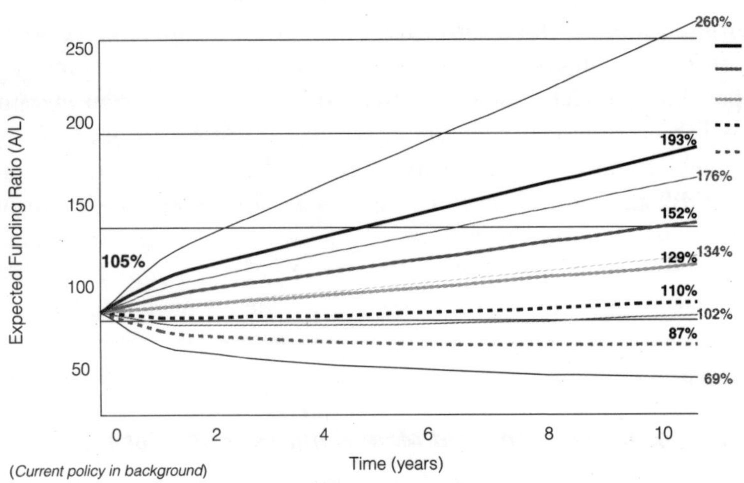

FIGURE 3.17 *Improved Funded Ratio (A/L) Distributions over Time*

Source: Barclays Global Investors

So, more equities might pay for the plan, but they also might make it more expensive. It is not a one-sided decision, but a full risk-return trade-off not unlike any other that a well-informed investor might expect.

The other little bubble that needs to be popped is that equities and other risky assets don't always achieve the expected return "over the long term." Over the long term, these distributions show exactly the possibility set, and a full half of the time the results will be lower than expected, sometimes much lower. This is consistent with history. We have had, and likely will have again, very long periods of equity returns that are well below expectations. Let me make the point more strongly by reminding us all that the period of the 1980s and 1990s was two decades of above-average performance; if we can experience two decades of *beating* the expected return, then we can have two decades of *failing to beat* the expected return. This bit of wisdom is contradicted regularly by those that defend the use of the expected return assumption for the discount rate. Unfortunately, equity returns are simply not that substantially mean reverting. If they were, the tulips' line would come back together as we moved out in time! They wouldn't look like tulips any more.

Comparing Investment Policies

Let's use the A/L ratio version of these surplus tulip charts, in Figure 3.15, to discuss this sponsor's current investment-policy choice (the current policy was completely unhedged to the liability; see the lighter lines, in the background). The sponsor could grow to have a 134 percent funded ratio (A/L ratio) over the study period of ten years if its current investment policy realizes returns, which with whatever happens to the liability place it at the median of the distribution; but at the fifth percentile, the worst case, it could be down as low as 69 percent funded. This is a dramatically wide range of possible outcomes.[15] Unfortunately, this plan is all too typical of most DB plans in the United States today. No wonder sponsors are experiencing more risk than they would prefer. These downsides, when they happen, cause a great deal of accounting pain. And they seem to occur too often.

What if we changed from the current policy, moving just onto the surplus frontier? What I mean by this is continuing to hold the same percentage (75 percent) of equities and other risky assets, but fully hedging the interest-rate risk of the liability by holding the liability-matching portfolio. What would that do for this sponsor in risk and return space?

Well, we've already shown this, in the heavy lines on the same chart that represent the distribution of A/L ratios, but we haven't yet interpreted it within the context of the case study. Notice that the median hardly changes at all with this change in policy; the expected A/L ratio is about the same in either case at the end of ten years. The geometric surplus returns are just about identical (the arithmetic returns are a bit different, but the different risk levels moderate the return differences).

But at the downside, at the one-in-twenty, worst-case level, we improve from a very low 69 percent funded ratio all the way up to an 82 percent funded level. This is a 13 percent improvement on what was a 31 percent underfunding spread, eliminating something like half of the downside exposure. Note, however, that we did give up something on the top end of possible future performance at the same time—we won't be as well off in extremely favorable markets. We can't ignore the upside loss, but there's been substantial improvement on the downside. And this is probably where more sponsors focus their concerns and attentions.

Dialing Down the Equity Exposure

This sponsor's exposure to equities and other risky assets is currently at 75 percent. This is very normal for a U.S. plan sponsor. But what does this mean? What effect does it have on this plan? Is this the right exposure level?

An equity exposure of 75 percent may generate too much downside risk for many sponsors, even if they are also holding a liability-hedging portfolio. If we dial down the equity just a bit—to say, 60 percent, continuing to hold the liability-hedging portfolio—how would that change this plan's risk and return trade-off?

Figure 3.16 shows the full surplus efficient frontier for this sponsor again, this time with arrows indicating the alternative investment positions that we are exploring. Figure 3.17 compares two surplus tulip charts again. The faint lines representing the sponsor's current policy are in the background just like before, but boldly in the foreground is an alternative, slightly lower-equity (60 percent; also fully hedged) policy for our consideration. How do they compare? We see from the surplus tulip that the median (our proxy for the expectancy) is now lower, down from 134 percent funded ratio to 129 percent. This should not be too much of a surprise—we expect a lower median for a more conservative investment policy. But there is good news also: the one-in-twenty worst case is now at an 87 percent funded ratio, up from the prior example's 82 percent and the current policy's 69 percent. So this slightly more conservative policy is truly more conservative and avoids a great deal of downside risk.

It is worth stopping and noticing that this substantial improvement in the downside exposure can be gained simply from fully hedging the liability's interest-rate risks and from dialing down the equity percentage a relatively modest amount, just 15 percent. And a look back to the surplus efficient frontier graph shows that the improvement carries into the other, progressively more conservative, positions (having even less equity) on the surplus frontier. This is the logically expected pattern. The median expectation for future levels of surplus continues to drop, but the downside risk continues to tighten up.

This is the real risk-return trade-off that a pension plan faces. Just how much risk is the sponsor willing to take in the effort to see the investment portfolio help pay for the plan?

Communicating with Plan Constituents

Asset-only return and risk still has some importance, even if it isn't correct theoretically, and it will for some time. Its importance is largely a practical one, a result of historic practice and the expectations of constituents. After all, sponsors have been reporting asset-only results for years, and it takes time to retrain expectations.

A successful surplus-based investment policy will hold a lot of long duration bond exposure because that is the necessary characteristic of the liability-matching portfolio, and this in turn means that we can expect increased asset-only volatility relative to current portfolios. For example, in Figure 3.12 we see that the asset-only risk for this sponsor goes up from 12 percent to 16 percent (while its surplus risk goes down a comparable amount), the increase occurring because of these longer duration bond exposures (risky-asset class exposures are the same as they would be today in both cases). In all fairness, this is a lot of asset-only risk. If the plan's constituents aren't refocused on the meritorious reduction in *surplus* risk, and the consequences of this for the future good health of the plan, they would be very concerned the first time rates went up and the portfolio went down commensurately, regardless of the fact that the liability had simultaneously also gone down.

If this sponsor, or any others, were to go to a surplus management approach, it is clear that they would have to prepare periodic reports that, in contrast to today's reports, have a very different emphasis. They would need to communicate first about economic surplus results during the period, showing the stability of the plan "despite market turmoil." The supporting material in the back of their reports would provide next the detail about the economic liability results, and only then the detail about the portfolio's results. It wouldn't be prudent to switch to a surplus-based policy otherwise; but it is probably not prudent not to switch!

Should Corporate Pension Plans Hold Any Equity at All?

Some people argue that pension plans in corporations and even in public bodies should not be holding equities at all, because investors can acquire and hold equities themselves—citing the Miller-Modigliani indifference propositions. But the fact is that the indifference propositions don't forbid pension plans or corporations from holding equities. The key word is "indifference": Stockholders may be *indifferent* about whether corporate pension plans hold equities in their portfolio, but indifference simply means that they are *neither opposed to nor in support of* such a plan. And in the real world, as opposed to the perfect world of theory, it may well be that there are advantages to holding securities through corporate agents: Many sponsors can hold equities less expensively than can the shareholders, and perhaps there is a better chance for more skillful efforts to add alpha than most shareholders might have on their own. So, while in theory the shareholders may be indifferent, in the real world with transactions costs and taxes and other imperfections, it is certainly possible that shareholders could have a modest preference for such holdings.

Perhaps it is just a management preference to hold equities, presenting an "agency issue." It isn't a surprise that many corporate executives want to hold equities: They wake up in the morning trying to make their own company's equity more valuable; they believe in equities, they believe in the markets, and they believe that holding equities is a good thing. They are fully paid up members of the equity ownership system, and they like to be consistent in their beliefs by holding equities in the pension plan. And there is no harm in this under the indifference propositions.

They do need to think through the organization's risk tolerance carefully before making the allocation decision. We don't want the downside risk from holding equities to hurt the company when or if it is experienced. Too much risk is not a good thing.

The Relationship Between Pension Expense and Equities (and Other Risky Assets)

When we say to a sponsor, "Why don't we reconsider being at 75 percent equity," the sponsor's first response might often be a hesitant "no." The immediate reasoning is that if the sponsor were to reduce the portfolio's equity and risky-asset exposure, it would have to reduce its expected-return assumption. In turn, this would cause its pension expense to go up. So the reluctance to reduce equity seems to come, at least in some significant part, from accounting concerns.

But is this reasoning correct? If the sponsor changes its investment policy to one with less equity and other risky-asset exposure, will it really have higher pension expense?

Well, at first blush, it does seem to be true. Certainly the expected return assumption would need to be reduced, and the *first* and most direct effect of that reduction is to increase pension expense.

But there is a *second* effect that must be considered if the discussion is to be complete. Each year, the actual, realized returns are observed. If they are above or below the expected return assumption, then the excess or shortfall over or under the stated expected return assumption (expressed in terms of dollars) is placed in the "accumulated actuarial gains and losses account."

What happens to persistent positive or negative balances in this gains and losses account? They are amortized back into expense, over time! So over the amortizing period, the income statement feels the effects of the actual, realized returns on the assets, not the expected returns.

So the bottom line is that actual realized returns are what affect pension expense over time, not the expected return assumption. The accounting convention based on expected returns merely acts as a smoothing mechanism for actual realized returns. As I've said above, although in another context, the accounting will always follow the economics, sooner or later.

This means that an organization can and should feel free to make its investment-policy decision—and, in particular, to decide on its exposure to equities and other risky assets—completely free of any concern about the effect of the expected return assumption on pension expense. The appropriate focus is on trading off the desire for higher returns against the risk that this may result in a downside experience that is larger than the company wants to carry. A downside experience will increase pension expense, and it will also (as discussed earlier) increase contributions.

Yes, I suppose it is true that in the first and maybe the second year after going to a new and less aggressive investment policy, there might be an upwards blip in pension expense even if the market's returns were at expectation. But remember, if there are downside returns in these or any future years, the new lower-risk investment policy will have smaller swings, and the bad news that shows up later in the smoothed accounting won't be as bad as it otherwise would have been. Only if the firm has a very short-term "survival" focus, as we might imagine United Airlines had in its last few years before bankruptcy, might the chance of higher pension expense in the immediate future outweigh the mild long-term effect. But, given a long-term focus, reducing the expected-return assumption really should not create a pension expense concern. Further, one can imagine any negative earnings impact would be completely and satisfactorily explained to analysts by a disclosure footnote. This is easy to communicate.

As we discussed earlier at length, the right way to make the decision about the plan's exposure to equities and other risky assets is as a risk-tolerance decision. Seeking higher expected returns by increasing the plan's exposure to equities and other risky assets really does increase the likelihood and magnitude of unpleasant downside experiences. These downside risks are real, and when they happen, they cause increased contributions and greater pension expense. Higher expected returns from holding more equities is certainly a good thing—when they are actually realized!—and in that case they would indeed help pay for the plan. But we do not want to take so much risk that we expose ourselves to the chance that the plan could become more expensive and

Managing Pension Funding Risk

Prescription: Use core teachings from modern portfolio theory to control true pension funding risk.

Investment-related pension funding risks are manageable with three investment policy tools, all implied by the nature of a total return (beta plus alpha) surplus efficient frontier:

1. Hold a liability-hedging portfolio: Dual duration liability-hedging techniques manage both types of *interest-rate risks* (real interest rate, and inflation).
2. Hold a consciously determined exposure to equities and risky assets. This exposure can be "dialed" up or down, to match the sponsor's tolerance for risk.
3. While we haven't discussed this item in depth in this chapter, hold a carefully determined exposure to active management. If skillfully employed, this also has the potential for improving future surplus levels. See Waring et al. (2000), and Waring and Siegel (2003).

To develop a surplus efficient frontier, it is necessary to use an economic measure of the liability. This measure benefits the sponsor not only by assisting with making improved surplus-based investment policy decisions, above, but also by more fully informing the sponsor about the cost of each benefit policy decision and the consequences of any contribution policy decision.

Pension funding risks, and costs, *can* be managed.

cause damage to the financial health of the sponsor. "Feeling lucky" is a poor substitute for making a calculated decision based on reasonable expectations.

Conclusions

Pension cost and expense can be better controlled, pension contributions can be better controlled, and pension-funding risk—volatility in either pension expense or contributions—can be better controlled, merely by looking at the liability in an economically appropriate way and letting one's pension benefit policy, pension investment policy, and pension contribution policy follow.

The big decisions are always the same: The first part of the discussion has to be about setting benefit levels that the sponsor is really willing to pay for and that it can afford. This can only be done meaningfully through economic views of the true present value of the benefits promised in that policy—the liability—and of changes in the liability resulting from proposed changes in the benefit formula. This is important because it is the economic liability that is in reality charged out as "normal costs" year after year. I know that this sounds wrong, as it appears to be the accounting liability and the accounting normal cost that are charged out, but the accounting always follows the economics over time, and the sponsor will in fact pay the full economic liability over time, plus—or minus—any special gains or losses from its investments.

And these economic normal costs will show up and be experienced by the sponsor in the form of pension expense and contributions—and these are also in their turn perfect functions of the benefit-level decision, that is, of benefit policy. Benefits that are too large invite accounting manipulation in the short term, but in the long term they cost what they cost, and the "surprises" related to any effort to understate this cost will come marching in, perfectly predictably, year after year. Only an economic measure of the liability will lay a basis for an accurate evaluation of what these costs will be.

For the next part of the discussion, we turn our attention to managing pension-funding risk, which we've implicitly defined as the volatility of the pension surplus (or nearly, but not completely equivalently, of the asset/liability ratio). This volatility in turn generates the volatility of contributions and of pension expense.

We manage these risks first by considering benefit policies that try to avoid, or at least minimize, the amount of unhedgeable risk in the liability. Mortality risk can be reduced if it is unacceptable, simply by using more thoughtfully adjusted mortality tables that incorporate improvements in future mortality. The risk in estimating final pay can be reduced by moving from final pay benefit formulas to final average pay to career average pay formulas, or even to absolute dollars of benefits determined year by year and accumulated into a final award. This isn't a recommendation, and frankly I don't think that these forecasting risks are that huge, but the sponsor that is especially concerned about these unhedgeable nonfinancial risks does have some choices.

More importantly, we manage volatility of contributions and of expense by managing the volatility of surplus. And we do this through a carefully crafted investment policy that fully incorporates the economic liability: The first requirement of the investment policy is that it has to hedge the interest-rate risks (and any other hedgeable risks that we can identify in the liability) by holding a liability-hedging portfolio to the full extent that it is practicable to do so. This should go without saying, but it is a complete departure from today's practice and is the single biggest risk-reducing opportunity for investment-policy improvement.

The second investment-policy decision the sponsor must make is on the degree of equity and other risky-asset exposure; this is a decision about risk tolerance. The risk that these equity and equity-like investment assets might have disappointing returns, which in turn force the sponsor to call on other corporate assets for remediation, is one that cannot be taken lightly. The smaller the plan is in relation to the sponsor organization, and the healthier the sponsoring organization is financially, the more risk the organization can arguably tolerate, and vice versa. Remember that bad times for the pension plan may also be bad times for the sponsoring organization.

The overarching and most critical point is that pension plans are being managed today with poor technologies that do little of what is required for good risk control and cost control, and as a result most sponsors are experiencing much more risk than is remotely necessary and costs that are consistently higher than expected.

These risks and costs can be controlled, as I've set forth here and elsewhere. Let's adopt this technology, and let's reconsider the future of the DB plan favorably. DB plans are way too valuable to let fail due to risks and costs that can be fully controlled.

Corporate plan sponsors do not want high-cost pension plans; they do not want high-volatility pension contributions; they do not want high-volatility pension expense; and they do not want high-volatility pension-funding ratios. All these wishes can be granted. That's the message we need to get out there. We do not need to shut down pension plans to get rid of pension funding risk.

References

Arnott, Robert D., and Peter L. Bernstein. 1988. "The Right Way to Manage Your Pension Fund." *Harvard Business Review* (January/February): 95–102.

Black, Fischer. "The Tax Consequences of Long Run Pension Policy." 1980. *Financial Analysts Journal* (July/August).

Bookstaber, Richard, and Jeremy Gold. "In Search of the Liability Asset." 1988. *Financial Analysts Journal* (January/February).

Campbell, John Y., and Luis M. Viciera. 2002. *Strategic Asset Allocation.* Oxford: Oxford University Press.

Elton, Edwin J., and Martin J. Gruber. 1992. "Optimal Investment Strategies with Investor Liabilities." *Journal of Banking & Finance* 16 (September): 869–90.

Grinold, Richard C., and Ronald N. Kahn. 2000. *Active Portfolio Management,* 2nd ed. New York: McGraw-Hill (1st ed. 1995).

Leibowitz, Martin L. 1987. "Pension Asset Allocation Through Surplus Management." *Financial Analysts Journal* 43 (March/April): 29–40.

Leibowitz, Martin L., and Roy D. Henriksson. 1988. "Portfolio Optimization Within a Surplus Framework." *Financial Analysts Journal* 44 (March/April): 43–51.

———. *Investing: The Collected Works of Martin L. Leibowitz.* 1992. Ed. Frank J. Fabozzi. Chicago: Probus Publishing Company.

Leibowitz, Martin L., Stanley Kogelman, and Lawrence N. Bader. 1991. "Asset Performance and Surplus Control: A Dual-Shortfall Approach." Salomon Brothers Inc. (July).

Markus, Rudolf, and William T. Ziemba. 2004. "Intertemporal Surplus Management." *Journal of Economic Dynamics and Control* 28 (February): 975–90.

Michaud, Richard O. 1989. "Economic Surplus and Pension Management." Merrill Lynch Capital Markets (February).

———. *Efficient Asset Management.* 1998. Boston: Harvard Business School Press.

Mulvey, John M. 1989. "A Surplus Optimization Perspective." *Investment Management Review* 3.

Roll, Richard. 1977. "A Critique of the Asset Pricing Theory's Tests." *Journal of Financial Economics* (March): 129–76.

Ryan, Ronald J., and Frank J. Fabozzi. 2002. "Rethinking Pension Liabilities and Asset Allocation." *The Journal of Portfolio Management* (Summer).

Sharpe, William F. 1990. "Asset Allocation." In *Managing Investment Portfolios: A Dynamic Process*, eds. John L. Maginn and Donald L. Tuttle, chapter 7. Boston: Warren, Gorham & Lamont.

———. 2002. "Budgeting and Monitoring Pension Fund Risk." *Financial Analysts Journal* (September/October).

———. 1964. "Capital Asset Prices: A Theory of Market Equilibrium Under Conditions of Risk." *Journal of Finance* 19 (September): 425–42.

———. 2004. "Equilibrium." In *Macro-Investment Analysis*. Available at http://www.stanford.edu/~wfsharpe/mia/eq/mia_eq1.htm.

Sharpe, William F., and Lawrence G. Tint. 1990. "Liabilities: A New Approach." *Journal of Portfolio Management* (Winter): 5–10.

Siegel, Laurence B., and M. Barton Waring. 2004. "TIPS, the Dual Duration, and the Pension Plan." *Financial Analysts Journal* (September/October).

Tepper, Irwin. 1981. "Taxation and Corporate Pension Policy." *Journal of Finance* (March).

Tobin, James. "Liquidity Preference as Behavior Towards Risk." 1958. *Review of Economic Studies* 25(2).

Treynor, Jack [Walter Bagehot, pseud.]. 1972. "Risk and Reward in Corporate Pension Funds." *Financial Analysts Journal* 28 (January/February): 80–84.

Treynor, Jack L., Patrick Regan, and Willam W. Priest Jr. 1976. *The Financial Reality of Pension Funding Under ERISA*. Homewood, IL: Dow Jones–Irwin.

Waring, M. Barton. 2004a. "Liability-Relative Investing: Be Dual Duration Matched and on the Surplus Efficient Frontier." *Journal of Portfolio Management* (Summer).

———. 2004b. "Liability-Relative Investing II: Surplus Optimization with Beta, Alpha, and an Economic View of the Liability." *Journal of Portfolio Management* (Fall).

———. 2004c. "Liability-Relative Strategic Asset Allocation Policies." Presented at The New World of Pension Fund Management: Finding Solutions to the Pension Funding Crisis, CFA Institute, March 16, 2004. Conference proceedings, September.

Waring, Barton, and Laurence Siegel. "Understanding Active Management." Investment Insights, Barclays Global Investors, San Francisco, April 2003. Part I republished as "The Dimensions of Active Management," *The Journal of Portfolio Management*, Spring 2003. Part II republished as "Debunking Some Myths of Active Management," *The Journal of Investing*, Summer 2005.

Waring, Barton, Charles Castille, Duane Whitney, and John Pirone. 2000. "Optimizing Manager Structure and Budgeting Manager Risk." *Journal of Portfolio Management* 26 (Spring): 90–104.

Chapter Notes

1. In theory, there is no reason why a DC plan couldn't be set up that would be every bit as successful as any DB plan. But in practice this is very unlikely to happen; it requires very high mandatory and explicit contribution rates and the availability of fairly priced payout annuities.

2. Admittedly, my employer, Barclays Global Investors, has a strong interest in the ongoing health of defined benefit pension plans, although it also has a significant interest in its defined contribution business. But regardless of any bias that I might have from this perspective, I am happy to defend the accuracy and importance of these observations and recommendations.

3. The word *stochastic* is used a lot to describe these traditional processes, usually in a transparent effort to lend authority to the work. But all it means is that certain of the variables, and particularly the asset return variables, are allowed to vary as if being drawn from the same distributions as are often assumed for such variables. In some of the better models, the liability's discount rate is even allowed to vary stochastically, affecting the funding ratio. But none of them allow the mix of asset classes itself to seek the properly defined surplus-efficient frontier—or we would long have had larger long bond portfolios than we actually see in practice.

4. An approach that would optimize consumption utility on a multiperiod basis would probably be superior, but it isn't practical mathematically. Even so, surplus optimization is a special, albeit limited, case of consumption utility optimization, so we're in the right ballpark and we are mathematically tractable.

5. Different levels of aggregation of the components of the liability (ABO, PBO, TBO, and so on, if consistently calculated on economic principles), will result in different values, but they are all internally consistent with one another and all are market referenced. This is just a choice of how much to measure, from the total, and doesn't offend the law of one price. But taking multiple measures of, say, the PBO or a PBO-like value, using different assumptions—most of which are noneconomic—does. There isn't space here to discuss the level of inclusion we need for surplus optimization, which is an interesting and subtle discussion. Suffice it to say that the measure used should establish an agreed level of benefit security. It should be inclusive enough to include all benefits already accrued by all past and present plan participants, and the sense of accrual should be an economic one.

6. See also Jack Treynor (1972), written under the *nom de plume* Walter Bagehot.

7. Conventional practice uses different discount rates for different financial statements. Corporate accounting uses a fairly conservative discount rate for the *balance sheet* version of the liability (high quality corporate credits; not too far off of the risk-free rate curve). But when it comes to developing pension expense for the income statement, the expected rate of return on assets is still

used. Public employee pension plans surprisingly still use the expected return on the assets for all purposes.

8. Dual dollar durations can be viewed simply as risk factors; the general prescription is to identify all of the investable or market risk factors in the liability that you can, and then match them with asset exposures (Waring 2004a). Also, Markus and Ziemba (2004) similarly identify the liability-matching portfolio as a separate "fund" in this same sense.

9. This applies to the extent that the necessary hedging instruments are available in the market, and at responsible pricing. This isn't always true: note the shortage of long real-rate instruments in both the United Kingdom and the United States, and, with respect to other post-employment benefits (OPEB) liabilities, the total dearth of health care inflation hedges everywhere. Where ideal instruments are not available, the next best should be used, the goal being to hedge what can be hedged. Bad pricing can be reflected in the optimization through an appropriate negative rate of return penalty.

10. Assets minus liabilities here equals zero. For Tobin's original formulation, there were no liabilities to subtract.

11. Often I use a Sharpe (1990) or Sharpe and Tint (1990) approach, one that references the surplus return to the *liabilities,* rather than to the *assets* as I have done here. It has many excellent qualities. Leibowitz (1988) formed his version of surplus return by reference to the assets, as I do in this paper. A third choice is to reference the surplus itself: Although it has some problems (we can wind up with zero-divide or negative-divide problems that can make the returns look funny), defining the return in terms of surplus probably makes the most economic sense. This is the approach used by Elton and Gruber (1992), and for certain work I also use it. See Waring (2004b) for a more complete discussion of these alternative bases for a definition of surplus return.

12. "No solutions? Then no problems!"

13. As this piece is undergoing final editing, in April of 2008, rates have been going down again, and equity returns have been seriously negative, a double whammy hurting plan sponsors just as they were hurt in 2001–2002. Yet most of them have been believing, along with most Wall Street prognosticators, that rates would be going up soon—for the last four years! These sponsors would be better off today, again, if they had hedged the liability and reconsidered the risk of their large equity positions.

14. I don't include the impact of future contributions and future normal costs, to isolate the effect of today's investment policy decisions on future plan health without recursive effects. Because bad investment performance does feed into tomorrow's required contribution, a chart that showed the distribution of surplus *after* contributions would show a picture whose risk spread was dampened. And the dampening would have been a result of the very concern that the sponsor is trying to manage, that is, the contribution volatility! To

avoid this circularity and show a clearer picture, contributions must be left out. And if contributions are left out, future normal cost accruals should be left out also. Think of the chart as a pictorial of what will happen over the future to the underlying wealth and health of the plan based on today's investment policy decision. And let's recognize that if there were no volatility at all in the surplus, a fully funded plan's contributions would be equal to its normal cost, and thus showing contribution is unimportant to today's investment policy decision.

15. The prior chart shows this same plan's surplus distribution with the same current investment policy, but in surplus dollar rather than A/L space. It starts out with a positive surplus of $300 million. With median realizations, it grows to a surplus of $6.8 billion, but at the fifth percentile, the worst case, the deficit will be –$9.6 billion.

avoid this circularity and show a clearer picture, contributions must be left out. And if contributions are left out, future normal cost accruals should be left out also. Think of this as a projection of what will happen over the next [illegible] ... [illegible] ... that if there were no [illegible] ... a fully funded plan ... contributions would be enough [illegible] ... and thus the [illegible] ... important to today's investment [illegible]

CHAPTER 4

A Simple Model for Pricing Securities with a Debt-Equity Linkage

SANJIV DAS

Who—Sanjiv Das is professor of finance at the Leavey School of Business at Santa Clara University. He previously held faculty appointments at the Harvard Business School and at the University of California, Berkeley. Sanjiv serves on the editorial boards of several journals, and is a senior editor of the *Journal Of Investment Management* and coeditor of the *Journal of Derivatives*. His current research interests include the modeling of default risk, algorithms for harvesting financial information from the Web, and derivatives pricing models. Prior to entering academia, Sanjiv worked in the derivatives industry throughout the Asia-Pacific region. He holds a PhD and an MPhil in finance from New York University and an MS in computer science from the University of California, Berkeley.

New Thinking—The model presented in this chapter provides a framework for pricing securities whose values depend simultaneously on inputs from more than one capital market. Sanjiv Das and Rangarajan Sundaram (Das's coauthor on another paper on pricing securities) construct a reduced-form security-pricing model that incorporates equity, interest-rate, and default risks. The model extracts both equity- and debt-market information to price hybrid debt-equity securities, such as convertible bonds. The model can also be used to value credit portfolios for which correlated default risk is a critical concern.[1] In the early days of derivatives, the typical scenario involved one underlying security based on a single company or credit. Today, the price of securities is based on a number of underlying risk factors, and the securities are often multiple-credit portfolio-type securities, such as a collateralized debt obligation. The market has evolved from a one-name, one-factor setting to an n-name, n-factor setting posing an often complicated pricing challenge because many of the factors tend to interact.

Adding Credit Risk to Standard Pricing Models

The simple model presented in this chapter looks at how credit risk can be added to equity and interest-rate risk to price a security, such as a distressed convertible bond, as a function of all three types of risk. Our goal was to construct a simple model that did not stray far from existing models, such as the models for pricing equity or interest-rate options. At the same time, we had to be completely cognizant of the fact that credit risk would interfere with the predictability of the other factors.

Consider, for example, the impact of a credit-risk variable on the pricing of a convertible security. At first thought, one might assume that as credit risk increases, the value of the convertible will drop. But as it turns out, that does not necessarily have to happen. Increasing credit risk can actually increase the price of a convertible because of the two types of options embedded in it—a warrant-type feature and an interest-rate call feature. As credit risk increases, both of these options are diminished in value. But if the interest-rate call feature diminishes in value faster than the warrant feature, the convertible may slightly appreciate in price. We were unaware of this relationship until we built the model and began to analyze the output.

The warrant-type option associated with credit risk also plays a role when, for example, two callable convertible bonds of different issuers, identical in terms of underlying equity and bond prices, have different default risks. The bond with the higher default, or credit, risk has a higher-priced, or at least a theoretically higher-priced, call option than the bond with the lower default risk. The reason for this is simple; it is purely mathematical. The risk-neutral distributions under both of these equity processes exhibit a greater upward drift for the bond with higher default risk because of the jump compensation in the model. The model must account for a greater degree of jump-to-default risk for the bond with the higher likelihood of default. This induces positive skewness that causes the equity options on these bonds to have higher values.

Credit risk also injects a volatility or pseudovolatility effect into the pricing of convertible securities that can result in their embedded options having higher values in higher credit-risk scenarios. So injecting credit risk into standard interest-rate and equity risk models mandates dealing with these types of issues.

Features of the Model

One of the basic features of our model is that it is a hybrid debt-equity model, useful for pricing securities that combine features of both markets. Our starting point is an equity model—a constant elasticity of variance (CEV) model—that is slightly different from the standard Cox-Ross-Rubinstein (CRR)-type model typically used to price equity options. We chose the CEV model because it can incorporate leverage effects, and as credit risk is often associated with leverage effects, this aspect of the model is particularly valuable.

We layer the CEV model onto the standard Heath-Jarrow-Morton (HJM 1990) model, which binds together the interest rate and equity features of the two models. Next, we layer on a jump-to-default process for equity when the convertible bond goes into default. This provision follows that of standard reduced-form models.

Our lattice design allows recombination so that implementation of the model is simple and efficient. The model can also be used to extract implied default functions in a manner similar to that used in deriving implied volatilities for trading equity options. An entire default function, not just the probability of default, can be extracted to characterize the role that default plays for a particular firm, based on the evolution of its equity value and the evolution of the interest-rate market. This ability distinguishes our model from others that rely completely on exogenously specified default. Our model deals with endogenously specified default.

The model supports debt-equity arbitrage trading and allows for the arbitrage-free simulation of correlated default. A practical extension of this model is the ability to apply it across a portfolio of names, or credits, to manage correlated default.

It is also easily calibrated to market-observable data. All inputs to the model can readily be found by looking, for example, no farther than the nearest Bloomberg screen. Embedded in the model are other models used as special cases, so that if we switch off the interest-rate portion of the model, we are left with the standard equity option model. If we switch off the equity part of the model, we revert back to the HJM model. In summary, the model is a reduced-form model with structural model features and can account for the leverage effect often associated with credit risk.

A very practical application of our model is convertible arbitrage. Today, when convertible bonds are overpriced relative to credit default swaps (CDS), a convertible arbitrageur shorts the convertible bond, writes CDS contracts, and delta hedges to remove unwanted interest-rate and equity risk. In our model, because the different market risks are allowed to interact, in contrast to being isolated as is the case today, the arbitrage analysis can be done comprehensively in a single step without making too many unnecessary assumptions.

Spreadsheet Model

The entire model runs on a spreadsheet. **FIGURE 4.1** is a screenshot of the model spreadsheet that shows the inputs to the model. This is a basic version of the model, for illustrative purposes only. However, it is computationally efficient because the model is based on a recombining tree.

Figure 4.1 shows a pared-down version of the model with inputs at the top and outputs at the bottom. On the left side of the spreadsheet is a four-year-maturity forward-rate curve with interest rates and volatilities specified for different points along the curve. On the right side of the spreadsheet, the inputs include stock price, stock volatility, correlation between stock price and interest rates, number of steps in the hexanomial tree used in the model, recovery rate on default, coupon on the bond, strike price, and so on. These inputs are consistent with the inputs required to price a convertible bond or any other kind of debt instrument.

Notice the four parameters at the upper left of the spreadsheet: a_0, a_1, a_2, and a_3. These are calibratable parameters that define the implied default function of the model. The implied default function is fitted to the credit markets and runs all the option pricing with defaultable characteristics. The model is calibrated to the prices of equity, forward rates, and interest

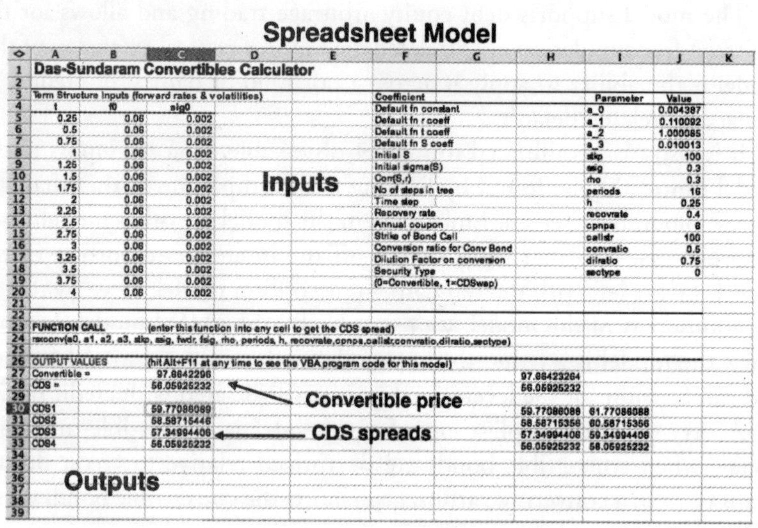

FIGURE **4.1** *Inputs and Outputs of Model*

rates, and the credit parameters are calibrated to CDS spreads. For example, using four CDS spreads of different maturities, four parameters on the credit part of the model are calibrated. Once that is done, the convertible can actually be priced with the correct amount of default risk. Because the model embeds default risk, it can readily handle distressed convertibles.

Application to Risk Premia and Credit Portfolios

The model can also be extended to extracting risk premia and to managing credit portfolios. Using data from CreditGrades for the period from January 2000 to June 2002, for the 30 issuers in the Dow Jones CDX INDU (CDX) Index, we calibrated the model to daily CDS spreads. Using the fitted parameters, we computed one-year, risk-neutral default probabilities, and quantified the risk premia by dividing the risk-neutral default probability by the default probability from CreditGrades. **FIGURE 4.2** shows the plot of the average default probabilities (equally weighted across 30 firms) over the period.

The difference between the two lines in Figure 4.2 indicates the risk premia for default on the stocks in the CDX Index. The black line and the gray line represent the statistical and risk-neutral probability of default, respectively. Prior to the big spike on September 11, 2001, the premia are rather small, but after that date they widened significantly with subsequent similar spikes linked to market shocks.

The other major extension of the model is its ability to differentiate between two types of credit correlation. One is the correlation induced by

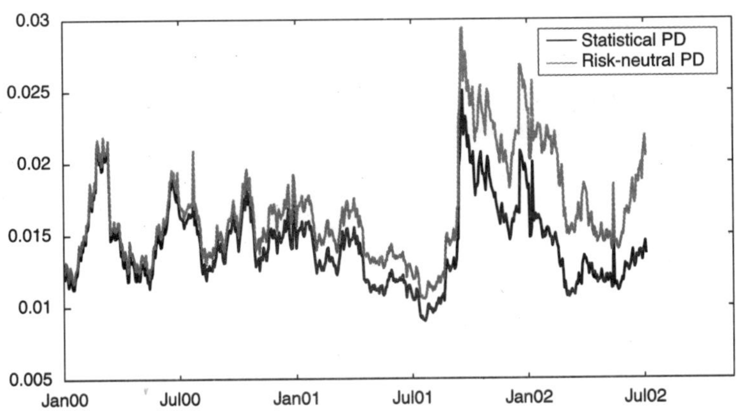

FIGURE 4.2 *Average Probabilities of Default, Dow Jones CDX INDU Index, January 2000 to June 2002*

Source: "An Integrated Model for Hybrid Securities," *Management Science* 53, 1375–1388.

correlated default probabilities. The other is contagion correlation. The structure of our model allows the calculation of both types of correlation. We can induce the correlation of the probabilities of default, and then, conditioning on the probabilities of default, can induce contagion correlation using a copula function.

Reduced-Form Model Concept

The model is useful in a range of applications even though it is extremely simple and straightforward. The basic concept behind the model is illustrated by the diagram in **FIGURE 4.3**, which illustrates how a stock's price reacts to risk in a standard CRR model, rising to uS (up-branch price), dropping to dS (down-branch price),[2] or jumping to zero in the case of a default.

This addition is also present in the jump-to-default model of Carr and Linetsky (2006) and assumes a special case—that the stock's price does not recover any value. Embedding the default branch in the standard model of a binomial tree, we arrive at the following model:

$$S(t+h) = \begin{cases} uS(t) & w/prob \quad q\exp(-\xi h) \\ dS(t) & w/prob \quad (1-q)\exp(-\xi h) \\ 0 & w/prob \quad 1-\exp(-\xi h) \end{cases}$$

where

S = stock price
t = time
q = risk-neutral probability of an up move in S, conditional on no default
ξ = continuous arrival intensity of the risk of default
h = time interval on the pricing lattice

The next expression, which is very similar to the CRR model, represents the probabilities under the risk-neutral measure:

$$q = \frac{\exp[(r+\xi)h] - d}{u - d}$$

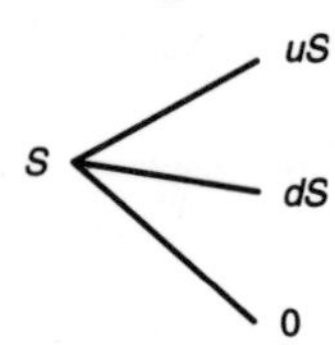

FIGURE 4.3 *Binomial Tree with Jump-to-Default Branch*

The Firm Variable

The underlying, driving variable in our model is the readily observable stock price, in contrast to the unobservable value of the firm. The model tracks the evolution of a convertible bond issuer's stock price, allowing for a jump in the price to zero should the issuer default on its debt. The model writes down debt directly as a function of the stock price, as in the following equations, which begin with the process for the stock price, and then develops the pricing equations for debt:

$$dS(t) = (r + \xi(S(t), t))S(t)\, dt + \sigma S(t)\, dZ(t) - S(t)\, dN(\xi(S(t), t))$$

$$dD = \left[D_S (r + \xi)\, S + \frac{1}{2} D_{SS}\, \sigma^2 S^2 + D_t\right] dt + D_S\, \sigma S\, dZ + [\phi\, D - D]\, dN(\xi)$$

$$E[dD] = rD\, dt.$$

$$D[r + \xi(1 - \phi)] = D_S(r + \xi)S + \frac{1}{2} D_{SS}\, \sigma^2 S^2 + D_t$$

Note that this is the standard fundamental asset pricing PDE with the adjusted risk-free rate as $[r + \xi(1 - \phi)]$. Its solution is:

$$D(S(t), t) = E\left\{\exp\left(-\int_t^T [r(u) + \xi(S(u), u)(1 - \phi)]\, du\right)\right\}$$

The percentage loss in value of the firm when it defaults is expressed as follows:

$$Y - 1 = \frac{\phi D - V}{V} = \phi \mathcal{L} - 1$$

The term $\mathcal{L}$ represents the level of leverage, or the ratio of debt to firm value, and ϕ is the recovery rate of debt. Thus, upon default, the firm value jumps from V to ϕD. The entire derivation occurs in a risk-neutral context. The result is an expression for debt that maps nicely to the reduced-form Duffie-Singleton model (1999), so that since $dV = dS + dD$, we have,

$$\frac{dV}{V} = \mu\, dt + \eta\, dZ + (Y - 1)\, dN(\xi)$$

where μ, η are functions of the parameters of S and D. The specification implies a lognormal firm value with stochastic volatility.[3]

The value of the firm, V, is equal to the value of the firm's equity, S, less the value of its debt, D. Therefore, a change in V will equal the net change in the value of the firm's equity and the value of its debt. So by starting with the value of a firm's equity S, and deriving the value of debt D, we can

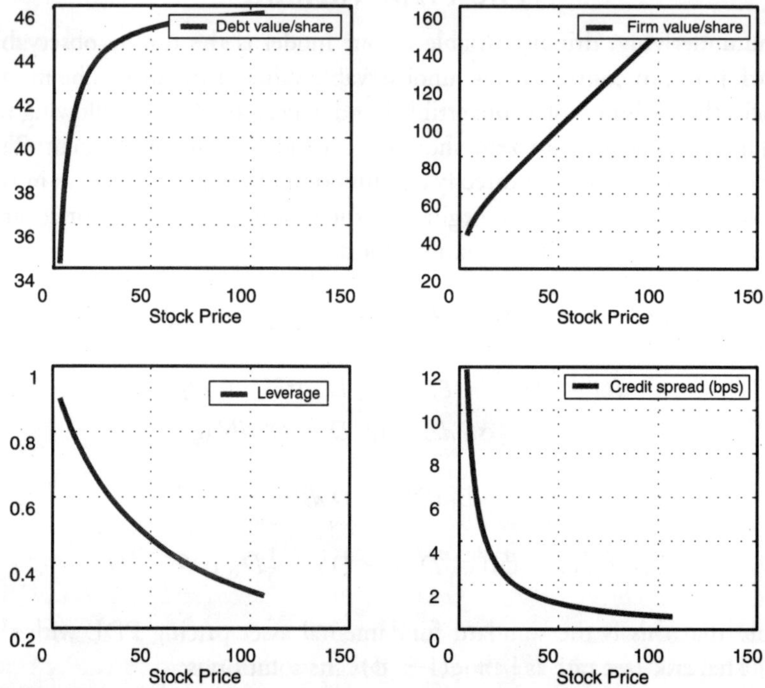

Debt, firm asset value, leverage, and spreads in the jump-to-default equity model plotted against equity value. We implemented the solution using a lattice integration approach. The plots are based on the following parameter values: stock price $S = 100$, zero-coupon debt face value per share $F = 50$, maturity of debt $T = 5$ years, volatility coefficient $\sigma = 0.3$, default intensity $\xi(S(t)) = \exp(-0.1)/S(t)$. The recovery rate is $\phi = 0.4$. The plots present range of 2.5-year forward the values of debt, firm value, equity, leverage, and credit spread on the bond with remaining 2.5-year maturity.

FIGURE 4.4 *Impact of Changes in Stock Price on Value of Firm Variables*

Source: "An Integrated Model for Hybrid Securities," *Management Science* 53, 1375–1388.

back out the value of the firm V as the sum $S + D$, thus demonstrating the connection of our model to structural, as well as reduced-form, models.

The four graphs in **FIGURE 4.4** illustrate that the model has the correct relationships of the security values to the underlying stock price. As the stock price on the x-axis changes, the other variables in the model—value of debt per share, firm value per share, leverage, and credit spread, as shown on the y-axis—also change. Each relationship exhibits the anticipated convexity or concavity.

For example, in the top left graph of Figure 4.4, the concave relationship between a change in stock price and a change in the value of debt is consistent with one's intuition. When the stock price increases from a low baseline, the corresponding value of debt rises very quickly, but when the stock price increases from a high baseline, the change has much less of an impact on the value of debt. The decreasing marginal change in the value of the debt is a function of the nature of debt as a claim on a fixed payment.

The top right graph in Figure 4.4 shows the linear relationship between firm value and stock price. Figure 4.4 also illustrates how leverage tends to decrease in a convex fashion (bottom left graph) and credit spreads (in basis points [bps]) decrease before leveling off, as stock prices increase. The relationship between stock price and both leverage and credit spread is convex. Similar relationships may be seen when the x-axis variable is the firm value instead.

The relationships are nearly identical regardless of whether stock price or firm value is on the x-axis. The benefit of using the former variable to drive our model is that it is readily observable, while a firm's value is not.

Model Elements

The model incorporates three components—the term structure model, default risk model, and equity model which, in this case, is a CEV model.

The first layer of the model is a process that describes equity price movements prior to default. We use a standard risk-neutral CEV process, which is described by the following:

$$dS(t) = r(t)\, S(t)\, dt + \sigma S(t)^{\gamma}\, dZ(t)$$

where for $\gamma < 1$ this specification exhibits the leverage effect and for $\gamma = 1$, a Black-Scholes geometric Brownian motion. We modify the process by allowing for default using probability $\lambda(t)$, and we discretize the resulting jump-to-default model.

The equity model is based on the Nelson and Ramaswamy (1990) approach in which they show how to discretize the CEV process in a recombining binomial tree. Our addition is a third branch from each node of the binomial tree, which represents a jump-to-default value for equity and is expressed by the following set of equations:

$$S[Y_S(t)] = \begin{cases} [\sigma_S(1-\gamma)\, Y_S(t)]^{\frac{1}{1-\gamma}} & \text{if } Y_S(t) > 0 \\ 0 & \text{if } Y_S(t) \le 0 \end{cases}$$

$$Y_S(t+h) = \begin{cases} Y_S(t) + \sqrt{h} & wp \quad q(t)[1-\lambda(t)] \\ Y_S(t) - \sqrt{h} & wp \quad [1-q(t)][1-\lambda(t)] \\ 0 & wp \quad \lambda(t) \end{cases}$$

$$q(t) = \begin{cases} \dfrac{R(t)/[1-\lambda(t)] - b(t)}{a(t) - b(t)} & \text{if } Y_S(t) > 0 \\ 0 & \text{if } Y_S(t) \leq 0 \end{cases}$$

$$a(t) = \frac{S[Y_S(t) + \sqrt{h}]}{S[Y_S(t)]}$$

$$b(t) = \frac{S[Y_S(t) - \sqrt{h}]}{S[Y_S(t)]}$$

where

t = generic node on the tree
$S(t)$ = stock price at node t
h = length of one period on the tree
$\lambda(t)$ = risk-neutral likelihood of a jump to default at node t
$R(t)$ = gross one-period interest rate at node t

This is a tree for which all probabilities are risk neutral. The value $a(t)$ is the size of the up move in the stock tree, and the value $b(t)$ is the size of the down move. Because the standard CEV process allows for the stock price to be absorbed at zero, our model provides for both drifts to default and jumps to default. This is one of the innovations of our model.

The second layer of the model is a standard interest-rate model that incorporates the evolution of forward rates over time. We adopt the discrete-time, recombining form of the HJM model. This term structure model is as follows:

$$f(t+h, T) = f(t, T) + \alpha(t, T)h + \sigma(t, T)X_f\sqrt{h}$$

where for any given pair of time points (t, T) with $0 \leq t \leq T \leq T^* - h$, $f(t, T)$ denotes the forward rate on the default-free bonds applicable to the period $(T, T+h)$. At all times t, assume zero-coupon bonds of all maturities are available. The short rate is $f(t, T) = r(t)$, and forward rates follow the stochastic process. The drift in the process is represented by $\alpha(t, T)$ and the volatility by $\sigma(t, T)$ (both taken to be functions of time only, to preserve the computational tractability of the model), and $X_f(t)$ is a random variable taking values in the set $\{-1, +1\}$.

The time t price of a default-free zero-coupon bond of maturity $T \geq t$ is, as usual, defined by the following:

$$P(t, T) = \exp\left\{-\sum_{k=th}^{T/h-1} f(t, kh)\cdot h\right\}$$

To complete the risk-neutral lattice, let $B(t)$ equal the time t value of a money market account with an initial investment of \$1 for which the proceeds roll over at the default-free short rate, such that

$$B(t) = \exp\left\{\sum_{k=0}^{th-1} r(kh)\cdot h\right\}$$

Using Martingale arguments, we arrive at the following recursive expression that relates the risk-neutral drifts α to the volatilities σ at each t:

$$\sum_{k=t/h+1}^{T/h-1} \alpha(t,kh) = \frac{1}{h^2}\ln\left(E_t\left[\exp\left\{-\sum_{k=t/h+1}^{T/h-1} \sigma(t,kh)X_f h^{3/2}\right\}\right]\right)$$

Next, the equity and debt processes are joined together in a bivariate lattice with two goals in mind. The first is that the probabilities of the joint process will achieve the correct correlation between equity returns and changes in the spot rate, and the second is that the lattice will be recombining to ensure fast computation of derivatives prices.

The lattice model is hexanomial, meaning that emanating from each node are six possible branches, or states, as depicted in **TABLE 4.1**.

The table contains two free parameters, m_1 and m_2, in the probability measure. The correct values of both parameters are found in order to provide a default-consistent Martingale measure with the appropriate correlation between the equity and interest rate processes. This also ensures that the lattice recombines.

TABLE 4.1 *States and Hexanomial Probabilities*

X_f	X_s	PROBABILITY
1	1	$P_1=(1+m_1)(1-\lambda(t))/4$
1	−1	$P_2=(1-m_1)(1-\lambda(t))/4$
−1	1	$P_3=(1+m_2)(1-\lambda(t))/4$
−1	−1	$P_4=(1-m_2)(1-\lambda(t))/4$
1	$-\alpha$	$P_5=\lambda(t)/2$
−1	$-\alpha$	$P_6=\lambda(t)/2$

Source: "An Integrated Model for Hybrid Securities," *Management Science* 53, 1375–1388.

The default process is the third and final layer in the model. To facilitate implementation, we make default a function of the equity price and the interest rate at each node on the tree. The theoretical support for this approach is that equity prices should reflect credit risk, and default probabilities have been shown to be connected to the term structure.[4] We use an endogenous default approach, meaning that a conditional $\lambda(t)$ is specified at each node, with $\lambda(t)$ being a function of the state variables—equity and interest rates. Assuming a functional relationship between $\lambda(t)$ and the other variables, we are able to obtain a consistent and parsimonious lattice.

We define default intensity, $\xi(t)$, as follows:

$$\xi(t) = \exp[a_0 + a_1 r(t) - a_2 \ln S(t) + a_3 (t - t_0)]$$

which is a function of the spot rate $r(t)$ in the term structure of forward rates $f(t)$, stock price $S(t)$ at each node, and time t. A similar, but less general, endogenous default intensity extraction has been implemented by Das and Sundaram (2000), Carayannopoulos and Kalimipalli (2003), and Acharya, Das, and Sundaram (2002).

Default intensity $\xi(t)$ is a function of the four parameters—a_0, a_1, a_2, and a_3—introduced previously in Figure 4.1 as inputs to the model. Parameter a_0 determines the direction, up or down, on the tree. Parameter a_1 modulates default as a function of the interest rate, and parameter a_2 modulates default as a function of the stock price. Parameter a_3 is the coefficient of the total time from t_0 to current time t on the lattice. Thus, a_3 is a slope parameter, so that when a_3 is positive, default rates are rising, and when negative, default rates are falling.

In a construction such as this, if the stock price goes to infinity, $\xi(t)$ will be zero with no default output possible in the model. If, however, S goes to zero, $\xi(t)$ will go to infinity, and the model will indicate instant default.

So from every node there are six possible states—two default states and four nondefault states. The four possible states are (1) rise in equity price, S, and interest rate, r; (2) rise in S and fall in r; (3) fall in S and rise in r; and (4) fall in S and r. The two default states are both jumps to default to account for the separate cases of default in a rising and falling interest-rate scenario. However, these default states could be collapsed into one.

To ensure that the model maintains the correct correlation between interest rates and equity prices, we need to specify a correlation equation:

$$Cov(X_f(t), X_S(t)) = \left[\frac{1 - \lambda(t)}{2}\right][m_1 - m_2]$$

as well as a second equation for stock returns,

$$E\left[\frac{S(t+h)}{S(t)}\right] = \left(\frac{1-\lambda(t)}{4}\right)[a(t)(1+m_1) + b(t)(1-m_1)$$
$$+ a(t)(1+m_2) + b(t)(1-m_2)] = \exp[r(t)h]$$

to ensure the stock price is a Martingale under the risk-neutral measure.

Each of the six possible states on the tree corresponds to a probability (p_1 to p_6). These probabilities are defined by parameters m_1 and m_2 as shown in Table 4.1. This is a mathematical nicety that allows us to solve for the probabilities. Thus, m_1 and m_2 are two free parameters in the Martingale condition of the stock process as well as in the covariance calculation between interest rates and equity prices. In solving for these two parameters, the model actually solves for p_1 through p_6 in completely closed form. The result is a six-way tree instead of the standard equity-option binomial tree in completely closed form.

Essentially, this completes the description of the model. The probability of default in the model is driven by the intensity of default, so that defining the values of a_0, a_1, a_2, and a_3 defines the default function and indicates how default will occur in the model. This entire model can be written in about two and a half pages of VBA program code in an Excel spreadsheet and runs quickly enough that it can be calibrated easily.

Calibrating the Model with Credit Default Swaps

The increasing amount of trading in credit default swaps (CDS) offers a source of empirical data for calibrating the model. All of the model parameters come directly from Bloomberg screens with the exception of the four parameters a_0 to a_3. The term structure of CDS is available for cross-sectional fitting of the model parameters. To illustrate how changes in the parameters have an impact on the term structure of CDS spreads, **FIGURE 4.5** shows the plots of four curves for maturities from one to five years with quarterly time steps.

Keeping all other parameters fixed, the parameters a_1 to a_3 are varied, with a_0 held constant in all scenarios. The effect of parameters a_1 (impact of the short rate) and a_2 (the coefficient of the equity price) can be observed in Figure 4.5. Parameter a_1 has a level effect on the spread curve, but as parameter a_2 increases, default spreads decline. And when $a_3 > 0$, the term structure of CDS spreads is upward sloping, and when $a_3 < 0$, default spreads are declining, which is consistent with a reduction in premia over time.

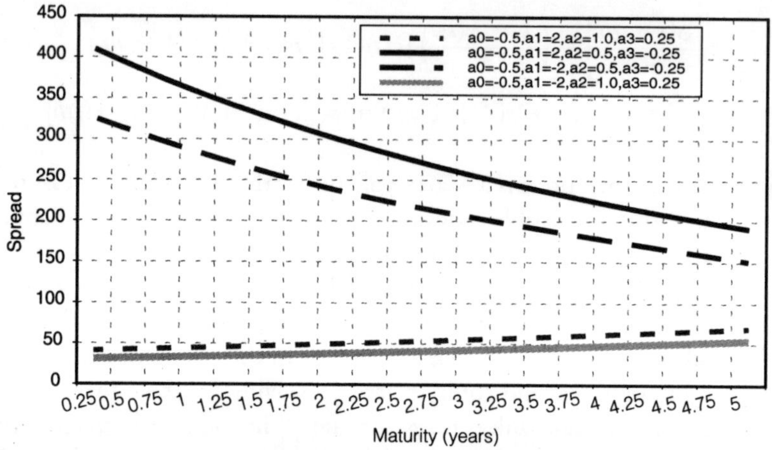

Term structure of default swap spreads for varied default function parameters. This figure presents the term structure of default swap spreads for maturities from 1 to 5 years. The figure has 4 plots. The default intensity is written as $\xi(t) = \exp[a_0 + a_1 r(t) + a_3 (t - t_0)]/S(t)^{a_2}$. Keeping all the other parameters fixed, we varied parameters a_1, a_2, and a_3. Hence, the 4 plots are the result. Periods in the model are quarterly, indexed by i. The forward rate curve is very simple and is just $f(i) = 0.06 + 0.001 \ln(i)$. The forward rate volatility curve is $\sigma_f(i) = 0.01 + 0.0005 \ln(i)$. The initial stock price is 100, and the stock return volatility is 0.30, given $\gamma = 1$. Correlation between stock returns and forward rates is 0.30, and recovery rates are a constant 40%. The default function parameters are presented on the plots.

FIGURE 4.5 *Term Structure of Default Spreads*

Source: "An Integrated Model for Hybrid Securities," *Management Science* 53, 1375–1388.

Gamma, or the coefficient of the CEV model, can also be varied to reflect the impact of leverage in the model as shown in **FIGURE 4.6.** As gamma drops from 1.0 to 0.5, the curves move monotonically upward, and leverage increases. In this way, the model can be tuned to account for any required leverage effects.

The model can also be calibrated to CDS spreads. **FIGURE 4.7** presents the fitted term structure of CDS spreads for maturities from one to four years plotted against the original default spreads for the stock return of Ambac Financial Group, Inc.

The first and third graphs present the term structures for January 2, 2002, and June 28, 2002, respectively. The second and fourth graphs show the empirical and fitted CDS spreads for those dates. The fit is almost perfect. While our feedback was quite good regarding the model's potential usefulness for manufacturing firms, we questioned its practical application for firms in other industries. This example for Ambac shows that the model can be fitted to the CDS spreads of financial firms as well. This

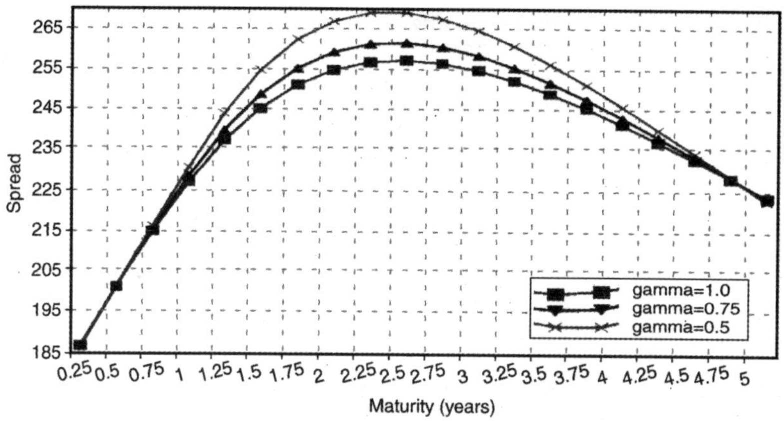

Term structure of default swap spreads for varying leverage. This figure presents the term structure of default swap spreads for maturities from 1 to 5 years. The default intensity is written as $\xi(t) = \exp[a_0 + a_1 r(t) + a_3 (t - t_0)]/S(t)^{a_2}$. Keeping all the other parameters fixed, we fixed parameters $a_0 = -1.814681$, $a_1 = 58.55167$, $a_2 = 2.16029$, and $a_3 = -0.37119$. Periods in the model are quarterly, indexed by i. The forward rate curve is very simple and is just $f(i) = 0.06 + 0.001 \ln(i)$. The forward rate volatility curve is $\sigma_f(i) = 0.01 + 0.0005 \ln(i)$. The initial stock price is 58.31, and the stock return volatility is 0.40, given $\gamma = 1$. Correlation between stock returns and forward rates is 0.0, and recovery rates are a constant 40%. We varied γ from 0.5 to 1.0. Since the stock volatility when $\gamma = 1$ is 0.4, as we change the CEV coefficient γ, we also adjust the variable σ so as to keep the conditional total volatility of the diffusion roughly the same, by the following equation: $\sigma_s S_0^{\gamma} = \sigma_{CRR} S_0$. This ensures that the total diffusion volatility in the CEV model is approximately the same as in the CRR model, and is the same approach as used by Nelson and Ramaswamy (1990) for comparisons in their paper. We notice very minor changes in CDS spread curves.

FIGURE 4.6 *CDS Spreads and the Leverage Effect*

Source: "An Integrated Model for Hybrid Securities," *Management Science* 53, 1375–1388.

capability is a definite advantage for a reduced-form model, as compared to the more common structural model, which may not properly account for the leverage effect.

Impact of Default Risk

The model may be easily used to price callable convertible debt. One aspect of considerable interest is the extent to which default risk has an impact on the pricing of convertible debt through its effect on the values of the call and convertible features via interest-rate risk and equity price risk, respectively. Comparing callable convertible bonds and plain defaultable bonds in environments with different volatilities, we show that default risk might make the convertible bonds more valuable. As the risk of default increases,

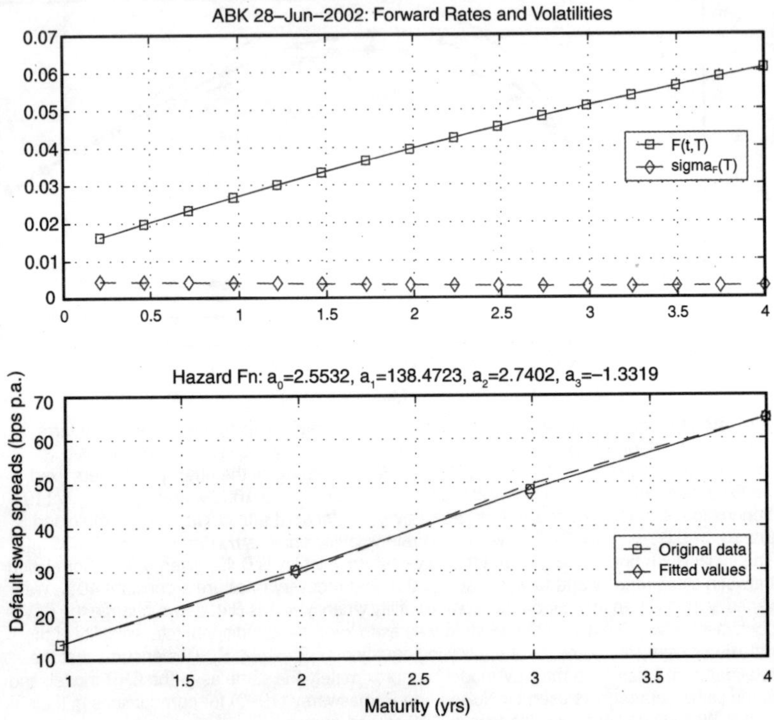

Fitted and Empirical Default Swap Spreads for AMBAC. This figure presents the fitted term structure of default swap spreads for maturities from 1 to 4 years, plotted against the original default spreads. The first graph presents the term structure for June 28, 2002. The second graph shows the empirical and fitted credit default swap spreads. The default intensity is written as $\xi(t) = \exp[a_0 + a_1 r(t) + a_3 (t - t_0)]/S(t)^{a_2}$. The fitted parameters of this function are provided in the figures below. The stock price on the 2 dates was \$58.31 and \$67.20 respectively. Stock return volatility was roughly 40% on both dates. Recovery rates on default were assumed to be 40% and the correlation between short rates (i.e., 3 months tbills) and the stock return of AMBAC was computed over the period January 2000 to June 2002; it was found to be statistically zero. The yield curves for the chosen dates were extracted from the historical data pages provided by the Federal Reserve Board.

FIGURE 4.7 *Calibration to CDS*

Source: "An Integrated Model for Hybrid Securities," *Management Science* 53, 1375–1388.

with the default parameter a_0 plotted on the x-axis in **FIGURE 4.8**, the convertible bond loses less value than the comparable nonconvertible bond.

At some point, both bonds converge in price because, as default risk continues to rise, it effectively snuffs out the value of both the warrant feature and the interest-rate call on the convertible until neither effectively exists; thus, the bond basically becomes the equivalent of a plain bond without callable and convertible features.

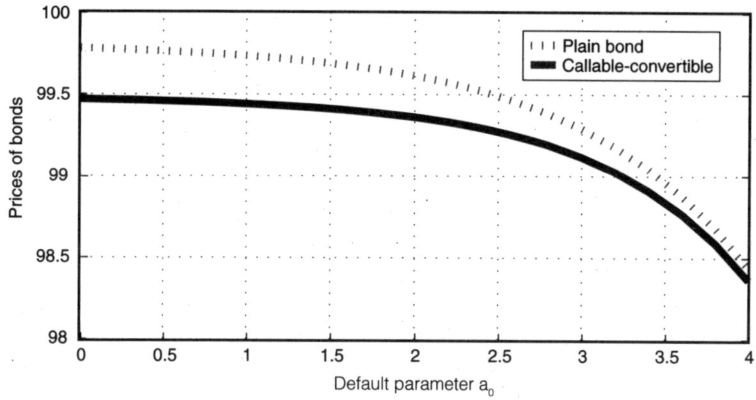

FIGURE 4.8 *Comparison of Bond Prices for Convertible and Plain Bonds, Example 1*

Source: "An Integrated Model for Hybrid Securities," *Management Science* 53, 1375–1388.

Another example is shown in **FIGURE 4.9**. Again, default risk is on the x-axis. As default risk increases, the values of both the plain and convertible five-year bonds drop in lockstep, but only to a certain point.

In this example, market conditions at the outset are such that the call and conversion features of the convertible bond essentially cancel each

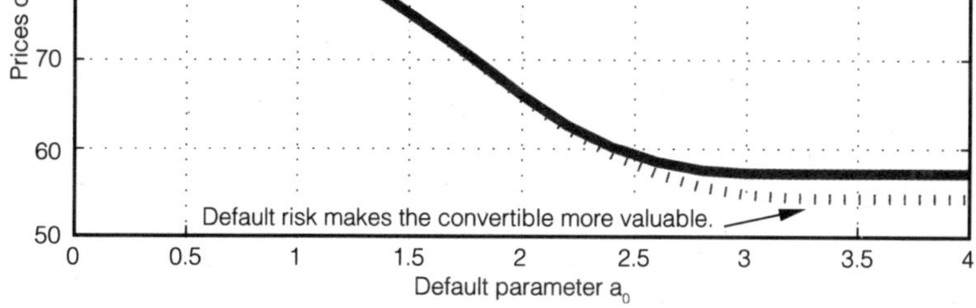

FIGURE 4.9 *Comparison of Bond Prices for Convertible and Plain Bonds, Example 2*

Source: "An Integrated Model for Hybrid Securities," *Management Science* 53, 1375–1388.

other out, causing the two bonds to be priced virtually identically in an environment with zero default risk. At a certain level of default risk, however, the convertible bond begins trading richer than the plain bond. This happens because the interest-rate call option is deteriorating at a faster rate than the warrant option, which, through its equity dependence, imbues the convertible with additional value.

A calibration of the model also permits the extraction of credit risk premia. A simple empirical illustration fits the model to the thirty names in the CDX Index. Using data from CreditGrades for the period from January 2000 to June 2002, we calibrated the model daily to the CDS spreads for each name in the index. A benefit of the model is that it can be fitted daily to the term structure of CDS spreads, so time series data are not required. This is the same approach that a trader would follow if he or she were trading based on this model. The trader would fit the model to the term structure and, using all the parameters for the day, compute the one-year probability of default.

FIGURE 4.10 plots the average risk premium ratio for the CDX Index from January 2000 to June 2002 and shows how the premium for default risk moves over time.

Using the fitted parameters, we computed the one-year risk-neutral default probabilities and quantified the risk premia by dividing the risk-neutral probability by the default probability from CreditGrades. Using the series of the different premia for each of the names in the index, we undertook a principal components decomposition of the premia that suggests two main components, or factors, that drive credit risk premia.

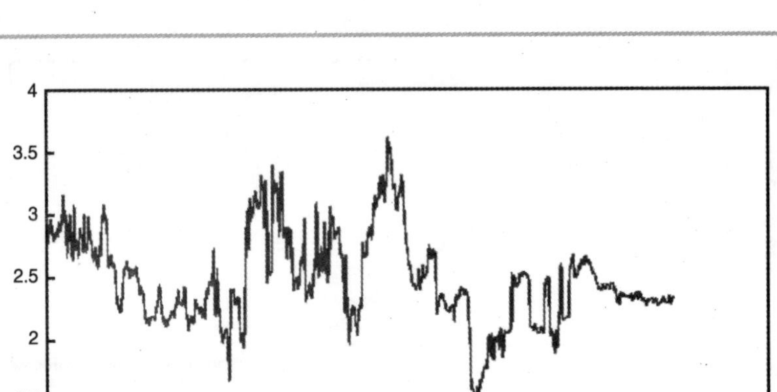

FIGURE 4.10 *Default Premia for the Dow Jones CDX INDU Index, January 2002 to June 2002*

Source: "An Integrated Model for Hybrid Securities," *Management Science* 53, 1375–1388.

The first principal component explains over 60 percent of the variation and the second explains nearly 30 percent of the variation. Comparing the time series of the main principal component to the time series of the S&P 500 Index, we find that they track closely, with a correlation of 50 percent. Therefore, the equity markets appear to be driving credit premia. We also compared the principal components to the time series of the VIX (volatility) Index, but the correlations were not statistically significant.

To this point, the model has considered a portfolio of only a single name. The next step is to test the model with a portfolio of multiple names. Basically, this involves fitting one hexanomial tree to each name in the portfolio. Each of the trees is on a recombining lattice, so a computer can easily describe with one tree all the risks related to that name. Suppose we have a portfolio of about forty-five names and want to know how it will behave. To model the risk-return probability of the portfolio, it is necessary to calibrate forty-five different trees. But each calibration takes only about fifteen to twenty seconds, so the computational effort is minimal. The next step is to put a correlation structure on the entire set of forty-five trees.

With credit models the correlation structure is obtained by reverse engineering various types of credit portfolio prices that exist in the market. In this case, that approach is not necessary. Since our model is driven by a combination of the equity process, the interest-rate process, and the implied default function of equity and interest rates, we can derive a covariance matrix that describes how equity and interest rates evolve over time.

The calibrated default function

$$\xi_i(t) = \frac{\exp[a_0^i + a_1^i r(t) + a_3^i (t - t_0)]}{S_i(t)^{a_2^i}}$$

is a function of the four parameters, a_0 to a_3. Once these four parameters are obtained for each name in the portfolio, the next step in determining the covariance matrix of default intensities is to take the Jacobian of this entire system. Letting the covariance matrix of $[r(t), S_1(t), S_2(t), \ldots, S_n(t)]'$ be Σ, we have the following process:

$$V(t) \approx J(t)\, \Sigma J(t)', \text{ where } J(t) \in R^{n\times(n+1)}$$

Jacobian

(jth row)

$$J_i(t) = \left[\frac{\partial \xi_i(t)}{\partial r(t)}, 0, \ldots, 0, \frac{\partial \xi_i(t)}{\partial S_i(t)}, 0, \ldots, 0\right]$$

$$= \left[a_1^i\, \xi_i(t), 0, \ldots, 0, \frac{-a_2^i}{S_i(t)}\, \xi_i(t), 0, \ldots, 0\right]$$

This process provides the entire covariance matrix for all forty-five names.

Another way of looking at this is that once we have the default functions for each name in the portfolio, and if we know the level of interest rates and the stock price, we can derive the default intensity for any name at any point in time. So, by generating simulated samples of a stock's price movements over time, which is easily done, we can simulate a system of default probabilities for every point in time. If we insert the simulated stock prices in the equation for $\xi(t)$, the default probability for that name is rendered.

We can effectively calculate, in the risk-neutral world, an entire simulation of default probabilities by using stock prices as the driver for all the correlations in the model. The simulation is also consistently arbitrage-free under the risk-neutral measure. Therefore, we have a fully consistent, arbitrage-free, risk-neutral-measure-driven correlation design that allows us to correlate stock prices, simulate them, and derive the corresponding default probabilities.

Contagion

Default risk includes two types of correlation. One is the correlation of default probabilities, which is driven by the correlation of stock prices. A second type of correlation is related to contagion. When contagion is present, even after the impact of default probability correlation is accounted for, further correlation in price movement is induced among the various names in the portfolio, initiated by the occurrence of defaults. Empirical evidence from previous research indicates that contagion does exist.[5] A copula function can capture the additional contagion. The model can be used to trade portfolios that might be susceptible to contagion.

Based on the entire data set of defaults from the last twenty-five years, we identified the contagion events, and after removing the default probability correlation, found that about 4 percent to 5 percent correlation remained. Thus, we injected this approximate level of additional correlation into the model, which was easily accomplished in the tree-framework. We did this by running the simulation after all the different trees had been calibrated. Each default probability, at every node on the tree or at each point in time, was actually drawn with an additional correlation to allow for the contagion correlation. The next section explores this further.

Three-Parameter Intensity Function

We created a version of the model that drops the interest rate component—in order to simplify the analysis—so that the default function consists of only three parameters: alpha, gamma, and beta. The default function is as follows:

$$\xi_t = \exp(\alpha + \gamma t) S_t^{-\beta}$$

Beta (β) has an impact on the curvature, gamma (γ) influences the slope, and alpha (α) modulates the level of the spread curve. This is exactly the same function described previously, with the exception of the interest-rate component, and therefore is a more compact version of the model. From a practical standpoint, almost all managers of fixed-income portfolios are already completely comfortable thinking in these terms—about the level, slope, and curvature of the yield curve as the three separate factors that drive fixed-income portfolios. Our model framework captures these three factors, mapping them quite nicely, not only in drawing the curves, but also in the mathematics behind the trees used to price the different securities.

We considered six names—General Motors Corp. (GM), Sun Microsystems, Inc. (SUNW), Barclays Bank PLC (BARC), Parmalat SpA (PRF), Amazon.com, Inc. (AMZN), and Northwest Airlines (NWAC)—through this basic default function. The first three names in Panel A of **TABLE 4.2** are of reasonably high quality with small CDS spreads. The next three names are of very poor quality with much wider CDS spreads; for example, the one-year spread for PRF is 16,383 bps.

TABLE 4.2 *Calibrated Default Functions for Six Firms*

PANEL A: INPUT DATA

TICKER	STK(S)	σ	ϕ	CDS SPREADS (BPS) 1 YR	2 YR	3 YR	4 YR	5 YR
BARC (UK)	5.2	33.40%	0.5	9.21	12.5	15.7	18.4	20.6
SUNW	3.95	61.20%	0.5	5.07	48.6	109	161	200
AMZN	34.95	59.60%	0.5	0.07	5.0	23.5	50.7	79.1
GM	30.93	34.50%	0.5	3723	1954	1364	1069	892
PRF (Italy)	0.11	86.20%	0.5	16383	8546	5775	4430	3605
NWAC	6.33	65.50%	0.5	5603	2988	2115	1677	1414

PANEL B: CALIBRATED PARAMETERS

TICKER	PARAMETERS α	β	γ	PD (5 YRS) MODEL	CREDIT GRADES
BARC (UK)	−3.2	1.89	0.15	0.21	0.10
SUNW	−3.93	1.16	0.65	0.52	0.19
AMZN	2.45	1.44	0.73	0.32	0.08
GM	−0.8	−0.37	−3.17	0.83	0.46
PRF	0.87	0.53	−2.37	0.99	0.77
NWAC	3.9	1.49	−1.93	0.91	0.59

Source: Bandreddi, Santhosh, Sanjiv Das, and Rong Fan, 2007. "Correlated Default Modeling with a Forest of Binomial Trees." *Journal of Fixed Income*, Winter, 1–20.

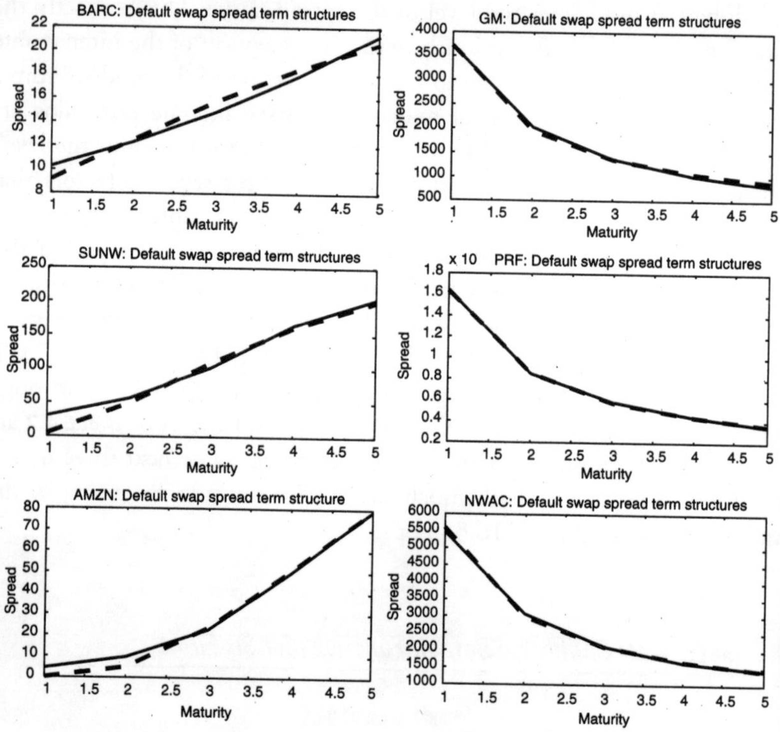

FIGURE 4.11 *CDS Curves for Weak and Strong Credits*

Source: Bandreddi, Santhosh, Sanjiv Das, and Rong Fan, 2007. "Correlated Default Modeling with a Forest of Binomial Trees." *Journal of Fixed Income*, Winter, 1–20.

We fitted the parameters α, β, and γ for each of the six stocks. These parameters are shown in Panel B of Table 4.2.

The CDS spread curves drawn from this model are given in **FIGURE 4.11**. The spread curves for the three high-quality names—SUNW, BARC, and AMZN—are on the left side and are upward sloping. This is a standard feature of almost all high-quality credits. Current spread levels tend to be smaller than future spread levels due to mean reversion and the potential for quality deterioration. Likewise, mean reversion and the potential for quality improvement affect the poorer quality names—GM, PRF, and NWAC—whose downward-sloping default spread curves are shown on the right side of Figure 4.11. Because they are conditional on the firms' surviving the short term, the default spread levels of the poorer credits should fall substantially. The model fits this intuition fairly well. The solid lines in each graph plot the actual, market-driven CDS spread curve, and the dashed lines represent the fitted spread curve.

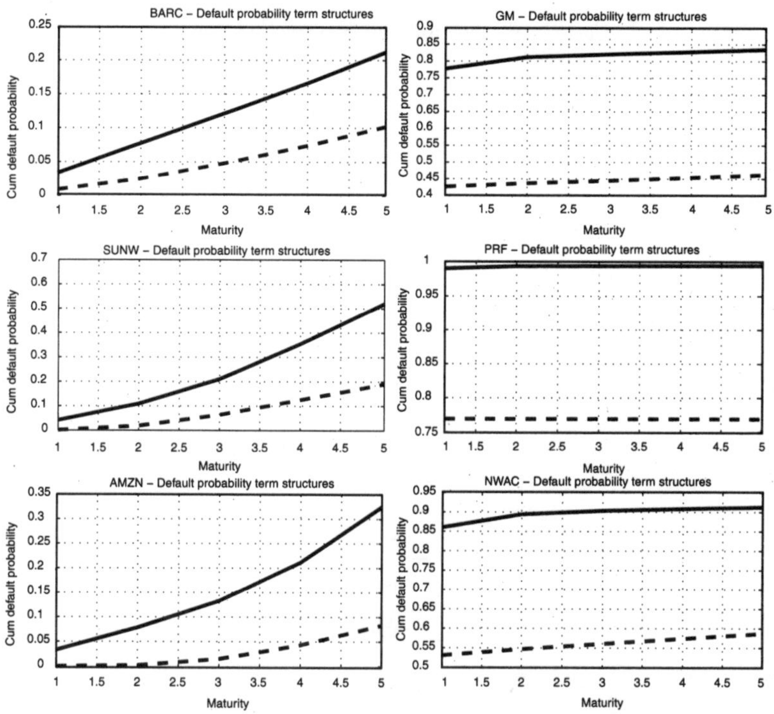

FIGURE 4.12 *Risk Premia for Weak and Strong Credits*

Source: Bandreddi, Santhosh, Sanjiv Das, and Rong Fan, 2007. "Correlated Default Modeling with a Forest of Binomial Trees." *Journal of Fixed Income*, Winter, 1–20.

The next set of graphs in **FIGURE 4.12** shows the default risk premia for the six credits. The solid line is the risk-neutral spread curve, and the dashed line is under the physical measure. The difference between the two lines indicates the premia for credit risk. Again, the stronger credits are in the graphs on the left side of the figure, and the weaker credits are on the right side. The difference between the two lines is smaller for the stronger credits than it is for the weaker credits, evidence of the larger default premiums the market demands on the weaker credits.

Correlated Default

To illustrate how the model estimates correlated default, we created a portfolio of ten credits for which we induced both types of correlation—for the probability of default and for contagion. **TABLE 4.3** describes the differences between the two types of correlation in the test portfolio. The process

TABLE **4.3** *Correlated Default and Basket Contracts*

CORR S	CORR PD	1ST DEF	2ND DEF
Panel A:	**Intensity**	**Corr = p**	**Conditional Corr = p**
0.00	−0.0006	0.025660	0.000158
0.40	0.3952	0.024665	0.001228
0.80	0.7965	0.021124	0.005046
Panel B:	**Intensity**	**Corr = p**	**Conditional Corr = 0**
0.00	−0.0015	0.025605	0.000139
0.40	0.3953	0.025753	0.000167
0.80	0.7971	0.025726	0.000162
Panel C:	**Intensity**	**Corr = 0**	**Conditional Corr = p**
0.00	0.0005	0.025611	0.000177
0.40	−0.0004	0.026013	0.000178
0.80	0.0004	0.025556	0.000169

Source: Bandreddi, Santhosh, Sanjiv Das, and Rong Fan, 2007. "Correlated Default Modeling with a Forest of Binomial Trees." *Journal of Fixed Income*, Winter, 1–20.

involved pricing two types of basket default contracts—the first to default and the second to default. A first-to-default contract gives the buyer of the contract a certain payoff if any one name in a basket of securities defaults within one year. A second-to-default contract is one for which payoff occurs when two or more securities default within one year.

The first column in Table 4.3 gives the correlation of stock returns, *Corr S*; the next column lists the correlations of default probabilities, *Corr PD*; and the last two columns provide the probabilities of the first-to-default, *1st def,* and second-to-default, 2nd *def,* outcomes. The three panels in Table 4.3 show how default intensity correlation, *Corr,* and contagion correlation, *Conditional Corr,* have an impact on the probabilities of default in the portfolio under each of the three scenarios described in the first column.

Interestingly, the two types of correlation affect the two types of contracts in different ways. When the default probability correlation is high, the first-to-default contract becomes less valuable. The reason for this is that either all or none of the securities is likely to default, and the probability of the payoff being triggered declines. The second-to-default contract increases in value when the default correlation increases, because the probability of more than one default occurring at the same time, or within a given period of time, is higher.

If both types of correlation are assumed to exist, as is illustrated in Panel A, the value of the second-to-default contract increases sharply as correlation among the securities increases. When the correlation among the securities is 80 percent, the probability of payoff of the second-to-default contract is 0.005046, compared to a value of 0.000158 when the correlation is zero. The opposite is true for the value of the first-to-default contract but by a lesser degree. When the correlation among the portfolio securities rises to 80 percent, the probability of payoff of the first-to-default falls to 0.021124 from 0.025660, its value when the correlation of the securities in the portfolio is zero.

If either of the correlations is "switched off" so that, as in Panel B, default correlation is present, but contagion correlation is not, the values of the second-to-default contracts drop substantially compared to their values under the conditions described in Panel A. And Panel C presents the results in the opposite case, when contagion correlation is present, but default correlation is not. Here again there is not much effect on the values of either the first- or second-to-default contracts.

We did not anticipate this result when we built the model; that is, both types of correlation need to be present to effect meaningful changes in the value of the contracts because the correlations interact. If either type of correlation is absent in a portfolio, meaning that the assets are truly uncorrelated or contagion effects are assumed away, the prices of the contracts exhibit only minimal variation with changing correlation. We were surprised to discover this unexpected relationship.

Summary

Thus, our model offers a promising approach for pricing securities with equity, interest-rate, and default risk, in particular, convertible bonds. The model incorporates two types of correlation and is easily calibrated to derive return probabilities for a range of products. Technically, the model is a hybrid in the reduced-form framework that matches the stylized features of structural models and can be viewed as a bridge between two broad classes of models. The methodology we have developed is a risk-neutral, arbitrage-free correlation model implemented using a forest of default-embedded trees, rather than a single hexanomial tree. And the basic model for each name runs quickly and easily on an Excel spreadsheet.

One of the economic benefits of the model is its ability to price hybrid derivatives. Any security with a debt-equity linkage can be priced using observable market data with easy calibration for relative pricing. This approach could not have been undertaken until three or four years ago, simply because there were not enough CDS trades on which to base the model. With the growth of the CDS market, this approach is now possible. Another benefit of the model is that it supports correct, risk-neutral, arbitrage-free simulation of credit portfolio defaults and thus can be used to manage credit portfolios.

The model can also generate implied default functions. Endogenous default functions allow for the translation of equity correlations into default intensity correlations. We use a Cox process framework to decompose credit correlations into standard default probability correlations and contagion correlations, both of which have important portfolio effects for practitioners, particularly those running fixed-income portfolios.

Finally, credit portfolio losses are sensitive to conditional correlations, or contagion correlations, over and above standard probability-of-default, or intensity, correlations. Loss distributions are most sensitive when both types of correlation are present.

References

Acharya, Viral, Sanjiv Das, and Rangarajan Sundaram. 2002. "Pricing Credit Derivatives with Rating Transitions." *Financial Analysts Journal* 58 (May/June): 28–44.

Carr, Peter, and Vadim Linetsky. 2006. "A Jump to Default Extended CEV Model: An Application of Bessel Processes." Working paper. New York University and Northwestern University.

Carayannopoulos, Peter, and Madhu Kalimipalli. 2003. "Convertible Bond Prices and Inherent Biases." *Journal of Fixed Income* 13: 64–73.

Cox, John, Stephen Ross, and Mark Rubenstein. 1979. "Option Pricing: A Simplified Approach." *Journal of Financial Economics* 7 (September): 229–63.

———. 2000. "A Discrete-Time Approach to Arbitrage-Free Pricing of Credit Derivatives." *Management Science* 46 (January): 46–62.

Das, Sanjiv, Darrell Duffie, Nikunj Kapadia, and Leandro Saita. 2007. "Common Failings: How Corporate Defaults Are Correlated." *Journal of Finance* 62: 93–117.

Duffie, Darrell, Leandro Saita, and Ke Wang. 2005. "Multi-Period Corporate Default Probabilities with Stochastic Covariates." Working paper, Stanford University (September).

Duffie, Darrell, and Kenneth Singleton. 1999. "Modeling Term Structures of Defaultable Bonds." *Review of Financial Studies* 12: 687–720.

Heath, David, Robert A. Jarrow, and Andrew Morton. 1990. "Bond Pricing and the Term Structure of Interest Rates: A Discrete Time Approximation." *Journal of Financial and Quantitative Analysis* 25 (December): 419–40.

Nelson, Dan, and Krishna Ramaswamy. 1990. "Simple Binomial Processes as Diffusion Approximations in Financial Models." *Review of Financial Studies* 3: 393–430.

Chapter Notes

1. Sanjiv R. Das and Rangarajan K. Sundaram, "A Simple Model for Pricing Securities with Equity, Interest-Rate, and Default Risk," Working paper, July 2006. This article has been subsequently revised and published as "An Integrated Model for Hybrid Securities" in *Management Science* 53 (September 2007): 1439–1451. This rendition is based on a talk given on this paper at the *Journal Of Investment Management* conference in the fall of 2006. Rangarajan Sundaram is the Yamaichi Faculty Fellow and an associate professor of finance at the Stern School of Business at New York University. The talk also contains results from the paper "Correlated Default Modeling with a Forest of Binomial Trees" by Santhosh Bandreddi, Sanjiv Das, and Rong Fan published in the *Journal of Fixed Income*, Winter 2007, 1–20.

2. μ is the upshift parameter for stock increases and d is the downshift parameter for stock declines.

3. The implemented version of our model is more general and uses the Nelson and Ramaswamy (1990) CEV model for the equity process in order to account for the leverage effect.

4. See Duffie, Saita, and Wang (2005).

5. See Das, Duffie, Kapadia, and Saita (2007).

CHAPTER 5

Correlation in Daily Equity and Fixed-Income Returns

Implications for a Cross-Asset Factor Model

TERRY MARSH

Who—Terry Marsh is cofounder and CEO of Quantal International, Inc., and a member of the board of managers of Quantal Asset Management, LLC. He is emeritus professor of finance at the University of California at Berkeley. He has been awarded the Batterymarch Fellowship and the Hoover Institution National Fellowship and is a CPA and Fellow, CPA Australia. Marsh has consulted for the New York Stock Exchange, Options Clearing Corporation, Industrial Bank of Japan, New Japan Securities Co., Ltd., and Banamex, and was appointed to the Presidential Task Force on Market Mechanisms that investigated the 1987 stock market crash. In 1993, he was a Yamaichi Fellow and Visiting Professor of Economics at the University of Tokyo. An author of numerous studies, Marsh has published in the *Journal of Finance, Journal of Empirical Finance, American Economic Review, European Economic Review, Journal of Business, Journal of Financial Economics, Japanese Journal of Financial Economics*, and the *Wall Street Journal* among other widely read industry periodicals. Marsh received his MBA and PhD degrees from the University of Chicago.

New Thinking—Terry Marsh and his coauthors (2006) propose modeling the relation between equity and fixed-income returns to extend the literature on factor structure to cross-asset factors with explanatory power for returns in both global equity and fixed-income markets.[1] The authors study both the general trends in realized correlation of U.S. equities and Treasury bonds over the last ten years, and also the day-to-day "jumps" in equity and fixed-income returns. They find some evidence that the longer-run changes in correlation between equity and fixed-income factors are associated with a Fama-French HML "factor" and macrovariables, but the explanatory power is quite weak. With respect to the day-to-day jumps in comovements, the authors report that there seem to be two distinct regimes: one a flight-to-liquidity/quality, and the second, macroeconomic surprises; it is not clear that events in both regimes have the same relationship to market volatility. The authors also provide tentative evidence of a regime-like, long-run persistence in equity–fixed-income return comovements in the last half of the ten-year sample period that is likely associated with the management of interest rates by the U.S. Federal Reserve. The research presented here is intended to provide a basis for construction of a conditional factor model for *daily* global equity and term-structure movements.

Introduction

The motivation for undertaking this study was our interest in building a model that could explain the daily comovements in returns on equity and fixed-income instruments and that would in turn be useful in investment decisions that involve allocation and hedging across these asset classes. The stylized facts for the realized correlation of equity and fixed-income returns over the last ten years are quite remarkable—the average level of realized correlation between U.S. equity and fixed-income returns moved from about positive 60 percent in the mid-1990s to negative 40 percent in 2002; in 2006 it was roughly zero. We begin by extending these stylized facts: Did the correlation shifts seem to occur equally in different sectors, in value-growth-style classes, and for different market cap equities? Was the sensitivity of equity returns to different term structure factors—level, slope, curvature—the same through time?

After describing the joint behavior of equity and fixed-income returns over the last ten years, we outline how we have fitted a multifactor model to equities and fixed income and present some evidence about whether this fitted relation between equity and fixed-income factors is explained by company characteristics and macrovariables. We find some evidence that the shifts in correlation between equity returns and fixed-income factors are associated with a Fama-French high-minus-low (HML) factor and macrovariables, but the explanatory power is quite weak.

We then shift focus to a more microscopic analysis of the day-to-day comovements between equity returns and bond returns, and in particular to days when there are big "jumps"—outliers in returns on equities and fixed-income instruments. We see these jumps occur in two distinct types of market environments: The first consists of big down days for equities where a "flight to quality" or "flight to liquidity" in bonds is said to occur. The second environment is one where a substantial surprise revision in a macro variable, such as expected inflation, results in a big up day for equities and a big down day for fixed income. These jump events seem to occur in volatile market conditions where a simple volatility measure tends to be inadequate.

After identifying "big event" days for the combined equity-bond markets that are outside the bounds of normal behavior, we were curious to see if we could identify any serial persistence in the unusual behavior. While we could find no significant persistence in jumps in the comovement between equity and bond returns in the short term—that is, in days adjacent to a jump event—there does appear to be a longer-term persistence in these comovements. This persistence may be attributable to the management of interest rates by the U.S. Federal Reserve, and it appears to exhibit regime shifts as Federal Reserve policy changes.

We define the fixed-income factors in this study solely in terms of default-free bond returns, thus setting aside credit risk for now. Also, although we have fitted the equity–fixed-income factor model globally, most of the analysis presented here is for the U.S. market.

Stylized Facts: Realized Correlation of U.S. Equity and Fixed-Income Returns over Time: What a Joint Equity—Fixed-Income Model Needs to Explain

The time series of realized correlation of equity and fixed-income returns from January 9, 1997, to July 1, 2006, displays some interesting behavior. We used a methodology similar to that of Li (2002) in which we graphed the realized correlation of the daily returns of a value-weighted index of the 500 U.S. stocks with the largest capitalization and an equal-weighted index of Treasuries with maturities of six months, one year, and two, three, five, seven, ten, and twenty years.[2] We rebalanced the indexes daily. **FIGURE 5.1** shows the jagged pattern of *monthly* realized correlations along with a smoothed curve, calculated using a Hodrick-Prescott filter, superimposed on the chart.

We calculated monthly correlations for nonoverlapping months, within which correlation was assumed to remain constant. This approach can be thought of as a bivariate extension of the Merton volatility estimator. We averaged joint squared daily returns for the twenty to twenty-five trading days in a calendar month to estimate correlation for that month.

The magnitude of realized correlation of equity and bond returns is shown on the y-axis of Figure 5.1. The migration in correlation over the ten-year period is stunning. In early 1997 the realized correlation of daily

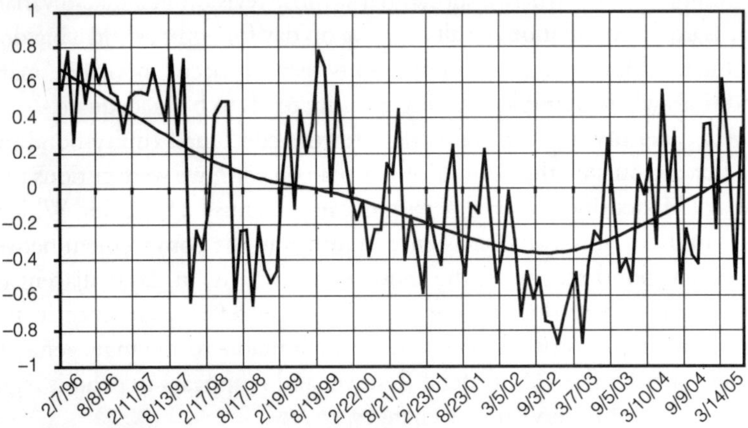

FIGURE 5.1 *Realized Correlation Between U.S. Equity and Bond Returns over the Last Decade*

Source: Quantal International

equity and bond returns was approximately 60 percent. This meant that, on average, if equity prices rose on a given day, bond prices would rise on average by approximately 60 percent of the equity price movement. After 1997 the correlation trended lower until it reached negative territory in mid-1999, bottoming out just above negative 40 percent around year-end 2002.[3] A negative 40 percent correlation means that if bond prices moved up in a day, equity prices on average moved down in an amount equal to roughly 40 percent of the bond price movement. Then, over the period extending from early 2003 to mid-2006, the correlation reverted back to basically zero in early 2005 and hovered around zero thereafter.

These movements in equity and bond return correlation over the ten years show up predictably as differences in subperiod results if you subdivide the ten years into two roughly equal subperiods. In the first subperiod, January 9, 1996, to December 29, 2000, the mean correlation between the equity and bond index returns is 0.18 with a *t*-stat of 3.23. By contrast, the mean correlation and the *t*-stat in the second subperiod are −0.25 and −5.19, respectively. The negative correlation of the second subperiod is "unusual" in that such sustained negative correlation has not been observed in the U.S. markets since the early to mid-1960s. Li (2002) and Scruggs and Glabadanidis (2001) found that from the mid-1960s to the mid-1990s—the thirty-plus-year time span preceding our sample period—the realized correlation trended upward and was in the 20 percent to 50 percent range.

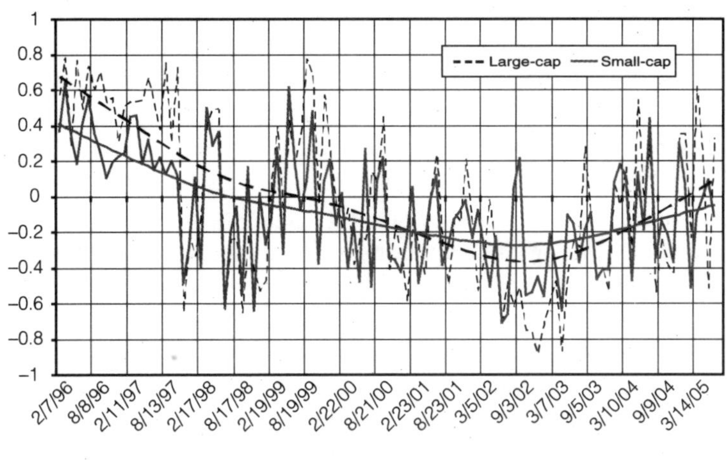

Source: Quantal International

FIGURE 5.2 *Realized Correlation Between U.S. Large-Cap and Small-Cap Equity Returns and Bond Returns over the Last Decade*

This positive trend was observed in almost all global markets, Japan being the most important exception.

The variation in realized correlation does not appear to be a "small-cap" or "large-cap" phenomenon. We define large-cap and small-cap stocks in terms of the value weighted indexes of stocks in the top and bottom deciles of the average 3,276 stocks used in the study.[4] **FIGURE 5.2** illustrates the realized correlation of both large- and small-cap stock returns with bond returns over the period of February 7, 1996, to July 1, 2006.

The mean correlation of the returns of large-cap equities with bond returns in the first subperiod was 0.19 (t-stat = 3.27), and the mean correlation of the returns of small-cap equities with bond returns was 0.04 (t-stat = 1.03). Guidolin and Timmermann (2004) report correlations of a similar magnitude for a longer sample period (January 1954 through December 1999) that overlaps our first subperiod. In our second subperiod the mean correlations for large-cap and small-cap equities with bond returns were −0.25 (t-stat = −5.17) and −0.23 (t-stat = −6.42), respectively. Thus, small-cap stock and bond returns share the same realized correlation as large-cap stock and bond returns over the last ten-year period, and in particular, the unusual negative correlation of the last five years.

We next turned our attention to an analysis of whether there were differences in comovements of equity and bond returns depending on whether the bond returns occurred due to changes in the level, or in the slope, of the term structure. We defined slope and level in three ways: (1) The level equals the ten-year yield, and the slope is the orthogonalized difference between ten-year and six-month yields;[5] (2) the level equals the six-month yield, and the slope is the same as in (1) but orthogonalized with respect to the six-month yield; and (3) both level and slope are implicitly defined by fitting principal components to yield changes in a manner similar to that of Litterman and Scheinkman (1991).

Interestingly, using the definitions in (1) above, we found that the comovement between equity returns (using Standard & Poor's 500 large-cap index) and (orthogonalized) slope differed in the first and second subperiods; that is, the relationship changed from one period to the other just as we had observed with the relation between equity and bond returns. Prior to 2001, when the slope or level of the term structure of yields decreased, equity prices typically increased. After 2000, however, changes in the term-structure slope or level were not associated with corresponding changes in equity prices.

When term-structure level and slope are implicitly defined as in (3) above, the results mirror the correlation estimated using the explicit definitions in (1) above. This makes intuitive sense in that the implicit level factor equally weights the yield at each maturity, while the ten-year yield used in definition (1) is basically a geometric average of zero-coupon yields at each maturity up to ten years.

We get a different result, however, when level and slope are defined as in (2) above. In this case, the comovements between equity returns and changes in level roughly equal those between equity returns and slope over time. A possible reason for the different outcome under definition (2) is that the six-month yield poorly measures the level of the term structure when the Federal Reserve manages short-term interest rates. The common perception is that in the post-2000 period the Fed has clearly managed interest rates in a very "hands-on" mode. Whatever the explanation, measurements of equity return exposure to a shift in the "level" of interest rates clearly depend on exactly how the "level" is defined.

We also examined, across ten equity sectors, the correlation of those sector equity and bond returns as well as the correlation of value and growth stock returns with bond returns. The ten sectors are those in the Dow Jones Industry Classification Benchmark (ICB) standard—basic materials, cyclicals, energy, financials, healthcare, industrials, noncyclicals, technology, telecommunications, and utilities—and value and growth stocks are proxied by the Dow Jones U.S. Value and Growth Indexes. The result, illustrated in **FIGURE 5.3**, is that the shifts over time in comovement between equity and bond returns tend to be quite uniform across all ten sector classifications and growth and value categories.

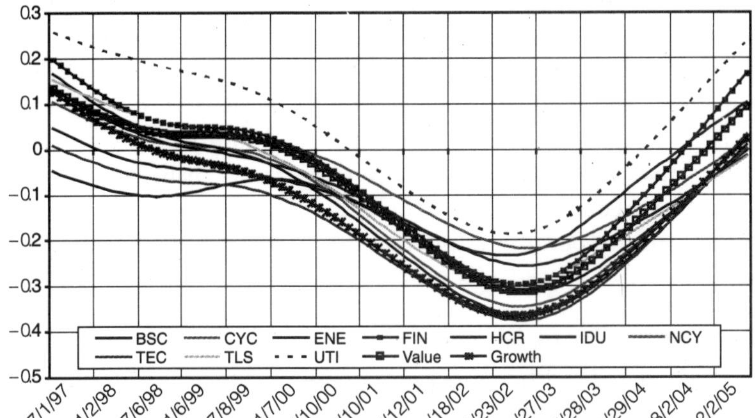

FIGURE 5.3 *Sectors and Value Growth*

Source: Quantal International

These findings suggest that the negative realized correlation between equity and bond returns after 2000 may not be strongly related to macro effects, such as inflation, since they would likely produce differing price effects across these different classes of stocks. Rather, the negative correlation is likely attributable to other determinants. We present more analysis of the connection between the equity-bond return correlation and macro variables later in this chapter.

It is interesting to note that prior to 2001 the sectors whose stock returns were most correlated with changes in yields—for example, utilities and financials—experienced increases in stock prices when either the level or slope of the yield curve decreased (and bond returns were positive). In the days when very traditional financial institutions "borrowed short and lent long," we might have expected the returns on their equities to be most strongly correlated with term-structure slope, in the sense that their equities did well when the term-structure slope increased. The fact that both the level and the slope of term structure covary with financial and utility returns is more consistent with the conventional wisdom that today's financial institutions (and utilities) do better in "strong markets" with low interest rates.

Nevertheless, in our second subperiod, after 2000, we detected little consistency in the correlation of equity returns in any sector and changes in the level of the yield curve. While equity returns of all sectors did covary with the slope of the yield curve, the covariation was in the opposite direction of that observed pre-2001; that is, a decrease in the slope of the yield curve was associated with a decrease in equity prices. The inversion of the covariation after 2000 was significant for some sectors, such as health care, technology, and industrials, but not for financials and utilities. This disconnect in the comovement of financial and utility equity returns with changes in the yield-curve slope again appears to challenge conventional wisdom based on the traditional behavior of these sectors; perhaps it again simply confirms our impression that the business models of companies in both sectors have broadened substantially in recent years.

Building the Factor Model

We began the model-building process with the Quantal conditional linear multifactor model for equities. The N equities each have exposures to ks systematic factors, as in the following equation:

$$\underset{N\times 1}{\tilde{R}_{St}} = \underset{N\times 1}{E_t(\tilde{R}_{St})} + \underset{N\times ks}{B_{St}}\ \underset{ks\times 1}{\tilde{F}_{St}} + \underset{N\times 1}{\tilde{\varepsilon}_{St}} \tag{1}$$

where:

N = number of stocks;

$\tilde{R}_{St}$ = vector of returns on the N stocks at time t;

$E_t(\tilde{R}_{St})$ = vector of expected return on the N stocks at time t;

B_{St} = matrix of exposures of each of the N stocks to each of the ks factors;

$\tilde{F}_{St}$ = vector of "shocks" to common factors that impact stock returns;

$\tilde{\varepsilon}_{St}$ = stock-specific component of return.

A similar conditional linear factor model can be applied to returns on fixed-income securities at key maturity points:

$$\underset{M\times 1}{\tilde{R}_{Bt}} = \underset{M\times 1}{E_t(\tilde{R}_{Bt})} + \underset{M\times kb}{B_{Bt}}\ \underset{kb\times 1}{\tilde{F}_{Bt}} + \underset{M\times 1}{\tilde{\varepsilon}_{Bt}} \tag{2}$$

where M is the number of fixed-income maturities and kb represents the number of fixed-income factors.

A joint factor structure involves a combination of the two models:

$$B_t\Omega_t B_t' = \begin{bmatrix} B_{St} & B_{SBt} \\ B_{BSt} & B_{Bt} \end{bmatrix} \begin{bmatrix} \Omega_{St} & \odot \\ \odot & \Omega_{Bt} \end{bmatrix} \begin{bmatrix} B_{St} & B_{SBt} \\ B_{BSt} & B_{Bt} \end{bmatrix}' \tag{3}$$

where for simplicity in (3) we reuse the symbols B_{St} and B_{Bt} in the joint factor structure to represent the "own-factor exposures" of equities to equity factors, and fixed-income securities to fixed-income factors, respectively; these own-factor exposures will generally be different numbers from those in the single equity and fixed-income factor models (1) and (2).

In the Quantal model, the factor structure is updated daily and the number of equity factors *ks* is dynamically determined, but is generally around twenty. The number of term structure factors *kb* across global markets, as represented by the U.S., Canada, Japan, U.K., Euro, and Switzerland, is also dynamically determined, but is generally around twelve (if the model were fitted just to the U.S., *kb* would equal 3, as in Litterman and Scheinkman [1991]).

The critical parameters in assessing the risk of a multiasset portfolio are the off-diagonal blocks containing the conditional covariances between the equity and term structure factors in (3). The evidence discussed in the last section points to substantial realized variation in these conditional covariances over the last ten years; moreover, ignoring the covariance altogether—that is, setting it to zero—would have been inadvisable except perhaps in the 2005–2006 time interval (2005–2006 would be covered by the "broken clocks are correct twice a day" exception). The conditional coefficients in the Quantal model are updated daily—hence the *t* on the factor exposures—and the model copes well in a day-by-day out-of-sample prediction of the shifts in the covariances realized in Figure 5.1.

Attribution of the Shift in Equity–Term-Structure Covariation to Macro Variables and Stock Characteristics?

The Quantal model permits the conditional covariance risk to be attributed to user-defined sets of macroeconomic variables or company characteristics. A priori we know that "reasonable persons" (reasonable experts) could disagree over the most meaningful set of variables—as a Goldman Sachs (2005) report put it: "The reality is that the drivers of volatility in general, and the links between macroeconomic variables and volatility, in particular, are not well understood." That said, term-structure factors (interest rates) are endogenous macrovariables in our model, so in this sense we are already relating equity volatility to this particular economic factor. At the same time, our analysis reported above reinforces the Goldman Sachs conclusion applied to joint equity–fixed-income return variation—the shifts over the last ten years in realized correlation between equity returns and fixed-income returns don't, at first glance, seem to have much to do with cross-sectional equity characteristics like company size, sector, or style. We now look more thoroughly at this conclusion.

Presumably if a pattern emerges in the properties of returns on equities and their covariation with term structure when the equities are sorted according to characteristics of the underlying companies, such as high-minus-low book-to-market ratios, momentum/reversal, dividend yield, and so on, the hypothesis is that the cross-sectional sorting criterion is merely a proxy for exposure to a time-series risk factor—that is, a cross-sectional characteristic like HML is not *per se* a "factor." In recent work, Aretz, Bartram, and Pope (2005) sort portfolios on the basis of the book-to-market ratio and look at monthly returns from 1971 through 1998 for HML portfolios. They find positive exposure of HML portfolios to changes in the slope of the term structure. This result is roughly consistent with what we illustrate in Figure 5.3 above, where the correlation between equity returns and term-structure changes does differ for value and growth stocks (using the difference between value and growth styles as a rough proxy for HML). However, just a glance at Figure 5.3 suggests that the variation over time in the correlation between bond returns (changes in term structure) and equity value or growth is more substantial than the difference in sensitivity of value and growth (HML) equity returns to term-structure changes.

Petkova (2002) also regresses a shift in the slope of the term structure against the monthly returns on an HML portfolio over two back-to-back periods—1963 to 1991 and 1992 to 2001, while including the Fama-French SML portfolio returns and market returns (MKT):

1963–1991 (Monthly):

$$\hat{u}_t^{TERM} = -0.02 + \underset{(2.83)}{2.74}\, HML_t - \underset{(-0.69)}{0.39}\, SMB_t + \underset{(2.30)}{1.53}\, MKT_t + \varepsilon_t$$

$$R^2 = 4.7\%$$

1992–2001 (Monthly):

$$\hat{u}_t^{TERM} = -0.01 + \underset{(2.47)}{1.74}\, HML_t + \underset{(0.74)}{0.29}\, SMB_t + \underset{(2.05)}{1.11}\, MKT_t + \varepsilon_t$$

$$R^2 = 2.75\% \qquad (4)$$

In both subperiods, she identifies a statistically significant relationship between shifts in the term structure (in our analysis, fixed-income factors) and the returns on HML portfolios, although the explanatory power is not strong. Most interesting perhaps, Petkova finds that the relationship between HML portfolio returns and changes in the term structure seems rather stable between the two periods that she studies. Petkova finds little connection between firm size and term-structure shifts—thus the return on a portfolio that is long small firms and short large firms seems not to be highly correlated with fixed-income returns. It seems fair to say that we don't have a good theory for why book-to-market or value and growth firm returns would plausibly be correlated with term-structure shifts while small-firm versus large-firm returns aren't.

Our approach is slightly different. We determined HML portfolio exposure to three Quantal fixed-income factors: level, slope, and curvature.

In the following three equations, fitted to the U.S. market, level is the first factor, slope is the second factor, and curvature is the third factor:[6]

$$\begin{aligned}&(1996.01.09-2005.06.22)\\ &HML_t = 0.02 + \underset{(3.06)}{2.74}\, F_{B1,t} + \underset{(3.68)}{2.48}\, F_{B2,t} + \underset{(2.36)}{1.59}\, F_{B3,t} + \varepsilon_t\\ &AdjR^2 = 1.0\%\end{aligned} \tag{5}$$

$$\begin{aligned}&(1996.01.09-2000.12.29)\\ &HML_t = 0.01 + \underset{(0.50)}{0.38}\, F_{B1,t} - \underset{(-2.18)}{1.65}\, F_{B2,t} + \underset{(2.62)}{1.98}\, F_{B3,t} + \varepsilon_t\\ &AdjR^2 = 1.0\%\end{aligned} \tag{6}$$

$$\begin{aligned}&(2001.01.03-2005.06.22)\\ &HML_t = 0.03 + \underset{(4.49)}{2.57}\, F_{B1,t} + \underset{(2.78)}{1.59}\, F_{B2,t} - \underset{(-0.61)}{0.35}\, F_{B3,t} + \varepsilon_t\\ &AdjR^2 = 2.0\%\end{aligned} \tag{7}$$

The regression looks potentially interesting insofar as the coefficients in equation (5) are significant for the entire sample period from 1996 to 2005. Equations (6) and (7), for the subperiods 1996 to 2000 and 2001 to 2005, further suggest that while the fixed-income factors have some explanatory power for the HML, or growth-to-value, portfolio returns, the relationship itself shifts between the subperiods. The level coefficient changes from strongly positive in equation (5) to slightly positive in equation (6) to strongly positive again in equation (7). The slope coefficient moves from strongly positive to negative to positive, and the curvature coefficient is positive in equations (5) and (6), and negative in equation (7). Notice, however, that the adjusted *R*-squareds at 1 percent and 2 percent are certainly nothing to write home about.

To expand our analysis we formed tracking portfolios, each of which was a linear set of Quantal's U.S. equity and fixed-income factors, and then tested whether these factors have any relation to various U.S. economic variables. We regressed the realized value of the economic variable against the tracking portfolio prediction, with the realized value defined as

$$y_{t,t+m} = \delta_y + \beta_y \hat{y}_{t,t+m} + \eta_t \tag{8}$$

and the prediction defined as

$$\hat{y}_{t,t+m} = a + \underline{b}'_S\, \underline{F}_{St} + \underline{b}'_B\, \underline{\overline{F}}_{Bt} \tag{9}$$

A strong, positive coefficient, b', is an indicator of a relationship between the equity and fixed-income factors and the realized economic variable that we are trying to track.

The tracking portfolios actually yielded sensible results for inflation (CPI), employment growth, and Fed funds rate, but the results for industrial production growth were puzzling. For the first three macro variables, the *R*-squareds were high—8 percent for CPI and the Fed funds rate, and 5 percent for employment growth—and the coefficients were positive and statistically significant. The coefficient is negative for the fourth economic variable, industrial production growth, and the equity factors. Since intuitively we know that the stock market is predicting future macroeconomic states, we should expect that it will only react to realized macro variables insofar as they have some portent for the future. Nevertheless, based on the results thus far, it seems that our factor model is performing relatively well if judged by the tracking portfolio connection between equity and fixed-income factors and macroeconomic variables.

Finally, in studying the relation between stock returns and the different "macroeconomic" components of term structure—level, slope, and curvature—we wanted to check whether the results were sensitive to the precise definitions of these components.

In **FIGURE 5.4**, the realized correlation between equity returns and the three term structure factors, level, slope, and curvature, is plotted for the case in which the term-structure factors are defined implicitly (as, for example, in Litterman and Scheinkman [1991]), and then for the case in which the term structure factors are defined explicitly in terms of key rates.

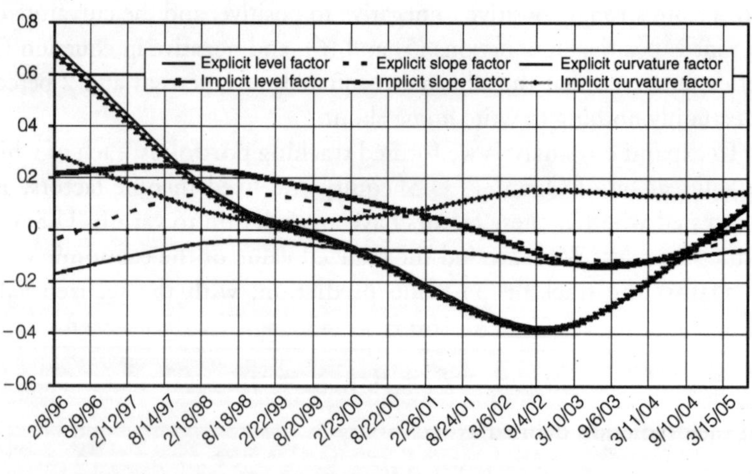

FIGURE 5.4 *Realized Correlation Between U.S. Equity Returns and Shift in Term Structure Factors over the Last Decade*

Source: Quantal International

In this chart, the slope component is actually the negative of the slope of the yield curve so that one can more easily compare this figure with earlier figures. The bottom line is that one draws much the same conclusion about the shifting correlation of equity and term-structure factors whether one is using an implicit or explicit factor model to estimate those term-structure factors, provided that the yield curve level is defined in terms of long-term yield in the explicit model.

A Closer Look at the "Spikes"

The monthly realized correlations between equity and bond returns over the sample period are very "spiky." In the analysis of the previous sections, we have largely ignored that spikiness and focused on the trend over time in the time series of these realized correlations. We now look at these spikes in more detail, and we examine in particular whether we can learn anything from them about the day-to-day determinants of the comovements in equity and bond returns.

Connolly, Stivers, and Sun (2004) try to model the shifting correlation between equity and fixed-income returns over time, relating the shift to the CBOE Volatility Index (VIX). Their objective is to test whether the level of uncertainty in the markets might determine the correlation between equity returns and fixed-income returns. If the VIX is indeed a good measure of that uncertainty, it essentially becomes a state or regime variable that can forecast when the correlation might be shifting.

Connolly and the coauthors regress bond returns against stock returns over the period January 9, 1996, through December 31, 2000 (also roughly the first half of our ten-year sample period), as in the following equation:

$$B_t = a_0 + [a_1 + a_2 \ln(VIX_{t-1})]S_t + v_t \tag{10}$$

In their regression, they find a statistically significant negative coefficient for the market uncertainty proxy, VIX, as a determinant of the correlation between equity and bond returns. Their results are as follows:

$$\hat{B}_t = \underset{(0.269)}{0.004} + [\underset{(11.244)}{1.866} - \underset{(-11.056)}{0.568}\ \ln(VIX_{t-1})]\ S_t \tag{11}$$

The findings of Connolly and the coauthors at first seem to provide evidence of a viable relation between the volatility in the stock market and bond returns based on the large negative coefficient and an R-squared of 9 percent.

To dig into the results of Connolly and the coauthors, we began by plotting the daily equity index returns against the daily comovement in equity and bond index returns over our sample period, shown here in **FIGURE 5.5.**

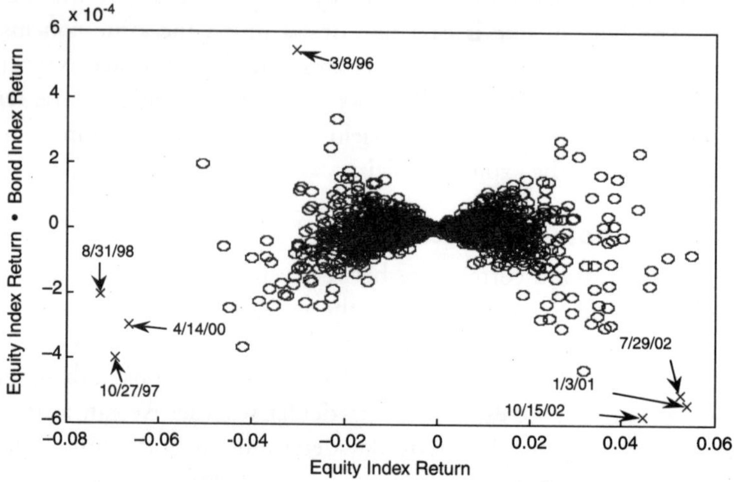

FIGURE 5.5 *Daily Comovements in U.S. Equity and Bond Returns: The Informative Observations*

Source: Quantal International

The daily equity market return is on the x-axis with a range of almost −8 percent to 6 percent; that is, there were a number of big up and down days in the market over the time period. The y-axis is the daily realized comovement between, or the cross-product of, the return on the equity index and the return on the bond index. The striking feature of Figure 5.5 is how much it looks like a bow tie or an hourglass on its side. It is very symmetric with only a few outliers, which are the potentially instructive points on which we want to concentrate.

The outliers of 10/27/1997, 04/14/2000, and 08/31/1998 occurred on days when equity returns fell dramatically and the correlation between equity and bond returns was negative—in other words, equity prices fell and fixed-income prices rose (yields fell). We think of these market events as a flight to quality or a flight to liquidity.

The outliers of 07/09/2002, 10/15/2002, and 01/03/2001 occurred on days when equity returns rose dramatically and the correlation between equity and bond returns was negative, with equity prices rising and fixed-income prices falling (yields rising). On these days, the market appeared to receive an announcement that would be negative news about expected real interest rates and/or inflation (that is, inflation and interest rates would rise and bond prices would fall), but equities actually held their own or increased when investors interpreted the news to imply that company cash flows, and thus equity values, would improve in tandem with higher interest rates and a growing economy.

Figure 5.5 includes observations of both flight to quality (bad news for stocks, good news for bonds) and of the reverse. However, the bad-news-for-stocks events occur pre-2000 and are associated with shocks like the Russian debt/Long-Term Capital Management crisis and the Asian markets crisis. The post-2000 good-news-for-stocks events tend to be associated with Fed announcements and macroeconomic events. It seems better model-wise to differentiate the two sets of events as belonging to two different volatility regimes, rather than to attempt to explain both sets of events in terms of the same volatility as a measure of market uncertainty.

One indication of movements in volatility of returns, or different volatility regimes, is "fat tails," that is, a high frequency of outliers like those in Figure 5.5. We now examine whether the joint events are truly outliers in a bootstrap distribution of equity and bond returns, and then whether these "big market return" days were preceded by some unusual behavior or whether they foretold unusual market behavior on subsequent days. To do this we first categorize the equity and bond returns into four quadrants. Quadrant 1 is located in the upper right quadrant of a scatter plot of equity returns against bond returns (with zero returns at the origin) and includes days when both equity and bond prices rise by greater than a one sigma event. Quadrant 2, days when equity prices fall and bond prices rise, both by greater than a one-sigma event, is located in the lower left quadrant of the figure. This is the flight-to-quality scenario. Quadrant 3 denotes a market in which both equity and bond prices fall dramatically (again by greater than a one-sigma event) and is located in the upper left quadrant of the figure. And quadrant 4 captures an event in which equity prices rise and bond prices fall, once again greater than one sigma; it is located in the lower right quadrant of the figure.

FIGURE 5.6 shows the frequency with which the events in each of the four quadrants occurred in the first subperiod, September 1, 1996, through December 29, 2000. The strings of white circles in Figure 5.6 mark the range of frequencies we observed when the series of daily stock returns were randomly paired (1,000 times) with the series of daily six-month bond returns. The length of these strings of white circles thus represents the range of outcomes that would be expected if daily stock and bond returns were unrelated.

The black dot in each string of white circles indicates the observed number of respective quadrant events that actually occurred in the sample period. We see in the figure that there is an unusually high number of quadrant 2 events—when equity prices fall and bond prices rise,

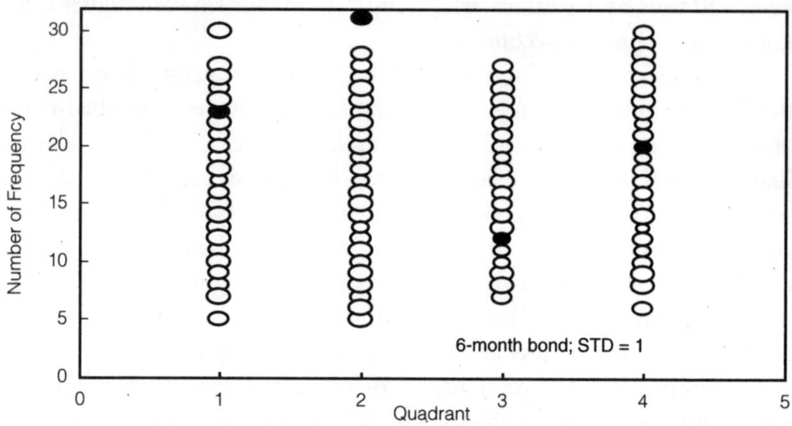

FIGURE 5.6 *Daily Comovements in U.S. Equity and Bond Returns: Bootstrap 1/9/1996–12/29/2000*

Source: Quantal International

characterized as a flight to quality or liquidity—more so than would be expected if the returns were independent.

FIGURE 5.7 plots the range of frequencies for each quadrant event in the second subperiod, from March 1, 2001, through June 13, 2005.

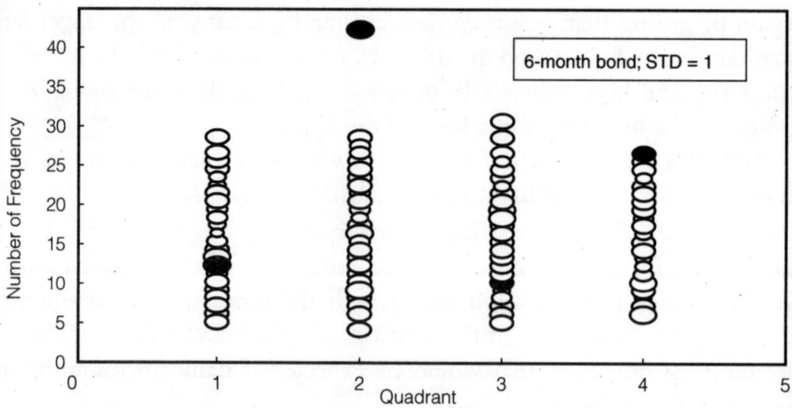

FIGURE 5.7 *Daily Comovements in U.S. Equity and Bond Returns: Bootstrap 1/3/2001–6/13/2005*

Source: Quantal International

The same negative correlation of equity and bond return events that we see to be significant in quadrants 2 and 4 for the first subperiod is repeated in the second subperiod.

In the midst of a flight to liquidity, it might be expected that short-term securities would benefit most from the liquidity demanded by the market. **FIGURE 5.8** suggests that this is not true, in that the same relation between equity and bond returns is observed with (say) ten-year bonds as with six-month bonds. In this case, then, the explanation for this type of correlation might actually be better termed *flight to quality* than *flight to liquidity*.

An unusually high number of frequencies of quadrant 4 events—stock prices up significantly while bond prices are down—is also evident in the second subperiod for both six-month and ten-year bonds. It is reasonable to describe this type of event as a "macro" surprise that is interpreted by the market as good for corporate revenues and/or depreciating the value of fixed-rate corporate debt obligations—both these events would explain the increase in equity prices concurrent with a decrease in bond prices.

The results of this analysis indicate that the spikes in the comovement of equity and bond returns are indeed unusual relative to the volatility in those returns. But are they persistent? Will a flight to quality on, for example, a Monday, have any fallout on equity and bond returns on Tuesday? We ran the gamut of statistical tests and could not find any level of persistence, not even a GARCH (Generalized Autoregressive Conditional Heteroskedasticity)-like persistence of a shock into the future or of conditional volatility.

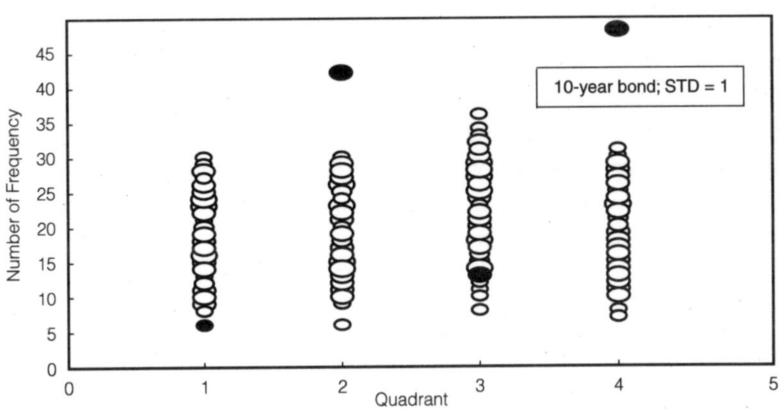

FIGURE 5.8 *Daily Comovements in U.S. Equity and Bond Returns: Bootstrap 1/3/2001–6/13/2005*

Source: Quantal International

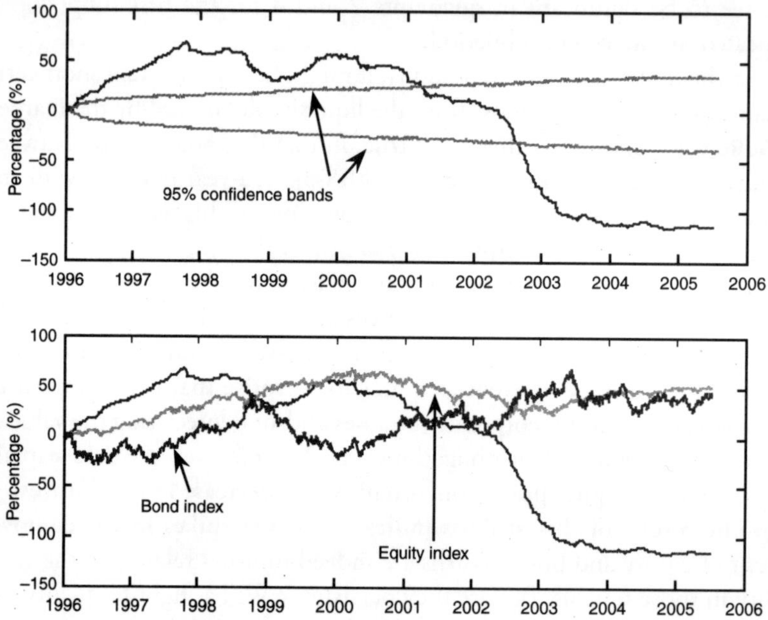

FIGURE 5.9 *Cumulative Daily Comovements in U.S. Equity and Bond Returns: 1/9/1996–6/13/2005*

Source: Quantal International

We also calculated a CUSUM (Cumulative Sum Chart)-like statistic to test for longer-term serial dependence. The charts shown in **FIGURE 5.9** graph the cumulative daily comovements over the entire sample period, with time period on the x-axis and the cumulative comovement statistic on the y-axis. We calculate the cross-product of the bond return today and the equity return today and compound that cross-product forward to tomorrow, continuing in this manner through the entire period to produce a cumulative cross-product total.

The 95-percent confidence intervals shown in the top chart in Figure 5.9 are those expected from randomizing or bootstrapping from the joint distribution of returns. The actual cumulative sum of the cross-product is well outside the 95-percent bootstrapped confidence interval bounds. This result unquestionably enriches the puzzle, a puzzle to which we do not yet have a perfect answer. Although we don't seem to be able to detect GARCH-like serial dependence in the correlation between equity and bond returns on a day-to-day basis, when we analyze the dependence using a nonparametric CUSUM-like statistic we seem to detect longer-term persistence.[7]

The bottom chart in Figure 5.9 plots the cumulative sum of the cross-product of the daily returns on equities and bonds along with the U.S. equity and stock indexes. The dependency is obviously strongest through 2001, 2002, and 2003, which is the well-known period when the Fed was "strongly" manipulating short-term interest rates; the Greenspan-led Fed continuously forced down the short end of the term structure in those years to stimulate the economy, resulting in a steep yield curve. At this juncture, then, if we have to pick a candidate state variable by which to classify the behavior of joint daily equity-bond returns into regimes, it would be Fed policy; perhaps this is obvious. Moreover, it is plausible that the temporal pattern of Fed intervention ("long-term intervention") creates a long-run dependency rather than a shorter-term GARCH-like dependence.

History provides some support for our conjecture. James Bullard (2005), writing in the Federal Reserve Bank of St. Louis's *National Economic Trends*, notes that the financial environment of the early 1960s bears a remarkable resemblance to that of the latter part of the preceding ten years that we've examined here, with low inflation, low interest rates, and so on. A reversal of the correlation between equity and fixed-income returns took place in the 1960s as well.

It is one thing to conjecture that the regime shifts and long-run serial dependence in equity-bond returns are attributable to the Fed; it is quite another to actually quantify that policy effect in, say, a regime-switching model that is not simply fitted to past data. We leave this to a follow-up paper.

Conclusion

Our study of the realized correlation between daily U.S. equity and Treasury bond returns over the last ten years—the first step in building a global cross-asset factor model—has led us to several interesting observations. First, substantial shifts have occurred over the last ten years in the realized levels of correlation between U.S. equity and bond returns. Second, when we define yield curve slope and level as they are most commonly defined in the market—*level* being the long-term yield and *slope* the difference between long-term and short-term yields—changes in both level and slope pre-2001 covary with equity returns across all sectors and value and growth categories in a manner consistent with conventional wisdom: that is, when slope and level increase, equity prices decrease. Interestingly, if the "level" of interest rates is instead defined as the *short-term* rate, explanatory power drops substantially; we believe that this occurs because the short-term rate was "Fed-managed" over much of our sample period. Third, the evidence suggests that some of the shift in correlation between equity and bond returns or yield changes is concentrated in equities that are sensitive to the cross-sectional Fama-French HML "factor" and to macro variables such as the CPI and employment growth; however, the explanatory power of these explicit factors is quite weak, even more so compared to the shifts themselves in the equity-bond return correlation. Fourth, the jump behavior of joint daily equity and bond returns over our sample period appears to be explained as either a flight to quality or as a reaction to surprise announcements of changes in macrovariable forecasts. Fifth, while there is little persistence in the jumps over the short term (that is, in the days adjacent to the jumps), there does appear to be persistence over the longer term, primarily as a result of interest rate management by the Fed after 2001. Part of our future research agenda concerns the extent to which we can model this longer-term dependence, perhaps using the time series forecasts of an "expert" Fed watcher as a benchmark. The important message at this point is that—given the movements over time in the correlation between equity and fixed-income returns—if we assume that equities will always exhibit the same exposure to the fixed-income markets, we will be making a serious error.

References

Arshanapalli, Bala, Lorne Switzer, and Alexandre Vezina. 2003. "Sources of Time-Varying Risk and Risk Premia in U.S. Stock and Bond Markets." Working paper. Concordia University (January).

Aretz, Kevin, Söhnke Bartram, and Peter Pope. 2005. "Macroeconomic Risks and the Fama and French /Carhart Model." Unpublished paper. Lancaster University (September).

Bullard, James. 2005. "Twist and Shout, or Back to the Sixties." *National Economic Trends*, Federal Reserve Bank of St. Louis (March).

Connolly, Robert, Chris Stivers, and Licheng Sun. 2004. "Stock Market Uncertainty and the Stock-Bond Return Relation." Working paper. University of North Carolina at Chapel Hill (February).

Goldman Sachs. 2005. "Is the Low-Volatility Regime Coming to an End?" *Global Economics Weekly* 5 (November 9): 37.

Guidolin, Massimo, and Allan Timmermann. 2004. "An Econometric Model of Nonlinear Dynamics in the Joint Distribution of Stock and Bond Returns." Working paper. University of Virginia and University of California San Diego (July).

Henry, Ólan, Nilss Olekalns, and Sandy Suardi. 2004. "Modelling Comovements in Equity Returns and Short Term Interest Rates: Level Effects and Asymmetric Volatility Dynamics." Working paper. University of Melbourne (October).

Lee, Jaime, Terry Marsh, Robert Maxim, and Paul Pfleiderer. 2006. "The Relation between Fixed Income and Equity Return Factors," *Journal Of Investment Management* 4 (Fourth Quarter): 52–72.

Li, Lengfeng. 2002. "Macroeconomic Factors and the Correlation of Stock and Bond Returns." Working paper, Yale University (November).

Litterman, Robert, and José Scheinkman. 1991. "Common Factors Affecting Bond Returns." *Journal of Fixed Income* (June): 54–61.

Petkova, Ralitsa. 2002. "Do the Fama-French Factors Proxy for Innovations in Predictive Volatility?" Unpublished paper. William E. Simon Graduate School of Business, University of Rochester (November).

Scruggs, John, and Paskalis Glabadanidis. 2001. "Risk Premia and the Dynamic Covariance between Stock and Bond Returns." Working paper. Washington University in St. Louis (March).

Chapter Notes

1. Jaime Lee, Terry Marsh, Robert Maxim, and Paul Pfleiderer. "The Relation between Daily Fixed Income and Equity Returns Factors," *Journal Of Investment Management* 4 (Fourth Quarter): 52–72.

2. The bond returns are constructed from an implied zero-coupon yield series. Using the constant maturity yield data on the Treasury securities, obtained from the Federal Reserve, we constructed the implied zero-yield curve and calculated the returns of the Treasury securities.

3. Li (2002) found the same trend in equity and bond return correlation for his sample period from 1996 to 2000.

4. The number of stocks in the sample universe was 2,150 at the beginning of the study, rose to 3,839 around the end of 2001, and declined to 3,511 at the end of the sample period. The universe included both nonsurvivor and new companies and was screened for illiquidity and other considerations. The Quantal database was the source of daily return data for the equity and fixed-income securities.

5. Orthogonalization is performed by regressing changes in the differences between the ten-year and six-month yields on changes in the ten-year yield.

6. We use U.S. Treasury return data going forward, but with the high degree of integration of the global markets, we would expect the Canadian, U.K., Euro, and Swiss fixed-income markets to produce similar results. The Japanese market would likely produce divergent results.

7. Arshanapalli, Switzer, and Vezina (2003) find persistence in the conditional covariance between S&P 500 returns and ten-year Treasury returns in a multivariate GARCH-M model that they fit over the period October 1, 1979, to July 5, 2000.

CHAPTER 6

Transaction-Cost Modeling as a Source of Alpha

MARK COPPEJANS AND ANANTH MADHAVAN

Who—Mark Coppejans is a research officer and member of the Global Trading Research Group at BGI, focusing on execution research and trading strategies across different asset classes worldwide. Before joining BGI in November 2003, Coppejans was an assistant professor of economics at Duke University. He received his PhD in economics from Northwestern University and a BA in economics and applied mathematics from the University of California, Berkeley.

Ananth Madhavan heads the Global Trading Research Group at Barclays Global Investors (BGI). He leads BGI's global trading research team with a focus on execution research and trading strategies across different asset classes worldwide. Madhavan also works closely with the global trading team and BGI's alpha research and product groups to design and implement trading strategies capturing liquidity-driven market opportunities. Before joining BGI in 2003 Madhavan was managing director of research for Investment Technology Group (ITG), Inc., and a member of the firm's management and executive committees. Previously, he was the Charles B. Thornton Professor of Finance at the Marshall School of Business at the University of Southern California and an assistant professor of finance at the Wharton School of the University of Pennsylvania. Madhavan is the author of numerous publications in leading academic and practitioner journals. He received his PhD in economics from Cornell University and his BA from the University of Delhi, India.

New Thinking—Ex ante transaction cost modeling can improve alpha by increasing skill and breadth, and optimizing turnover level and fund capacity. Madhavan and Coppejans have developed a quantitative formula to measure the impact of forecast costs on pretrade portfolio decision making—construction, turnover, and overall fund size—and to model the increase in alpha generated by a higher correlation of forecast costs to actual costs. Integrating cost information and its effects into active management increases investment returns.

Introduction

Investment managers do not usually think of transaction costs as being a source of alpha—unless, of course, they are the market makers. Traditionally, managers have considered the impact of realized transaction costs on investment returns after the fact. Posttrade (ex post) analysis focuses on how transaction costs reduce the returns of an investment strategy. There is, however, much to be gained by focusing on pretrade (ex ante) considerations, namely the impact of transaction costs on expected returns through portfolio construction and turnover level.

Three Essential Ingredients in Investment Management

Before we look more specifically at the ex ante impact of trading costs, we need to back up and look at the three essential ingredients in investment management. First, there is the expected return, or alpha forecasts. Second, there is risk, which quantitative managers usually think of in terms of risk models and variance matrices. Third, there are the transaction-cost estimates; that is, how much it will cost to get into or out of a position (see **FIGURE 6.1**).

We think about each of these three elements in the pretrade and posttrade investment process. At the research level, we look at a universe of securities and obtain signals correlated to the securities' returns, costs, and volatility. We build models, heuristics, or rules of thumb around these ingredients of risk, return, and cost to aid in the portfolio construction process. We then determine a set of optimal weights for each of the securities, again using different models or heuristics. Once the portfolio is built and traded, we look at each risk, return, and cost again. We determine which portion of the return was due to intended bets—that is, our measure of the robustness of our alpha model. We look at the deviation from the risk forecast—that is, our measure of the accuracy of our risk models. Finally, we compare the actual transaction costs to pretrade estimates. But until now, there have been no rigorous transaction-cost models against which to measure these results.

Risk and return and the trade-offs between the two have been studied extensively. The least-well-understood element of portfolio management

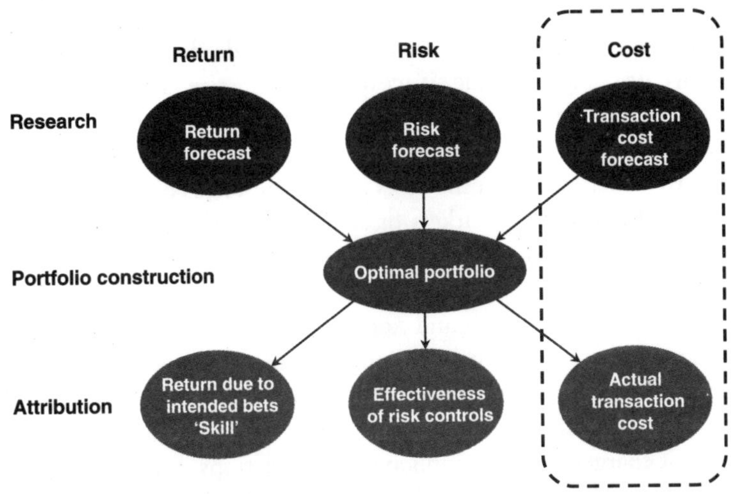

FIGURE 6.1 *Costs and the Investment Process*

Source: *Journal Of Investment Management*

is transaction costs and the role of trading costs in investment management, and, importantly, how modeling transaction costs can be used as a source of additional alpha.

Transaction Costs

Why do costs matter? Because there is a world of difference between great notional returns on a paper strategy and the actual delivery of returns to investors. Superior returns come from superior investment ideas, great signals, and great insights; in other words, strong alpha models and strong risk models. But that is not the whole story. While superior investment ideas are obviously a necessary condition for superior returns, they are not a sufficient condition. Much of the recent work on trading costs shows that trading costs can substantially erode or even wipe out altogether the notional profits of an investment strategy. Transaction costs are important, and it is important to get them right. Therefore, superior execution is the second necessary condition to achieve superior returns. We want to predict transaction costs and use this prediction to build better portfolios and to evaluate trading.

We cannot begin to analyze transaction costs until we define what we actually mean by "costs." Traditionally, trading costs were thought of as only the explicit costs of the transaction; the costs for which there is an actual paper ticket or expense, such as commissions, fees, stamp duties, ticket charges, and so on. More importantly, however, there are implicit costs. Implicit costs occur because a trade may not be placed or executed immediately, causing slippage from order or trade delays; or because we may move prices as we trade, if we're trading in size. There may also be opportunity costs, a failure to execute for example, and other such costs. In addition, these implicit costs can actually be negative, not positive charges, by which we mean the costs are manifested as diminished portfolio returns. In emerging markets or small-cap markets, for example, the implicit costs of slippage or market impact can be a substantial negative drag on performance. Explicit charges are the tip of the iceberg. The vast majority of costs are implicit and not easily measured.

When we think about how to measure costs, there are many possible candidates that traders and others propose. But the best method must have three key properties. First, the measure has to capture all relevant frictions, the explicit charges, and the implicit costs or frictions. Second, there needs to be alignment between the trading view of costs and the portfolio manager view of costs. Third, the measure must be game-proof. Traders—who know their compensation at year-end depends on the success of their trades, measured, at least in part, by the cost metric—must not be able to easily game the system to the benefit of their bonus.

The Implementation Shortfall

The correct measure, and a widely accepted metric of costs, is the implementation shortfall (IS), first developed by Jack Treynor (1981) and later rediscovered and further developed by Andre Perold (1988). Simply put, implementation shortfall (see **FIGURE 6.2**) measures the difference between the notional, or paper, and actual portfolio returns, and thus captures not just the explicit costs but also the difficult-to-measure implicit costs, such as market impact, slippage, and opportunity costs from failing to execute.

Implementation shortfall is a measure that exhibits the three key properties mentioned earlier: It captures all costs; it cannot be easily gamed, because the benchmark is set ahead of time; and it provides consistency between the trader's and the portfolio manager's views of performance because it measures the actual costs and slippage that both parties see in the actual return.

FIGURE 6.3 is an example of the performance impact of implicit and explicit costs in practice.

Imagine an order to purchase 1,000 shares of XYZ, which is trading at 100. Assume that commissions are 4 basis points and that the taxes, stamp duties, and ticket charges are another 36 basis points. For reasons having to do, perhaps, with portfolio systems being down or delays in the trading

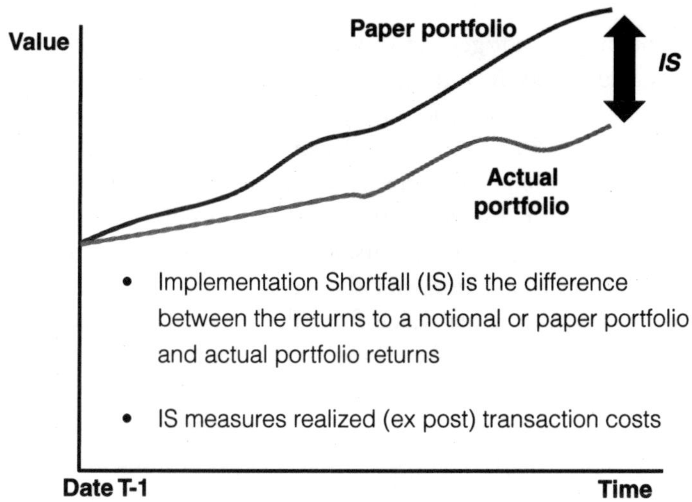

FIGURE 6.2 *Transaction Costs—Ex Post*

Source: *Journal Of Investment Management*

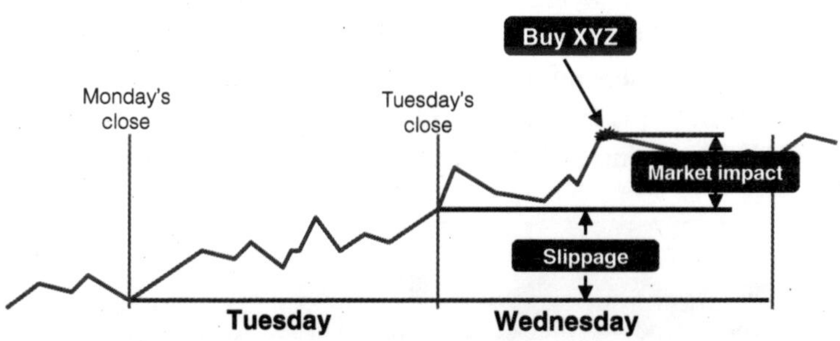

An order to buy 1,000 shares of XYZ is generated after the close on Monday; the closing price (benchmark) is $100.00.

No trades occur on Tuesday and the price closes at $100.50.

On Wednesday, all 1,000 shares are traded at $102.00 per share; commissions are 4 cents per share or $40; fees are $360.

FIGURE 6.3 *Implementation Shortfall Example*

process, the order is not generated until the close of business on Monday. No trades actually occur until Wednesday. From Monday close at 100 to Wednesday, when the trades occur, there is slippage due to the delay, which, in this example, is 50 basis points. When the trades are made, there is a market impact on top of the slippage, which pushes the prices up 150 basis points. So the explicit costs of the trade are 40 basis points, and the implicit costs of the trade are 200 basis points, for a total of 240 basis points.

The IS of this transaction, not shown in Figure 6.3, is the 240 basis points of deviation of actual value from the notional, or paper, portfolio when it was constructed by the manager. The 200 basis points of implicit costs generated by slippage and market impact is captured by the IS metric.

One caution with IS—it is important to get the units right. The 240 basis points in the example above is the cost to get into the position. It is a one-way trading cost. But we will have to exit and potentially get back in and get back out. Imagine a fund that is turning over at 200 percent. In one year, we buy and sell, and buy and sell again. The alpha returns are usually annualized. The one-way costs need to be annualized too, using a scalar that accounts for turnover, which is the transaction-cost amortization function (TCAF). The TCAF will be incorporated into our model later in this chapter. What follows is an interim example of its effect (see **FIGURE 6.4**).

Assume a fund for which the paper portfolio alpha is 200 basis points before costs. The correct ex post net return is the original paper portfolio alpha less the TCAF weighted costs, which is calculated as the turnover multiplied by two times the trading costs. Notice how the predicted post-trade alpha varies depending on turnover and costs. In the first example given, the turnover is 60 percent and the one-way costs are 50 basis points. The TCAF, 60 percent × 2 × 50 bps, is subtracted from the paper portfolio

Example

- Consider a fund with predicted annualized expected excess return of 2% (200 bps) and turnover of 60%. If (one-way) transaction costs are 50 bps, then predicted posttrade alpha is:

140 bps = 200 bps – 60% x 2 x 50 bps

If turnover were 200% and costs were 40 bps, we would have:

40 bps = 200 bps – 200% x 2 x 40 bps

FIGURE 6.4 *The Transaction-Cost Amortization Function (TCAF)*

Source: Journal Of Investment Management

alpha of 200 basis points, for a posttrade alpha prediction of 140 basis points. Similarly, in the second example, a portfolio with 200 percent turnover and one-way costs of 40 basis points yields a predicted posttrade alpha of 40 basis points. So annualizing costs with the correct scalar is a sensible approach for posttrade modeling and measurement of costs.

Modeling Transaction Costs

Once we know how to measure trading costs, the next step is to model, or forecast, the costs. This cost model does double duty. It is used to predict trading costs and to benchmark traders. For example, the best trader may generate an IS of 120 basis points, which, at first glance, seems like poor performance. Using the cost model, we can take into account the trade complexity of the orders the trader handles and forecast the annualized trading costs. The forecast might generate a predicted IS of 150 basis points, in which case the trader's performance has an added value of 30 basis points—bonus-worthy performance. This is the posttrade use of the transaction cost model.

The cost model is also used pretrade to build the portfolio, to select the right securities (breadth) and the appropriate trade size, and to determine the optimal turnover. As an intuitive analogy of this ex ante process, unrelated to active investing, consider online poker. It is an anonymous game. There are lots of different sites to choose from. Ideally, we want to pick the site dominated by the less skilled (a.k.a. alcohol-addled) college students, and we want to avoid the sites populated by the poker pros. How do we know which sites to avoid? We build a model based on our own empirical experience and/or based on information culled from chat rooms or blogs. Our model helps us to distinguish the pro sites from the rank amateur sites.

In a similar manner, we use cost models ex ante in portfolio construction to select the right investments. Transaction cost models, by linking order generation and trade execution, can act as a brake on entry or exit. So the model affects returns on a pretrade basis, because the cost forecasts impact the active investor's ex ante decisions.

The Information Ratio

We can start to build our model using the conceptual framework for thinking about active management formulated by Richard Grinold (1989), his *fundamental law of active management.* Grinold's formula (see **FIGURE 6.5**) starts by defining the information ratio (IR) as the ratio of active return to active risk. The IR is a commonly used measure that captures the expected return per unit risk.

Grinold's key insight into active management (see **FIGURE 6.6**) is that the information ratio can be viewed as the product of skill times breadth. *Skill* is

Information ratio (IR) - ratio of active return to active risk

$$IR = E[R_A]/\sigma_A$$

FIGURE 6.5 *Fundamental Law of Active Management*

Source: *Journal Of Investment Management*

Fundamental Law of Active Management (Grinold, 1989) states that IR is the product of skill (IC) and breadth (N):

$$IR = IC\ \sqrt{N}$$

FIGURE 6.6 *Fundamental Law of Active Management*

Source: *Journal Of Investment Management*

measured by a correlation coefficient, which we call the *information coefficient* (IC). It is a measure of how good an investor is at forecasting future returns. For now, we will take the IC as given, but later on we will see that the IC can be modeled as a function of time, allowing for natural decay in the signal. *Breadth* is the number of independent bets, or the proportional number of assets traded per unit of time. It describes the actual security selection.

An example will make this equation more concrete. Consider an IC of 5 percent. It means that the investor bets in the right direction 52.5 percent of the time, which is considered good performance in the investment management business. If the breadth is 100, then under Grinold's equation we take its square root, which is 10, and we end up with an IR of 0.5. With no constraints, a manager running a fund at 4 percent active risk will beat the benchmark by 2 percent. In other words, the manager will generate a paper portfolio alpha of 200 basis points.

IR with Constraints

The model was then extended (see **FIGURE 6.7**), by Grinold and Ronald Kahn (2000) and by Roger Clarke, Harindra de Silva, and Steven Thorley (2002), to capture constraints by adding the transfer coefficient (TC), which is a number between zero and one that measures the effects of a constraint. In other words, the TC measures a portfolio manager's effectiveness in transferring individual security return predictions into actual portfolio positions. In the absence of any constraints, the transfer coefficient is one.

$$IR = TC \quad IC \quad \sqrt{N}$$

FIGURE 6.7 *Effect of Constraints*

Source: *Journal Of Investment Management*

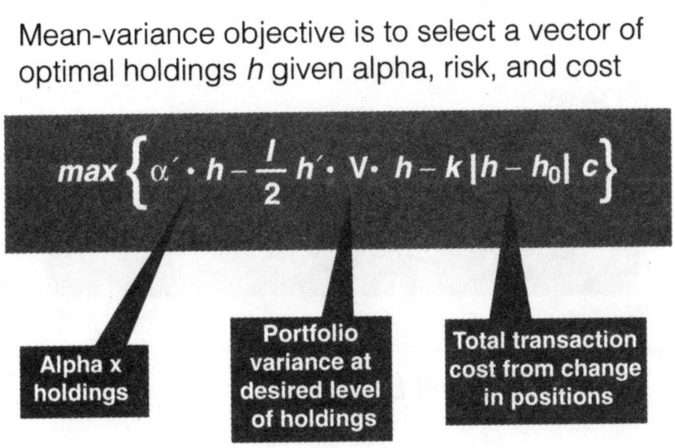

FIGURE 6.8 *Introducing Transaction Costs*

Source: *Journal Of Investment Management*

Constraints might include a restriction that an investor can go long only, restrictions as to sector or industry neutrality, and other similar limits. For our purposes, what is most important to note is that costs do not explicitly show up here. Instead they are assumed to be subtracted ex post.

Now we want to introduce transaction costs (see **FIGURE 6.8**) in the same ex ante sense as the other constraints. We set up a mean-variance objective function to maximize expected return and subtract a penalty on the variance of returns as well as transaction costs.

Different ingredients go into this objective function. There is a model for alpha, a model for risk, or the portfolio variance matrix (V), and one for transaction costs. For the purpose of this chapter, which is to develop the transaction-cost model, we'll take the risk model as given. The alpha model comes out of a forecasting process (see **FIGURE 6.9**).

The alpha model is simply the IC times the standard deviation times the signal, which is a normalized signal. If the IC is high and correlation is strong, then we can put a lot of weight on the signal, and the alpha is high. It is a linear regression that we can intuitively understand.

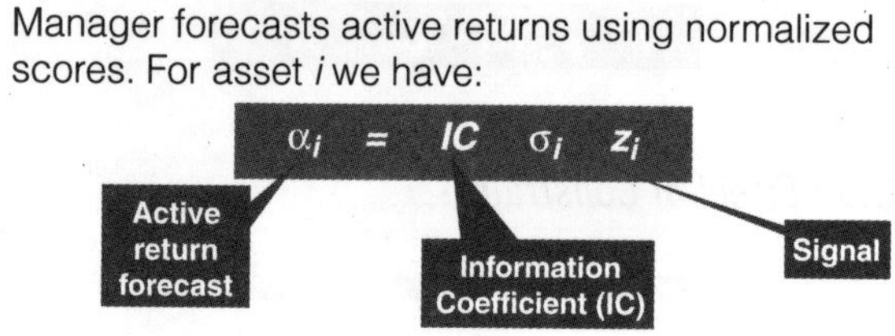

FIGURE 6.9 *Alpha and Risk Forecasts*

Source: *Journal Of Investment Management*

$$IS_i = a_i + bX_i + e_i \qquad i = 1,\ldots,N$$

FIGURE 6.10 *Factor Model Example*

Source: *Journal Of Investment Management*

The transaction-cost model follows the same format. Forecasting costs, as in forecasting alpha, is based on signals correlated with the realized implementation shortfall. That is, costs in any given asset are a function of some factor, and for our purposes we'll use a single factor model, although the model can easily be generalized to a multifactor cost model. **FIGURE 6.10** shows an asset's marginal transaction costs, its IS, as represented by a factor model.

This equation can be viewed as a vector that varies by stock, where a_i and b_i are security-specific constraints, X is the composite signal, and e_i is an error with a mean of 0. We can then move to model security-specific costs—stock by stock, currency by currency—using our model for transaction cost forecasts.

Here c_i is the expected cost, to distinguish it from the IS, which is the realized or posttrade cost. This equation forecasts asset-specific average transaction costs, which vary by stock, times a beta coefficient, times the liquidity signal. The liquidity factor explains deviations from the mean costs. Intuitively, for example, we might predict that illiquid stocks will incur costs higher than the mean.

FIGURE 6.11 illustrates the predictive model for transaction costs. Estimated costs for an order *i*, are modeled as a function of an average shortfall plus a term proportional to the liquidity signal.

Source: *Journal Of Investment Management*

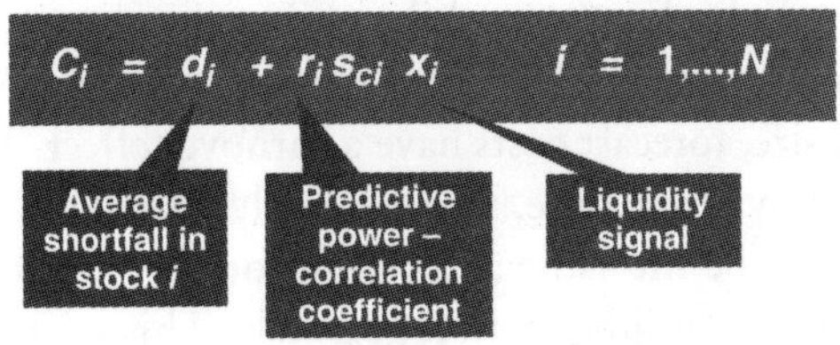

FIGURE 6.11 *Model for Transaction Cost Forecasts*

Transaction-Cost Impact

As has been pointed out earlier, our intuition is that costs affect which securities we buy or sell, and that those costs also affect the size of the trade. Now we can deal with this intuition quantitatively. The first effect is through the reduction in breadth caused by costs. There is a no-trade region in which annualized costs are higher than alpha, so it is not worth doing a trade there, no matter if we are buying or selling. Only if costs are small enough and alpha large enough will an investor buy. The higher our costs, the less we buy. Therefore, the no-trade region kills breadth. If we go back to Grinold's IR formula, which says skill times breadth equals the IR, then we can see that if costs reduce breadth, then performance, or the IR, is reduced. But the investor is also reducing the size of his bet, so the costs are ex ante damaging returns in two ways.

Another element of this no-trade region is the problem of portfolio backlog. **FIGURE 6.12** illustrates the no-trade region. As alpha deteriorates, we stop trading because of the transaction costs, and investments start to pile up. Portfolio backlog is analogous to driving on the freeway—when cars are slowing ahead, drivers will begin to slow down earlier than necessary. A type of wave effect occurs, and ultimately there is a gigantic traffic

Source: *Journal Of Investment Management*

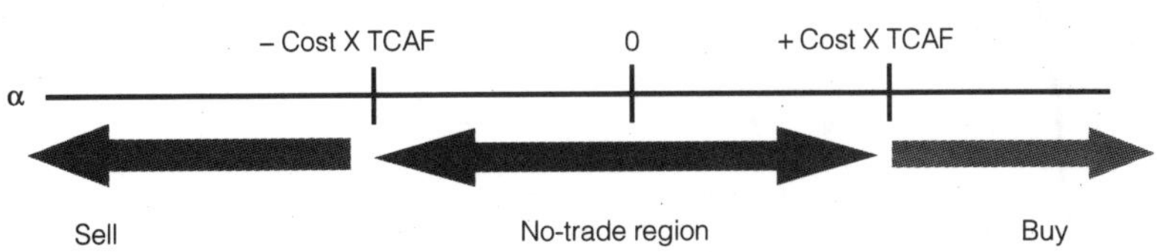

FIGURE 6.12 *No-Trade Region*

jam a mile long. This is a dynamic aspect of trading-cost management, which we will come back to toward the end of the chapter.

Looking again at our static model, we can see that in addition to reducing breadth and size, forecast costs have a turnover effect. This effect arises because alpha decays over time. It is generally true that a return forecast today is unlikely to be the same as a return forecast in the future. In fact, return forecasts decay as information gets stale. This relatively straightforward idea can be modeled by allowing the information coefficient, which measures the predictability of a signal, to decay over time. In our model, we allow for alphas to get stale, to account for the fact that the more we are inhibited from trading, the slower our turnover is and hence the staler our alphas. We balance capturing alpha through faster turnover against higher transaction costs. The decay rate of alpha provides the optimal decision points of when to trade and when not to trade. **FIGURE 6.13** shows the IC decay function suggested by Grinold and Kahn (2000). IC increases at first with time as information is first compounded in prices and then decays as this information gets stale.

Let's consider the dynamic model for a moment. Transaction costs slow the rate of entry or exit from positions, creating a portfolio backlog. We are inhibited from trading as quickly as we would like to by our transaction costs. The backlog is essentially positions we no longer want to hold, that are a drag on our portfolio performance (our alphas are getting so stale we do not even remember why we own certain securities), and the backlog eats up our capacity. A backlog portfolio is one in which we are actively long on assets that have negative alpha forecasts. Our investment positions are perverse.

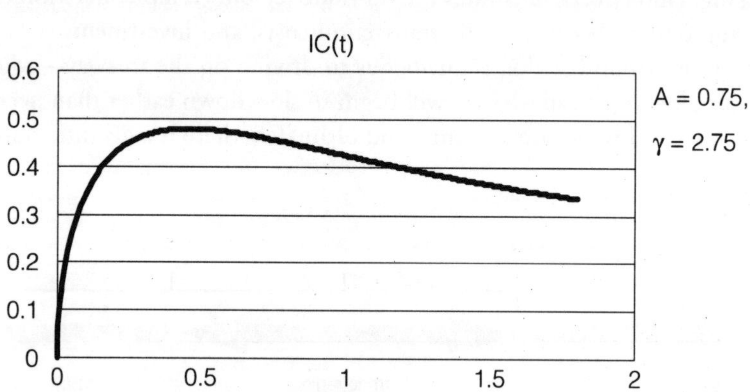

FIGURE 6.13 *Grinold and Kahn IC Decay Function*

Source: *Journal Of Investment Management*

Source: *Journal Of Investment Management*

$$IR = \psi(\rho, d, \kappa)\ IC\ \sqrt{N}$$

Where ψ is a function of the cost model's predictive power, ρ, average trading costs, *d*, and the amortization coefficient. The transfer coefficient can be below 1 even if there are no constraints.

FIGURE 6.14 *Ex Ante Transaction-Cost Effects*

Analytically, it is the difference between the portfolio we would hold if there were no transaction cost intimidation and the portfolio we actually hold. The backlog is a complex function of past alphas and costs, together with other portfolio constraints, which work together to increase the vintage of the holdings.

We derived the above expression (**FIGURE 6.14**) to capture the ex ante transaction-cost effects we have been considering.

As in Grinold's equation, the IR is the product of skill, the IC, and breadth, but there is an added factor now. We include a closed-form function that factors in the correlation between forecast costs (the cost model reviewed earlier including the liquidity factor) and actual cost (the IS); the mean level of costs, which varies by security; and the amortization coefficient. This new factor, ψ, is similar to the IC in the investment space, except that it is in the cost space.

We now have a model calibrated to include not only the traditional inputs of alpha and risk but also transaction costs. **FIGURE 6.15** is an example of how this calibration can be used to model a portfolio.

Source: *Journal Of Investment Management*

FIGURE 6.15 *Modeling a Portfolio*

Alpha & Risk	Cost
$s_a = 0.35$	$d = 0.004$
$IC = 0.045$	$s_c = 0.01$
$k = 4$	$r_c = 0.2$
$N = 500$	
$M = 250$	

$$IR = f(d, IC, r_c, k, N)$$

In this typical active fund, we assume a breadth of 500 bets per year (N), that is, 250 assets (M) turned over twice (turnover of 200 percent). Therefore, we set the TCAF (k) at 4. Volatility (s_a) is set at 0.35. The IC is 0.0447. The basic mean cost level (d) is 40 basis points (0.004), and the standard deviation of costs (s_c) is 0.01. The cost predictability correlation (r_c) is 0.20, or 20 percent, which is actually quite low. It is not uncommon for managers to achieve a cost-predictability correlation of around 40 percent. But for our purposes, we use the lower percentage to make the point that, in many instances, we spend too much time working to get this number high, when there is a lot of low-hanging fruit to be exploited by simply improving predictability on the negative alpha side of our investments.

Using these inputs, we can look at how the IR is affected by costs; in particular, we see how the IR increases as our transaction-cost forecasting becomes more accurate. For these parameters, as initially set, the IR is 0.478 when there are transaction costs and 1.0 when there are no costs.

In **FIGURE 6.16** we see that relatively small increases in costs can induce sharp declines in the IR (this tendency was demonstrated by the transfer

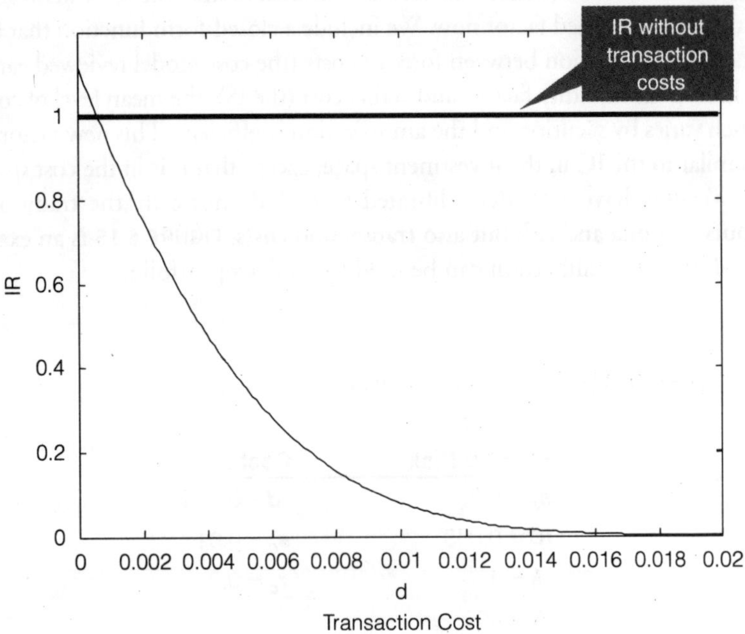

FIGURE 6.16 *Transaction Costs vs. IR*

Source: *Journal Of Investment Management*

coefficient modeled by Clarke, de Silva, and Thorley [2002] for other constraints, not including costs). So there is a clear and substantial deterioration in the IR, which comes from the erosion in breadth. In general, as costs become prohibitively large, the IR tends to zero; in the absence of costs, the formula is reduced to Grinold's original formulation (1989).

Interestingly, Figure 6.16 shows it is possible that for small transaction costs the IR can be above that in Grinold's original formulation. Intuitively, trading-cost forecasts are like a short-term return signal, and since both forecast and actual costs can be negative (for example, buying into a stock with negative short-term momentum), the additional "cost signal" acts to increase the information ratio. For all practical purposes, though, with realistic trading cost numbers, the actual IR is well below the theoretical maximum with no transaction costs.

Not only does the level of costs matter, the correlation between pretrade and posttrade costs, the predictive power (ρ_c), is an even more important factor in the IR. As we can see in **FIGURE 6.17**, increasing the correlation of forecast and actual costs from 0.15 to 0.20, a 33 percent improvement, increases the IR from 0.435 to 0.478, a 13 percent improvement. This is equivalent, in terms of the IR, to decreasing the mean cost level from 43.8 basis points to 40, a 9.5 percent improvement. Improved transaction-cost

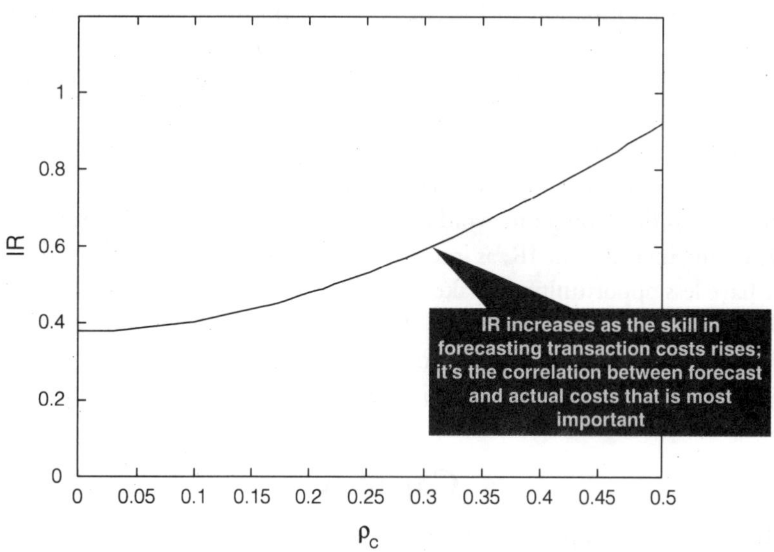

FIGURE **6.17** *Correlation of Forecast and Actual Costs*

Source: *Journal Of Investment Management*

forecasts can improve investment performance by an amount equivalent to a significant reduction in posttrade costs. Thus, increasing the precision of cost forecasts is tantamount to increasing skill, as measured by the IC. This should not be surprising, since the cost forecast is equivalent to a short-run, negative return forecast.

One of the surprising results of this analysis is that, as we develop better transaction-cost models, our actual costs may not go down. In fact, our costs may stay the same or even go up. Why? Because the real benefit of modeling might be realized in higher-cost securities. As we start modeling, we are not going to begin with securities in the large-cap space. They are the most liquid, so the IS on large-cap securities is generally smaller. We will start by modeling small-cap opportunities, emerging market currencies, and other less-active securities with higher frictions. As a result of transaction-cost modeling, we will take more bets in higher-cost securities and our realized costs will likely go up. So will our alpha.

Optimal Turnover

We have used our sample active fund to model how changes in the inputs affect the IR, and now we can turn to the problem of optimal turnover. Turnover enters the equation through the TCAF function. The question then is this: At what level of TCAF do we maximize our Sharpe ratio? A traditional solution sets the turnover based on average alpha duration, because the information coefficient depends on time. Holding a stock for only a few days lowers the IC because we fail to capture the underlying signal. Holding a stock too long lowers the IC because the signal becomes stale. So, for a certain length of holding time, the IC increases, and then at a certain point in time it declines again, approaching zero as the length of time grows longer. What happens to costs if we sacrifice some of the alpha by holding positions longer to avoid incurring transaction costs? A certain level of holding increases the IR, as it reduces costs. But it also reduces breadth, as we have less opportunity to make other investments. Optimal turnover (see **FIGURE 6.18**) is a function of the IC, breadth, and transaction costs. The inputs from our sample active fund, with the addition of a time factor in the calculation of IC, yield an optimal turnover of 2.2, or 110 percent.

Capacity

There is another application for our analysis, and that is to use it to think about capacity issues. As assets under management increase, trade size increases. Our alpha is linear, whereas our costs are not.

What we are really concerned with is the net alpha. In **FIGURE 6.19**, net alpha is represented as the gap between gross alpha, which increases

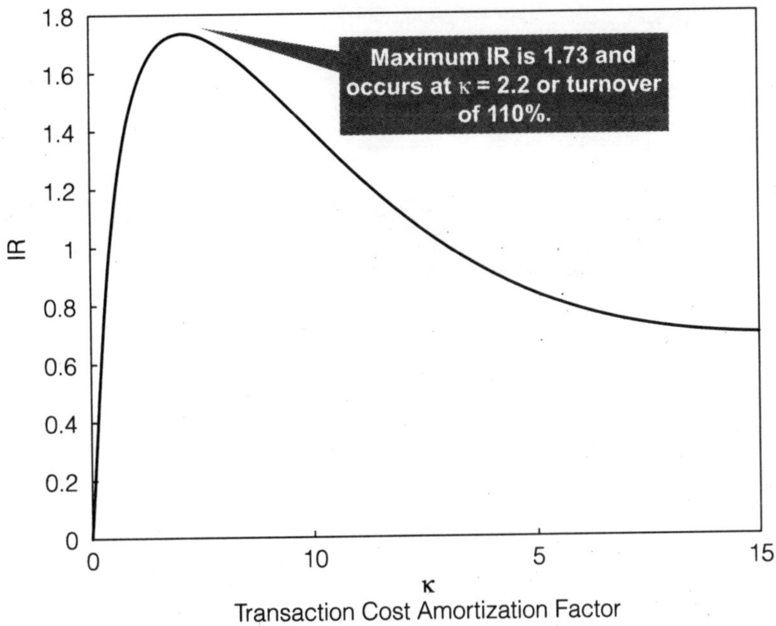

Source: *Journal Of Investment Management*

FIGURE 6.18 *Optimal Turnover*

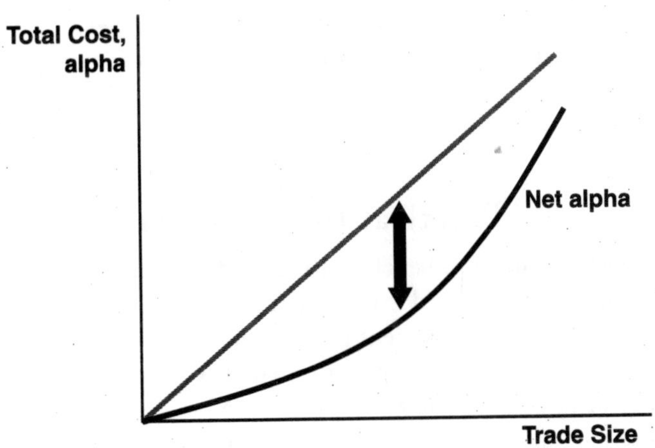

Source: *Journal Of Investment Management*

FIGURE 6.19 *Net Alpha*

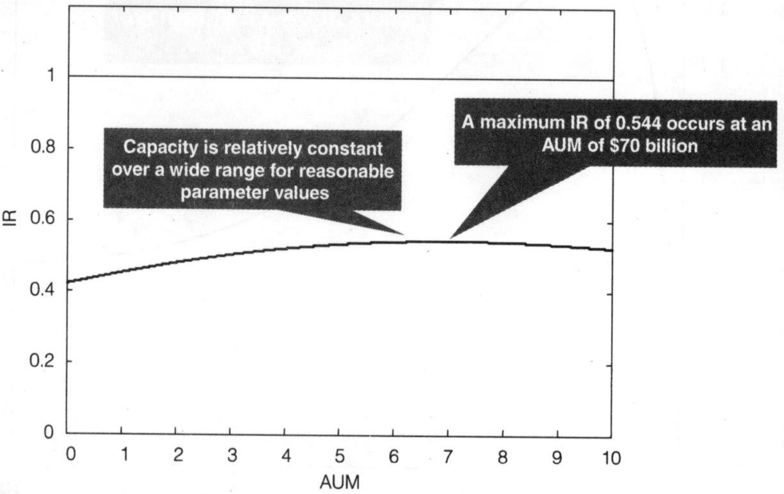

FIGURE 6.20 *Cost Forecasting and Optimal Capacity*

Source: *Journal Of Investment Management*

linearly with trade size (represented by the top line), and transaction costs (the lower line), which increase in a nonlinear fashion, because of the economies of scale associated with larger trades. So, capacity is ultimately a cost issue. Capacity depends on our costs of entry and exit, and, as such, can be influenced by our ability to forecast costs. As better cost forecasting increases our maximum information ratio, we can see, from **FIGURE 6.20**, how optimal capacity increases too.

Practical Implications

There are several practical benefits of the model we have worked through in this chapter. If measured correctly, transaction costs—both pretrade and posttrade—affect investment performance. Implementation shortfall is the best way to measure transaction costs. Our new transaction-cost model performs a double duty—it can be used to evaluate traders, and it can be used to build better portfolios. Trading-cost modeling is a source of alpha. Improved skill in modeling costs will improve investment return through better security selection and choice of order size. In addition, cross-sectional correlations between forecast cost and actual cost is what matters most, not the overall level of cost forecasts to actual outcomes. Our model improves that correlation.

There are also broader implications. Reducing trading costs (through the effective selection of venues, tactics, duration, and the like) increases realized returns and raises breadth and capacity while reducing backlog. Improvements in cost forecasting will appear in improved performance, not necessarily in lower transaction costs. And lastly, capacity is an elastic concept that is surprisingly responsive to relatively modest gains in transaction cost control or forecasting ability.

Transaction-cost modeling is a valuable and, until now, largely overlooked source of alpha.

References

Clarke, Roger, Harindra de Silva, and Steven Thorley. 2002. "Portfolio Constraints and the Fundamental Law of Active Management." *Financial Analysts Journal* 58 (September/October): 48–66.

Grinold, Richard. 1989. "The Fundamental Law of Active Management." *The Journal of Portfolio Management* 15 (Spring): 30–37.

Grinold, Richard, and Ronald Kahn. 2000. "The Efficiency Gains of Long-Short Investing." *Financial Analysts Journal* 56 (November/December): 40–53.

Perold, Andre. 1988. "The Implementation Shortfall: Paper Versus Reality." *The Journal of Portfolio Management* 14 (Spring): 4–9.

Treynor, Jack. 1981. "What Does It Take to Win the Trading Game?" *Financial Analysts Journal* 37 (January/February): 55–60.

There are also two key implications [illegible] trading costs through the [illegible] efficiency, [illegible] and the [illegible] increases [illegible] breadth [illegible] while reducing [illegible] [illegible] will appear in improved performance [illegible] in [illegible] transaction costs [illegible] capacity [illegible] [illegible]

[illegible]

[illegible] models. [illegible]

[illegible] Journal [illegible]

[illegible] Management [illegible]

[illegible] Costs of Long-Short [illegible] Journal [illegible] December [illegible]

[illegible] The Implementation [illegible]

[illegible] the Trading [illegible] Journal [illegible]

CHAPTER 7

Liquidity Risk in Financial Markets

GEORGE CHACKO

Who—George Chacko is a managing partner and chief investment officer of 6S Capital, a managing director of Trinsum Group, Inc., a professor at Santa Clara University, and an active board member of several firms. Chacko previously was a professor at Harvard Business School and a managing director of fixed income at State Street Bank in Boston. He has also held positions at Prudential Investments and Accenture. In his academic work he has published extensively on portfolio construction, complex financial securities, and the microstructure of financial markets. He holds a BS in electrical engineering from the Massachusetts Institute of Technology, an MBA from the University of Chicago, and an MA and PhD in business economics from Harvard University.

New Thinking—A great deal of work has focused on market microstructure, but relatively little work has been done on the risk associated with liquidity. The work that has been done has focused almost exclusively on U.S. equities, primarily because that market is liquid and so data are plentiful. Yet the corporate bond market is several orders of magnitude more illiquid than the equity market, and thus a more appropriate setting in which to study the effects of illiquidity. Chacko's work uses a database of U.S. corporate bond transactions and holdings, constructed from the Spectrum and National Association of Insurance Commissioners (NAIC) databases. He gets around the problem of a lack of trading in the corporate bond market (and therefore data) by constructing a new measure of liquidity, which does not require trading. With this, Chacko shows not only that liquidity risk is priced in the corporate bond market, but that the effects of liquidity risk are pervasive and need to be controlled for carefully when doing virtually any analysis of security returns.

Introduction

Any investor buying or holding a security or a portfolio of securities is exposed to liquidity risk. By *liquidity risk* we mean the gap between the fundamental value of a security and the price at which the sale of the security is actually transacted. High liquidity means this gap is small. As liquidity decreases, the size of the gap increases. Liquidity *risk* is the uncertainty of how wide or narrow this gap will be at any point in time. All investors and potential investors bear liquidity risk. Furthermore, this is a risk that is not fully diversifiable, as it is a systematic risk. The natural next question then is whether the systematic portion of liquidity risk is priced. In other words, do investors command a risk premium for bearing liquidity risk? We take a first look at how the liquidity risk premium is priced and open the topic for further, more rigorous analysis.

Why Does Liquidity Risk Matter?

Before we dive into the statistical and theoretical problem, let's look at the motivation behind this work. Why should we get into the topic at all? Think back to WorldCom in 2000, 2001, and 2002. The risk-neutral default probability of WorldCom (calculated here using the Merton model and information from the *equity* markets) rose from about 2 percent to approximately 7 percent or 8 percent, a nearly 300 percent increase (**FIGURE 7.1**). So the equity market was apparently getting information that there might be problems at WorldCom.

What about the credit markets? From November 2000 through January 2002 the credit spreads fluctuated but remained roughly flat. Which raises the question—why did the equity markets seem to be getting information, but the debt markets, or at least the credit markets, seem to be getting almost none of this information (**FIGURE 7.2**)?

Of course, this kind of information asymmetry is one reason that is widely discussed as a motivation for capital structure arbitrage, but why does it exist? It can't be that fixed-income managers are less intelligent than equity managers, or that they don't get information as fast as equity managers. That doesn't make sense. What then are the big differences between the equity markets and the credit markets? Well, one big difference is liquidity risk, which, once we understand it better, should be able to help us explain this WorldCom data. With this practical implication in mind, let's return to liquidity risk at a more general level.

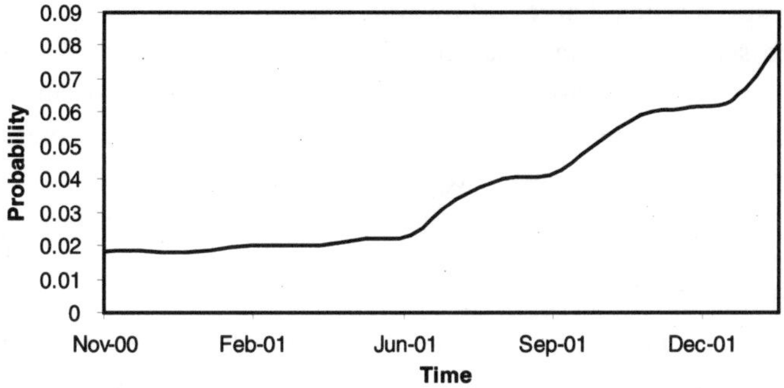

FIGURE 7.1 *WorldCom Risk-Neutral Default Probability*

Source: Data from G. Chacko, "Liquidity Risk in Corporate Bond Markets" (working paper, Santa Clara University, 2006).

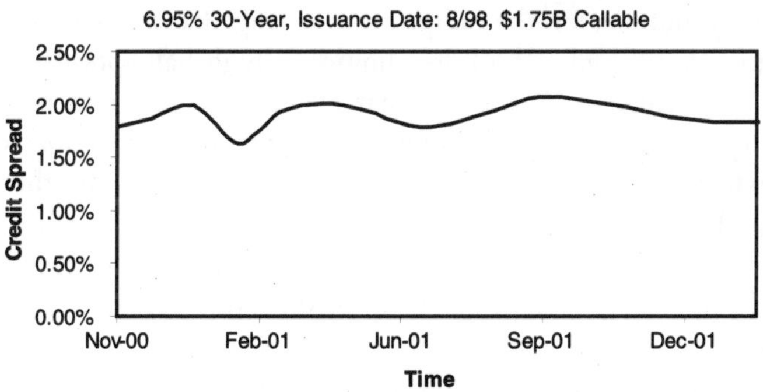

FIGURE 7.2 *WorldCom LT Credit Spread*

Source: Data from G. Chacko, "Liquidity Risk in Corporate Bond Markets" (working paper, Santa Clara University, 2006).

The Problem of Measuring Liquidity Risk

The gap between the transaction price of a security and its fundamental value is called the *half-spread.* The bid-ask spread is simply the sum of the buy half-spread (the buy price minus the fundamental value) and the sell half-spread (the fundamental value minus the sell price). Two factors give rise to half-spreads.

The first is that for a transaction to occur, there must be a match between a buyer and a seller. There is, however, a strong likelihood that when one wants to sell a particular quantity of a specific security, there will be no buyer who wants precisely the same security in the same quantity at the same time. Thus there are financial intermediaries—market makers. The role of a market maker is to bridge the gaps in security type, quantity, and time between buyers and sellers by storing securities on his balance sheet. The market maker charges a fee for this inventory service, which is collected through the half-spreads.

The second factor that gives rise to half-spreads is asymmetric information. In any given transaction, the parties can never be sure whether the counterparty is more or less informed. To compensate for the possibility of transacting with a more informed trader, market makers charge an additional fee to all traders (sometimes referred to as the *information-based transaction costs*), which is also collected through the half-spreads.

The question here is whether the bid-ask spread is time varying and whether this time variation is systematic. Is it priced? Intuitively, one might expect liquidity risk to be priced. Major "liquidity" shocks, such as the Long-Term Capital Management (LTCM) crisis, the bursting of the technology bubble, or the subprime mortgage-backed security (MBS) write-downs, resulted in both low liquidity (high half-spreads) and poor market performance. A security that experiences low returns precisely when an investor's wealth drops must offer a premium to investors to induce them to hold the security. While these are only two data points, they suggest that liquidity risk is priced.

Despite its importance to practitioners and academics, there has been relatively little empirical research devoted to this topic, and the results seem to be mixed. The main problem is almost a catch-22 in that liquidity is correlated to trading. The very securities that are thinly traded, where liquidity problems are profound, are the ideal candidates for examining liquidity and liquidity risk. However, these thinly traded securities by definition have very little trade data associated with them. There are no data because there is no trading, which is exactly the reason why one wants to study the liquidity risk of these securities. As a result, much of the empirical and theoretical research that has been done on liquidity risk has been done so in the highly liquid U.S. equities market. It is not surprising then that the question of whether liquidity remains an open question.

So the first task at hand is to construct a measure of liquidity that does not require trading. To begin with, we need to use data from an illiquid market, and the U.S. corporate bond markets are perfect for our purposes. From Chacko, Mahanti, Mallik, Nashikkar, and Subrahmanyam (2007)[1] we learn that while the median stock trades once every few minutes, the

FIGURE 7.3 *Corporate Bond Market Liquidity*

Frequency of Trading	2000	2001	2002	2003	2004	2005
> 200 days in year	0	2	5	5	3	6
150–200 days in year	11	15	33	42	25	14
100–150 days in year	38	80	152	146	149	116
50–100 days in year	273	401	621	786	730	739
30–50 days in year	502	675	774	940	1007	961
10–30 days in year	1862	2169	2377	2439	2722	2672
5–10 days in year	1544	1716	1568	1754	1742	1580
At least 1 day and almost 5 days in year	6191	5866	4987	5006	4786	4335
No trade in year	7872	6979	7163	8262	8397	8693
Total issues	18293	17904	17680	19380	19561	19116

Source: Data from G. Chacko, "Liquidity Risk in Corporate Bond Markets" (working paper, Santa Clara University, 2006).

median U.S. corporate bond trades less than once every two months—an order of magnitude difference (**FIGURE 7.3**).

Liquidity is not, however, just a function of number of trades. The average trade size matters, too; the larger the median trade size, the more liquid the market. But let's look at what happened in the corporate bond markets. From 1994 to 1998 the median trade size was increasing each year. Then from 1998 onward, the trade sizes decrease. So liquidity appears to be decreasing (**FIGURE 7.4**).

FIGURE 7.4 *Liquidity Trend in the Bond Market*

Average Trade Size Percentiles (millions of US dollars):

	YR94	YR95	YR96	YR97	YR98	YR99	YR00	YR01	YR02	YR03	YR04
MIN	0.00	0.00	0.00	0.00	0.00	0.00	0.00	0.00	0.00	0.00	0.00
10%	0.56	0.58	0.62	0.68	0.69	0.63	0.61	0.55	0.53	0.50	0.48
20%	0.89	0.96	1.08	1.13	1.21	1.19	1.19	1.06	1.03	0.98	0.94
30%	1.24	1.38	1.45	1.47	1.50	1.42	1.36	1.30	1.21	1.18	1.06
40%	1.71	1.91	2.17	2.39	2.38	2.30	2.21	2.02	1.89	1.80	1.68
50%	2.05	2.56	2.86	3.04	3.09	3.07	2.87	2.77	2.54	2.35	2.17
60%	2.69	3.18	3.88	4.24	4.50	4.38	4.18	3.94	3.61	3.32	2.99
70%	3.58	4.01	4.53	5.18	5.38	5.29	5.11	4.96	4.83	4.65	4.25
80%	5.04	5.79	6.11	6.13	6.89	6.71	6.53	6.47	6.30	6.11	5.84
90%	7.64	7.83	8.02	8.46	10.03	9.73	9.47	9.32	9.02	8.81	8.55
MAX	154.29	146.78	197.42	211.33	325.84	368.25	327.39	338.92	313.84	273.05	271.28

Source: Data from G. Chacko, "Liquidity Risk in Corporate Bond Markets" (working paper, Santa Clara University, 2006).

Why? What was going on? We could make a reasonable guess that it had to do with the start of the credit-default swap (CDS) market. Investors who traded credit actively left the credit market and moved to the CDS market, so the corporate bond market is now primarily traded by buy-and-hold funds, reducing liquidity, for reasons we'll look at it in more detail in a moment.

In summary, liquidity is a problem for most market participants in the U.S. corporate bond market. Therefore, to the extent investors command a premium for liquidity risk, it should be discernible in this market. But because corporate bonds are traded over-the-counter in a dealer market, getting data is difficult. No single dealer sees enough transactions to conduct a meaningful analysis. We could conduct research by going to an individual dealer and collecting and analyzing the transactions participated in by that dealer. But this leaves open the possibility of biases. For example, a dealer might be a market leader in executing high-yield transactions, in which case the dealer's transactions would be biased toward high-yield bonds.

To avoid biases, for our data set we turn to a custom database that is put together using a combination of Datastream 7i™ and a Wall Street bond dealer. While this combined database does not include all the transactions of the corporate bond market, the two cover a substantial portion. Even with this database, there is still the problem that trading volume is so low for most bonds that traditional methods of measuring liquidity can only measure small differences between most bonds.

A New Liquidity Measure

Because conventional liquidity measures are not appropriate for the corporate bond markets, we constructed a new liquidity measure that measures the *accessibility* of a bond rather than its trading volume; we call this measure *latent liquidity*. A bond is accessible if a dealer can call up any number of buy-side clients and easily obtain the bond. So, even if the bond does not actually trade much, it can be thought of as liquid, because it is readily available to a dealer. The location of the securities matters in this measure—if a bond is held primarily by investors with high-turnover portfolios, like hedge funds who buy securities to take advantage of mispricing, then it can be thought of as more accessible. By contrast, if long-term buy-and-hold investors, like insurance companies, primarily hold a bond issue, it is more difficult for a dealer to buy the bonds. The bond is, therefore, less accessible.

Thus, if we can figure out where a security is held, we can infer something about the characteristics of the owners of the security, and then from this learn something about its liquidity. Fortunately, we have access to holdings data through the NAIC and Spectrum databases. With this data we can look at who owns what on a quarterly basis, and we can see when transactions occur. With any particular bond issue, we can figure out what set of institutions (which we will generically call *funds*) owns the bond issue and what the average turnover is of those funds, and then we can calculate a weighted average turnover of the holders of that bond issue. The higher the weighted average turnover, the more accessible the bond, and vice versa. In this way, we construct a measure of latent liquidity (the weighted average turnover) that quantifies the accessibility of a bond to dealers based on the aggregate trading characteristics of investors holding bonds.

Let's see then if this does in fact measure liquidity. We can start with some simple tests. For example, measuring the liquidity of bond issues versus the principal amount, we find that when the principal amount is small, roughly \$400 million or less, the liquidity of that bond decreases. Similarly, when we have small bond issues, we intuitively think that they ought to be less liquid. The latent liquidity measure matches our intuition (**FIGURE 7.5**).

How about on-the-run versus off-the-run bonds? When a bond is first issued (*on-the-run*), we assume that it should be more liquid than a bond that has been sitting out in the markets for a long time (*off-the-run*). This is consistent with the casual evidence that many bonds are initially placed into high turnover funds, which then *flip* the bonds to lower turnover

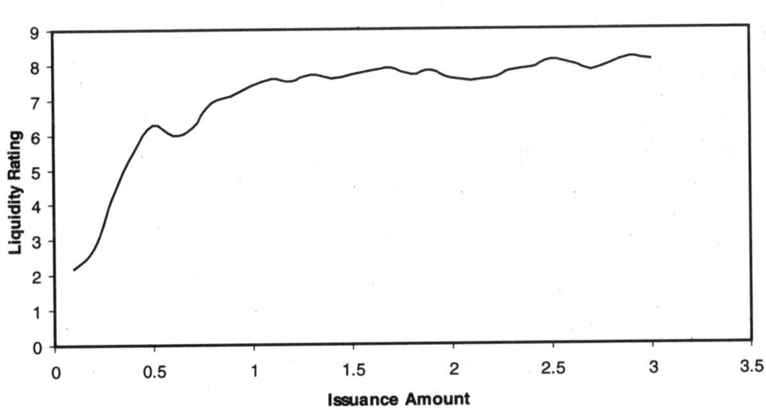

FIGURE 7.5 *Latent Liquidity of Bonds by Issuance Amount*

Source: Data from G. Chacko, "Liquidity Risk in Corporate Bond Markets" (working paper, Santa Clara University, 2006).

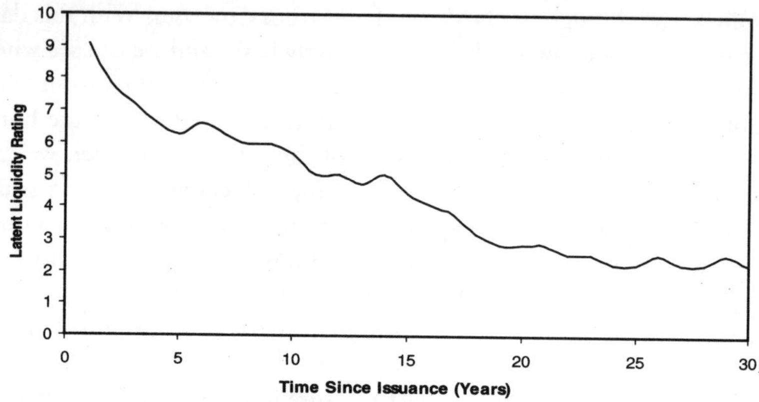

FIGURE 7.6 *Latent Liquidity of Bond vs. Age of Bond*

Source: Data from G. Chacko, "Liquidity Risk in Corporate Bond Markets" (working paper, Santa Clara University, 2006).

(usually buy-and-hold) funds. Again, this intuitive assumption is captured in the latent liquidity measure, the value of which is high when a bond is first issued and decreases as time passes (**FIGURE 7.6**).

We have not been terribly rigorous, relying on our intuition to test what the numbers are showing us, but at this stage of the research into liquidity risk in very illiquid markets, we have captured some important aspects of liquidity.

Liquidity Factor Construction

The next step is to run some tests to determine whether liquidity risk is priced or not. We can apply the standard process in asset pricing of constructing a risk factor building, in our case, a liquidity risk factor.

We begin by sorting our corporate bond database from over the last ten years, which is approximately 20,000 bonds (a number that excludes bonds with fewer than three trades in the entire thirteen-year period), into twenty-seven buckets. We sort first into three categories: duration risk, credit risk, and liquidity risk. Then within each of these three categories we sort again into three more categories—high, medium, and low duration; high, medium, and low credit risk; and high, medium, and low liquidity risk.

Once the sorting is done, we form three factor portfolios. In the duration factor portfolio we take a long position in high duration bonds and a

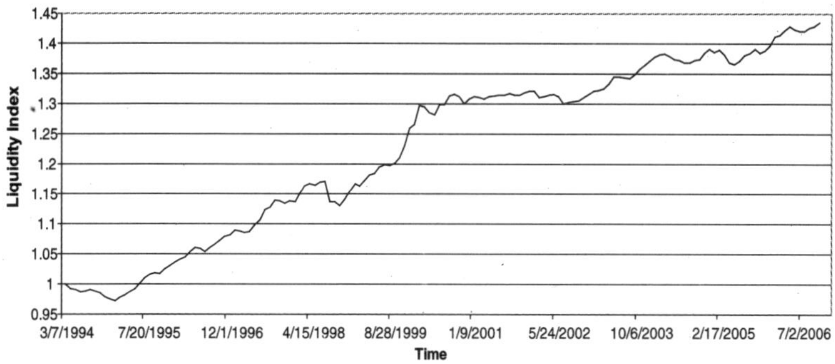

FIGURE 7.7 *Cumulative Liquidity Returns*

Source: Data from G. Chacko, "Liquidity Risk in Corporate Bond Markets" (working paper, Santa Clara University, 2006).

short position in low duration bonds, which we call HML (high minus low). This is our pure duration portfolio that tracks duration, or interest rate, risk. For the credit factor portfolio, we take a long position in the low credit bonds and a short position in high credit bonds, which we call LMH (low minus high). Here we've built a portfolio that tracks only credit risk. Finally, for the liquidity factor portfolio, we take a long position in the low latent liquidity bonds and a short position in the high latent liquidity bonds, which again we call LMH. We've now built a pure liquidity portfolio that gives us a time series of the liquidity risk factor (**FIGURE 7.7**).

In Figure 7.7 we see how $1 invested in a pure liquidity index would have performed over the thirteen years from 1994 to 2006. Specifically, the index rises in value to nearly $1.45, an annual compounded return of about 2.8 percent. The risk is reasonably steady and smooth, except for mid-1998 when the Russian default and subsequent LTCM crises hit the markets, and again in 2002 when the technology bubble burst. In both cases these were periods during which the liquidity premium increased substantially. These events caused, as we would have expected, liquidity crises. So the liquidity measure seems to be functioning, at least to the extent that we are getting the results anticipated.

Now that we have the measure, the question is whether liquidity risk is priced. In other words, is liquidity risk diversifiable? If it is diversifiable, then we wouldn't expect to earn a premium for taking the risk. But if it is systematic and cannot be fully diversified, then we should earn a premium.

FIGURE 7.8 *Alphas of Portfolios Sorted on Liquidity Betas*

	L	M/L	M	H/M	H	H − L
CAPM	−0.61%	0.18%	0.87%	1.46%	2.37%	2.98%
Duration	−0.47%	0.33%	1.02%	1.60%	2.58%	3.05%
Duration, credit	−0.70%	0.12%	0.69%	1.35%	2.19%	2.89%

Source: Data from G. Chacko, "Liquidity Risk in Corporate Bond Markets" (working paper, Santa Clara University, 2006).

To answer this question, we regress the bonds in our database on each of these three risk factors, to calculate a duration beta, a credit beta, and a liquidity beta for every bond. Once we have three betas calculated for each bond, we resort the bonds. First, we sort for five equal-weight liquidity portfolios—H, H/M, M, M/L, L—corresponding to high betas, high/medium betas, and so on through low betas. Then we sort each of the five liquidity portfolios into three credit portfolios—H, M, L—denoting high credit, medium credit, and low credit. Finally we take each of the now fifteen portfolios and sort each into three duration portfolios—H, M, L. Effectively we have done a 5 by 3 by 3 sort of the data.

The first thing we do to determine whether liquidity risk is important is run a regression of each portfolio against an asset pricing model (capital asset pricing model [CAPM]) and calculate the alpha. If liquidity is important, then we expect that the alphas will go up as we increase illiquidity. Again, the results match our intuition (**FIGURE 7.8**).

Next, in another informal test, we measure the *R*-squared, or increment in explanatory power, that we get from using the liquidity factor, by running factor regressions on the duration and credit portfolios with the liquidity factor included (**FIGURE 7.9** and **FIGURE 7.10**). Again we see that as liquidity decreases, the incremental *R*-squared produced by the liquidity

FIGURE 7.9 *Incremental R^2 of Liquidity Factor—Credit*

		Liquidity Portfolios				
		H	**H/M**	**M**	**M/L**	**L**
Credit Portfolios	**H**	5%	13%	20%	25%	33%
	M	5%	13%	22%	26%	35%
	L	5%	14%	23%	28%	37%

Source: Data from G. Chacko, "Liquidity Risk in Corporate Bond Markets" (working paper, Santa Clara University, 2006).

Source: Data from G. Chacko, "Liquidity Risk in Corporate Bond Markets" (working paper, Santa Clara University, 2006).

FIGURE 7.10 *Incremental R^2 of Liquidity Factor—Duration*

		Liquidity Portfolios				
		H	**H/M**	**M**	**M/L**	**L**
Duration Portfolios	**L**	3%	15%	22%	29%	37%
	M	3%	16%	24%	31%	38%
	H	4%	17%	25%	33%	40%

factor increases, as we would expect if liquidity is an important factor, which, of course, is our argument. An aside—one small thing to note in these tables is that we have not done the sorting perfectly. Notice that there seem to be patterns manifest between the high-to-low credit and high-to-low duration portfolios. But liquidity should not help to explain the differences between high credit or low credit, or duration levels. So that's an anomaly created by the slightly imperfect sort.

Practical Implications: Convertible Arbitrage and Treasuries

The tests we have done so far suggest that liquidity risk is an important risk factor and that it is priced. It is valuable at this point to look at whether this liquidity risk factor works in explaining the returns of other asset classes. It should, if it is in fact priced.

We start with the convertible arbitrage industry. First, think about what it is. Hedge funds employing a convertible arbitrage strategy go long a corporate bond and short the corresponding firm's equity. What are the liquidity implications? The corporate bond market is very illiquid. The equity market is liquid. When you construct this portfolio of long corporate bonds and short equities, even if you hedge out duration, or interest rate risk, and credit risk, you will still be left with a huge amount of liquidity risk. Your portfolio is long in illiquid securities and short in liquid securities—this liquidity mismatch results in an exposure to liquidity risk. Unless you explicitly match up the long and short positions on liquidity, you cannot eliminate this liquidity exposure.

Convertible arbitrage then should be a perfect candidate to illustrate high exposure to liquidity risk. Let's look at an example (**FIGURE 7.11**).

Rather than using the CSFB/Tremont Hedge Fund Index for Figure 7.11, we use a convertible arbitrage index created for our purposes. We have taken the universe of convertibles, put them together with the corresponding

FIGURE 7.11 *Benchmark Regressions*

Alpha	DEF	TERM	Rm-Rf	SMB	HML	UMD	Liq.	Adj.R^2
0.0036	−0.33	−0.47					0.92	28%
1.49	−1.07	−1.46					2.97	
0.0009	0.13	0.15	−0.21	0.04	0.03	−0.02	0.87	36%
0.42	0.48	1.20	−2.21	2.73	0.96	−0.35	3.22	
0.0014			−0.20	0.07	0.09	0.03	1.07	32%
0.79			−2.78	2.15	1.14	0.59	2.99	
0.0040	−0.66	−0.33						7%
0.58	−1.43	−1.21						
0.0026	−0.02	0.08	−0.15	0.07	0.08	−0.03		13%
3.51	−0.15	1.08	−2.74	2.44	1.26	−0.09		
0.0035			−0.17	0.06	0.09	0.01		11%
3.32			−2.07	1.8	1.51	0.25		

Source: Data from G. Chacko, "Liquidity Risk in Corporate Bond Markets" (working paper, Santa Clara University, 2006).

equities, and matched them up to hedge out credit risk and duration risk. We would, by the way, get very similar results using the CSFB/Tremont Convertible Arbitrage Index. The data are then regressed against the standard set of Fama-French factors—small minus big (SMB), HML, and up minus down (UMD)—as well as the equity market, a credit risk factor, and a yield curve slope factor.

The first thing to notice is that the convertible arbitrage market generally significantly outperforms the market, returning 10–12 percent alpha per year (based on the alpha of 26 basis points per week). The regression results are shown in the shaded region of the bottom panel in Figure 7.11. What happens to this extraordinary performance when we do the same regressions we've already done, but this time with the liquidity factor? These results are shown in the shaded region in the upper panel of Figure 7.11. The alpha comes down significantly. Now we have a 5 or 6 percent annualized alpha. Thus, one explanation for the seeming outperformance in the convertible arbitrage market appears to be simply that the returns are fair compensation for the liquidity risk held in convertible arbitrage portfolios. It turns out that the extraordinary returns, once adjusted for the liquidity risk factor, are not so abnormal after all. Convertible arbitrage, understood in these terms, is a way for investors to invest in liquidity risk, and by taking on this liquidity risk, they are in essence providing liquidity services to the market. In return for these services, they earn a fee—that's the alpha.

Convertible arbitrage is just an example. Any long-short position where there is a difference in liquidity between the long and short positions inherently has liquidity risk. Because most hedge fund strategies involve having both long and short positions, it should not be surprising that the regressions we have done for convertible arbitrage show the same results for other hedge fund strategies; namely, that most hedge fund strategies' alphas are due to their exposure to liquidity risk. In other words, most hedge fund strategies have large mismatches in liquidity between their long and short positions, and thus they take on substantial liquidity risk. Therefore, a significant portion of the alphas they earn is simply compensation for bearing this liquidity risk.

Some might wonder whether the fees charged by convertible arbitrage funds and other hedge funds are worth it if these funds are simply taking liquidity risk and earning returns for bearing this risk. However, you have to ask yourself whether liquidity risk is something that can be acquired easily. The answer is no. It takes a substantial amount of financial skill to put together long-short positions that are mismatched in liquidity and then to hedge out all of the major liquid beta exposures. For an investor seeking liquidity risk, this type of exposure is not easy to obtain (you could not simply call up an index fund provider and ask for a liquidity risk exchange-traded fund [ETF]). The high fees charged by hedge funds are compensation for doing the financial engineering to provide liquidity exposure to those investors who desire it with limited beta exposure.

And which investors want this liquidity exposure? The answer is long-horizon investors. For these investors, liquidity risk is not really much of a risk, due to their long investment horizon. So pension funds, endowments, and family offices are all (or should be) natural seekers of liquidity risk. They are willing to take this liquidity risk and thus provide liquidity services to the markets and earn a premium for doing so. In fact, one can argue that given their long investment horizon, it makes little sense for them to be investing in public markets, because when they do so they are essentially paying for liquidity services rather than being paid for these services.

Let's move to an out-of-sample test and look at the Treasury markets. There are three important factors in explaining bonds—level, slope, and curvature. The level factor is the level of the short end of the yield curve, in other words, the short rate. The slope factor is the return on the long end of the yield curve, the ten-year bond for example, less the return of, for example, the interbank overnight deposit rate at the short end of the yield curve. The curvature factor is a measure of the average convexity of the yield curve.

The Treasury market is generally thought of as a very liquid market. Despite this view, there are still significant differences in prices between on-the-run and off-the-run bonds. We might suspect then that liquidity risk is an important explanatory factor in the returns of these bonds. Let's

FIGURE 7.12 *Average Contribution of Individual Factors to Bond Yields (RMSE)*

Maturity	Curvature	Slope	Liquidity
0.5	1	2	4
1	2	5	8
2	4	8	13
3	9	12	19
5	22	33	45
7	33	45	64
10	19	58	78

Source: Data from G. Chacko, "Liquidity Risk in Corporate Bond Markets" (working paper, Santa Clara University, 2006).

go back to the slope factor. When we construct the slope factor, we are going long on one part of the yield curve and going short on another part of the yield curve. Sound familiar? Immediately you should be thinking about whether the two ends of the curve match up in liquidity risk, because if they don't, when you construct the slope factor, liquidity risk will be included in the measure.

To solve for this problem, we split the slope factor, to see how much is truly term premium and how much is liquidity premium. In **FIGURE 7.12**, you see that reflected in the separate term and liquidity columns.

What we see is that in fact the liquidity factor explains more about Treasury bond movements than the term, or even the curvature (though we already knew that slope was more important than curvature). In fact, the slope factor we have been constructing for years is mostly a liquidity factor, the liquidity difference between the long end and the short end of the yield curve.

Practical Implications: WorldCom, Again

We have come full circle now, back to WorldCom and the underlying motivation for this research. Recall that from late 2000 until spring of 2002, credit spreads in WorldCom stayed flat, even though we saw that the risk-neutral probability of default was being reflected in the equity markets (**FIGURE 7.13**).

But, based on our findings up until this point, we now know that the credit spread is in fact two spreads: a spread associated with default risk and a spread associated with liquidity risk. Without getting overly technical, we can split the spread in this fashion: We calculate the rolling beta of the WorldCom bonds with respect to the credit factor and to the liquidity

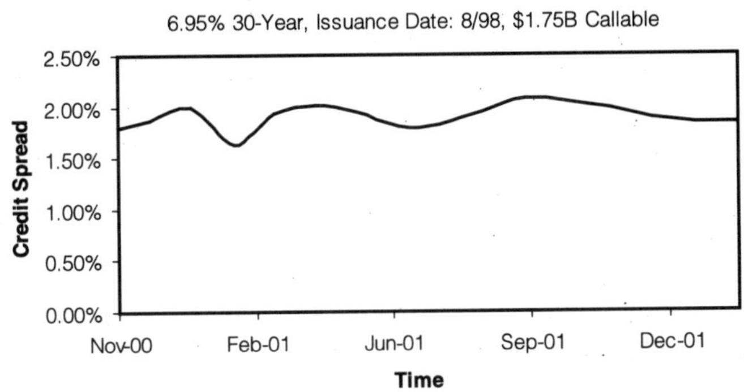

FIGURE 7.13 *WorldCom LT Credit Spread*

Source: Data from G. Chacko, "Liquidity Risk in Corporate Bond Markets" (working paper, Santa Clara University, 2006).

factor. Then, based on how the beta is split, we can split the spread proportionally (**FIGURE 7.14**).

What we see is that while the aggregate spread stays constant between November 2000 and February 2002, the liquidity spread actually decreases, and the default spread increases. Earlier we wondered how the bond market could have missed the picture. The answer is this: We had made a

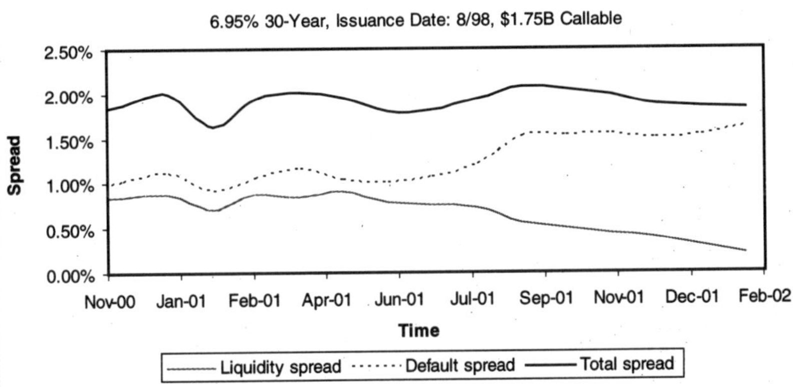

FIGURE 7.14 *Credit vs. Liquidity Spread for WorldCom*

Source: Data from G. Chacko, "Liquidity Risk in Corporate Bond Markets" (working paper, Santa Clara University, 2006).

mistake in assuming the total credit spread to be entirely due to default risk. In fact, the default risk component of the total spread increased; however, the decrease in the liquidity spread component masked the default spread increase. In fact, if you look closely at Figure 7.14, you can see a substantial decrease in the liquidity spread beginning in July 2001. This was when WorldCom conducted the largest issuance of corporate bonds in the history of the bond market to date. This issuance caused all WorldCom bonds trading in the markets to increase substantially in liquidity.

Let's push this methodology further and look at the Lehman Brothers Inc. indexes and split the aggregate spreads into liquidity and credit spreads, based on the liquidity and credit factors we constructed earlier. The results are interesting (**FIGURE 7.15** and **FIGURE 7.16**).

For BBB bonds we see that liquidity and default spreads are generally weighted about 50/50. Liquidity is sometimes more important. Default is sometimes more important. On average they are about the same, which means that liquidity is a key component of this index. If an investor interprets the entire credit spread as the return, or the premium, for default risk, it is a big mistake. Thus investors must be careful about drawing conclusions regarding credit based solely on the aggregate credit spread of bonds.

The story for BB bonds is similar. The liquidity spread component is a substantial component of the spread, but as you might expect here, the

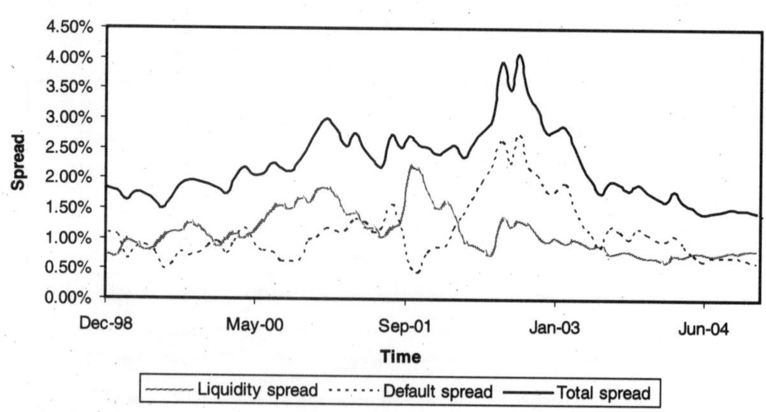

FIGURE 7.15 *Default Spread vs. Liquidity Spread for BBB Bonds*

Source: Data from G. Chacko, "Liquidity Risk in Corporate Bond Markets" (working paper, Santa Clara University, 2006).

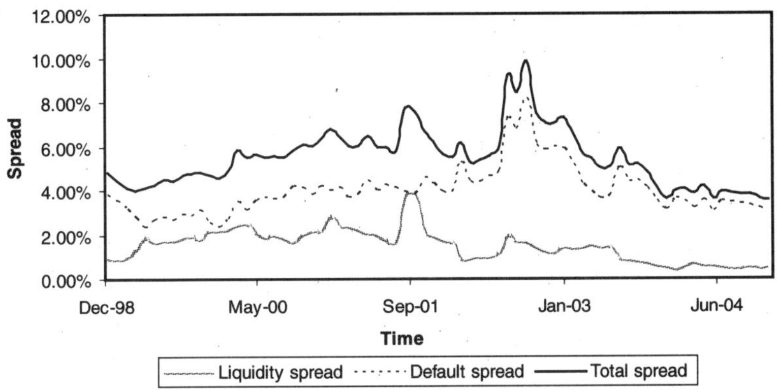

FIGURE 7.16 *Default Spread vs. Liquidity Spread for BB Bonds*

Source: Data from G. Chacko, "Liquidity Risk in Corporate Bond Markets" (working paper, Santa Clara University, 2006).

default spread is a larger component of the spread. In general, as we move to higher credit qualities, the liquidity spread becomes a larger and larger component of the spread, with very high credit qualities such as AAA and AA spreads being composed mostly of liquidity spread. On the other hand, as we go to lower and lower credit qualities, the default spread becomes the dominant component of the aggregate credit spread.

Practical Implications: Portfolio Construction

Our findings thus far should have an impact on the approach to portfolio construction. In deciding how we allocate assets, how we weight individual securities in our portfolio, we should be making the distinction between liquidity and credit risk. For example, an insurance company is willing to buy and hold a bond until maturity. The insurance company does not care whether the bond is illiquid or not. It can take on liquidity risk, because it is essentially not a risk due to its long investment horizon. Default risk, on the other hand, might be something the company is very concerned about. The portfolio composition for the insurance company that would result from isolating and optimizing the portfolio on credit risk and ignoring liquidity risk would be very different from the portfolio that would result from optimizing on total risk.

Conclusion

At the beginning of this chapter we asked, "Why does liquidity risk matter?" We take on liquidity risk in our portfolios, yet there has been no concerted investigation into whether there is a liquidity risk premium and, if so, how it is priced. In our investigation into why liquidity risk matters, we created a new measure of liquidity called *latent liquidity*, which quantifies the accessibility of a bond. From there we were able to develop a liquidity factor time series, which we used for our tests, extending our investigation to another asset class, to confirm that the liquidity risk factor is an important determinant of returns in other markets. Finally, we looked at how we might parse liquidity risk from credit risk in looking at a bond spread. In practical terms, once we have isolated liquidity risk, we can better hedge against unwanted risk and optimize our asset allocation, and thus our portfolio returns.

There is, of course, much more work to be done to develop the theory and models, but we've taken the first important step toward a deeper understanding of the impact of the liquidity risk factor in the markets.

Chapter Note

1. G. Chacko, G. Mallik, S. Mahanti, A. Nashikkar, and M. Subrahmanyam, "Latent Liquidity: A New Measure of Liquidity with an Application to Corporate Bonds," forthcoming in *Journal of Financial Economics,* 2007.

CHAPTER 8

Do Hedge Funds Increase Systemic Risk?

NICHOLAS CHAN, MILA GETMANSKY, SHANE M. HAAS, AND ANDREW W. LO

Who—Nicholas Chan and Shane Haas are senior research scientists at AlphaSimplex Group, LLC, in Cambridge, Massachusetts. Mila Getmansky is an assistant professor at the Isenberg School of Management at the University of Massachusetts. Andrew Lo is the Harris & Harris Group Professor of Finance at the Sloan School of Management at the Massachusetts Institute of Technology, the director of MIT's Laboratory for Financial Engineering, and the founder and chief scientific officer of AlphaSimplex Group. The authors thank Mark Carey, David Modest, René Stulz, Kevin Warsh, and participants of the National Bureau of Economic Research (NBER) conference on "The Risks of Financial Institutions" and the Atlanta Fed's 2006 "Financial Markets Conference—Hedge Funds: Creators of Risk?" for helpful comments and discussion. Thanks also to AlphaSimplex Group and the MIT Laboratory for Financial Engineering for research support. Parts of this article include ideas and exposition from several previously published papers and books of some of the authors—Getmansky, Lo, and Makarov (2004), Getmansky, Lo, and Mei (2004), and Lo (2001, 2002). This article is an abridged version of the paper presented at the Atlanta Fed's 2006 conference, held May 15–18; the longer version appears in *The Risks of Financial Institutions*, published by the University of Chicago Press in January 2007.

New Thinking—The term *systemic risk* is commonly used to describe the possibility of a series of correlated defaults among financial institutions—typically banks—that occurs over a short period of time, often caused by a single major event. A classic example is a banking panic in which large groups of depositors decide to withdraw their funds simultaneously, creating a run on bank assets that can ultimately lead to multiple bank failures. Banking panics were not uncommon in the United States during the nineteenth and early twentieth centuries, culminating with an average of 2,000 bank failures per year during the 1930–1933 period (according to Mishkin 1997), which prompted the passing of the Glass-Steagall Act of 1933 and the establishment of the Federal Deposit Insurance Corporation (FDIC) in 1934.

Although today banking panics are virtually nonexistent thanks to the FDIC and related central banking policies, systemic risk exposures have taken shape in other forms. In particular, the proliferation of hedge funds in recent years has indelibly altered the risk-reward landscape of financial investments. Unregulated and opaque investment partnerships that engage in a variety of active investment strategies, hedge funds have generally yielded double-digit returns historically, but not without commensurate risks, and such risks are currently not widely appreciated or well understood. In particular, we argue that the risk-reward profile for most hedge funds differs in important ways from more traditional investments, and such differences may have potentially significant implications for systemic risk. One example is what occurred in the aftermath of the default of Russian government debt in August 1998, when Long-Term Capital Management (LTCM) and many other fixed-income hedge funds suffered catastrophic losses over the course of a few weeks, creating significant stress on the global financial system and several major financial institutions—that is, creating systemic risk.

In this chapter, we consider the impact of hedge funds on systemic risk by examining the unique risk-and-return profiles of hedge funds—at both the individual-fund and the aggregate-industry level—and proposing some new risk measures for hedge fund investments. Two major themes have emerged from August 1998: the importance of liquidity and leverage, and the capriciousness of correlations among instruments and portfolios that were thought to be uncorrelated. The precise mechanism by which these two sets of issues posed systemic risks in 1998 is now well understood. Because many hedge funds rely on leverage, their positions are often considerably larger than the amount of collateral posted to support those positions. Leverage has the effect of a magnifying glass, expanding small profit opportunities into larger ones but also expanding small losses into larger losses. And when adverse changes in market prices reduce the market value of collateral, credit is withdrawn quickly, and the subsequent forced liquidation of large positions over short periods of time can lead to widespread financial panic, as in the aftermath of the default of Russian government debt in August 1998. The more illiquid the portfolio, the larger the price impact of a forced liquidation, which erodes the fund's risk capital that much more quickly. Now, if many funds face the same "death spiral" at a given point in time—that is, if they become more highly correlated during times of distress and if those funds are obligors of a small number of major financial institutions—then a market event like August 1998 can cascade quickly into a global financial crisis. This is systemic risk.

Therefore, the two main themes of this study are illiquidity exposure and time-varying hedge fund correlations, both of which are intimately related to the dynamic nature of hedge fund investment strategies and their risk exposures. In particular, one of the justifications for the unusually rich fees that hedge funds charge is the fact that highly skilled hedge fund managers are engaged in active portfolio management. It is common wisdom that the most talented managers are drawn first to the hedge fund industry because the absence of regulatory constraints enables them to make the most of their investment acumen. With the freedom to trade as much or as little as they like on any given day, to go long or short any number of securities and with varying degrees of leverage, and to change investment strategies at a moment's notice, hedge fund managers enjoy enormous flexibility and discretion in pursuing investment returns. But dynamic investment strategies imply dynamic risk exposures, and while modern financial economics has much to say about the risk of static investments—the market beta is a sufficient statistic in this case—there is currently no single summary measure of the risks of a dynamic investment strategy.[1]

To begin our discussion, we summarize the empirical properties of aggregate and individual hedge fund data used in this study: the Credit Suisse First Boston (CSFB)/Tremont Hedge Fund Indexes and the TASS individual hedge fund database. We then turn to the issue of liquidity—one of the central aspects of systemic risk—and present several measures for gauging illiquidity exposure in hedge funds and other asset classes, which we apply to individual and index data. Since systemic risk is directly related to hedge fund failures, we investigate attrition rates of hedge funds in the TASS database and present a logit analysis that yields estimates of a fund's probability of liquidation as a function of various fund characteristics such as return history, assets under management (AUM), and recent fund flows. We then present estimates of statistical regime-switching models for hedge fund indexes that capture certain nonlinearities unique to the hedge fund industry. We end by discussing the current industry outlook implied by the analytics and empirical results of this study. Our tentative conclusions suggest that the hedge fund industry may be heading into a challenging period of lower expected returns, and that systemic risk has been increasing steadily over the recent past. To address this growing concern, we put forward a modest proposal to establish a new entity patterned after the U.S. National Transportation Safety Board (NTSB).

Our preliminary findings must be qualified by the acknowledgment that all of our measures of systemic risk are indirect and therefore open to debate and interpretation. The main reason for this less-than-satisfying state of affairs is that hedge funds are currently not required to disclose any information about their risks and returns to the public, so empirical studies of the hedge fund industry are based only on very limited hedge fund data, provided voluntarily to TASS and which may or may not be representative of the industry as a whole. Even after February 1, 2006, when, in response to the U.S. Securities and Exchange Commission's (SEC's) Rule 203(b)(3)-2 (which was subsequently struck down by the U.S. Court of Appeals in June 2006), many hedge funds became registered investment advisers, the regular filings of those funds have not included critical information such as a fund's degree of leverage, the liquidity of a fund's portfolio, the identities of the fund's major creditors and obligors, and the specific terms under which the fund's investors committed their capital. Without this kind of information for the majority of funds in the industry, it is virtually impossible, even for regulatory authorities like the SEC, to construct direct measures of systemic risk. However, as the hedge fund industry grows, the number and severity of hedge fund failures will undoubtedly increase as well, eventually moving the industry toward greater transparency.

The Data

It is clear from our introduction that hedge funds exhibit unique and dynamic characteristics that bear further study. Fortunately, the returns of many individual hedge funds are now available through a number of commercial databases such as Altvest, Center for International Securities and Derivatives Markets (CISDM), HedgeFund.net, Hedge Fund Research (HFR), and TASS. For the empirical analysis in this chapter, we use two main sources: (1) a set of aggregate hedge fund index returns from CSFB/Tremont and (2) the TASS database of hedge funds, which consists of monthly returns and accompanying information for 4,781 individual hedge funds (as of August 2004) from February 1977 to August 2004.[2]

The CSFB/Tremont Indexes are asset-weighted indexes of funds with a minimum of $10 million of AUM, a minimum one-year track record, and current audited financial statements. An aggregate index is computed from this universe, and ten subindexes based on investment style are also computed using a similar method. Indexes are computed and rebalanced monthly, and the universe of funds is redefined on a quarterly basis.

The TASS database consists of monthly returns, AUM, and other fund-specific information for 4,781 individual funds from February 1977 to August 2004. The database is divided into two parts: "live" and "graveyard" funds. Hedge funds that are in the live database are considered to be active as of August 31, 2004.[3] As of August 2004, the combined database of both live and dead hedge funds contained 4,781 funds with at least one monthly return observation. Out of these 4,781 funds, 2,920 are in the live database and 1,861 in the graveyard database. The earliest data available for a fund in either database are from February 1977. TASS started tracking dead funds in 1994; hence, it has only been since 1994 that TASS transferred funds from the live database to the graveyard database. Funds that were dropped from the live database prior to 1994 are not included in the graveyard database, a circumstance that may yield a certain degree of survivorship bias.[4]

The majority of 4,781 funds reported returns net of management and incentive fees on a monthly basis.[5] We eliminated 50 funds that reported only gross returns, leaving 4,731 funds in the "combined" database (2,893 in the live and 1,838 in the graveyard database). We also eliminated funds that reported returns on a quarterly—not monthly—basis, leaving 4,705 funds in the combined database (2,884 in the live and 1,821 in the graveyard database). Finally, we dropped funds that did not report AUM, or reported only partial AUM, leaving a final sample of 4,536 hedge funds in the combined database (2,771 funds in the live database and 1,765 funds in the graveyard database). For the empirical analysis in this chapter, we imposed an additional filter—we required funds to have at least five years of nonmissing returns—leaving 1,226 funds in the live database and 611 in the graveyard database, for a combined total of 1,837 funds. This filter obviously creates additional survivorship bias in the remaining sample of funds, but since the main objective is to estimate measures of illiquidity exposure and not to make inferences about overall performance, the filter may not be as problematic.[6]

TASS also classifies funds into one of eleven different investment styles, listed in **TABLE 8.1** and described in the appendix at the end of the chapter, of which ten correspond exactly to the CSFB/Tremont subindex definitions.[7] Table 8.1 also reports the number of funds in each category for the live, graveyard, and combined databases, and these numbers show that the representation of investment styles is not evenly distributed but is concentrated among four categories: long/short equity (1,415), fund of funds (952), managed futures (511), and event driven (384). Together, these four categories account for 71.9 percent of the funds in the combined database.

TABLE 8.1 *TASS Funds Classifications*

CATEGORY	DEFINITION	NUMBER OF TASS FUNDS IN: LIVE	GRAVEYARD	COMBINED
1	Convertible Arbitrage	127	49	176
2	Dedicated Short Seller	14	15	29
3	Emerging Markets	130	133	263
4	Equity Market Neutral	173	87	260
5	Event Driven	250	134	384
6	Fixed-Income Arbitrage	104	71	175
7	Global Macro	118	114	232
8	Long/Short Equity	883	532	1,415
9	Managed Futures	195	316	511
10	Multistrategy	98	41	139
11	Fund of Funds	679	273	952
	Total	**2,771**	**1,765**	**4,536**

CSFB/Tremont Indexes

TABLE 8.2 reports summary statistics for the monthly returns of the CSFB/Tremont Indexes from January 1994 to August 2004 (see p. 180–181). Also included for purposes of comparison are summary statistics for a number of aggregate measures of market conditions.

Table 8.2 shows that there is considerable heterogeneity in the historical risk and return characteristics of the various categories of hedge fund investment styles. For example, the annualized mean return ranges from −0.69 percent for dedicated short sellers to 13.85 percent for global macro, and the annualized volatility ranges from 3.05 percent for equity market neutral to 17.71 percent for dedicated short sellers. The correlations of the hedge fund indexes with the Standard & Poor's 500 are generally low, with the largest correlation at 57.2 percent for long/short equity, and the lowest correlation at −75.6 percent for dedicated short sellers—as investors have discovered, hedge funds offer greater diversification benefits than many traditional asset classes. However, these correlations can vary over time. For example, consider a rolling sixty-month correlation between the CSFB/Tremont Multistrategy Index and the S&P 500 from January 1999 to December 2003, plotted in **FIGURE 8.1**. At the start of the sample in January 1999, the correlation is −13.4 percent, and then drops to −21.7 percent a year later, and increases to 31.0 percent by December 2003 as the outliers surrounding August 1998 drop out of the sixty-month rolling window.

Although changes in rolling correlation estimates are also partly attributable to estimation errors,[8] in this case, an additional explanation for the positive trend in correlation is the enormous inflow of capital into multistrategy funds and fund of funds over the past five years. As AUM increase, it becomes progressively more difficult for fund managers to implement strategies that are truly uncorrelated with broad-based market indexes like the S&P 500. Moreover, Figure 8.1 shows that the correlation between the Multistrategy Index return and the lagged S&P 500 return has also increased in the past year, indicating an increase in the illiquidity exposure of this investment style (see Getmansky, Lo, and Makarov 2004 and the next section). This increase in illiquidity exposure is also consistent with large inflows of capital into the hedge fund sector.

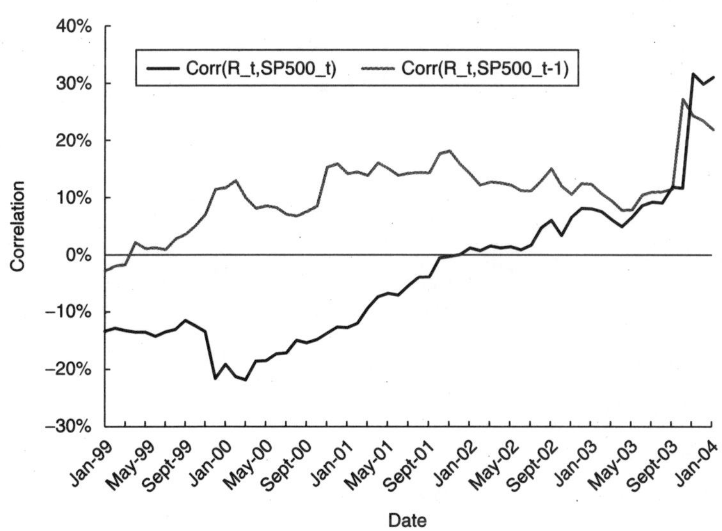

FIGURE 8.1 *Correlation Between CSFB/Tremont Multistrategy Index and S&P 500, January 1999 to December 2003*

TABLE 8.2 *Monthly Returns of the CSFB/Tremont Indexes, January 1994 to August 2004*

VARIABLE	SAMPLE SIZE	ANN. MEAN	ANN. SD	CORR. WITH S&P 500	MIN	MED
CSFB/Tremont Indexes:						
Hedge Funds	128	10.51	8.25	45.9	−7.55	0.78
Convertible Arbitrage	128	9.55	4.72	11.0	−4.68	1.09
Dedicated Short Seller	128	−0.69	17.71	−75.6	−8.69	−0.39
Emerging Markets	128	8.25	17.28	47.2	−23.03	1.17
Equity Market Neutral	128	10.01	3.05	39.6	−1.15	0.81
Event Driven	128	10.86	5.87	54.3	−11.77	1.01
Distressed	128	12.73	6.79	53.5	−12.45	1.18
Event-Driven Multistrategy	128	9.87	6.19	46.6	−11.52	0.90
Risk Arbitrage	128	7.78	4.39	44.7	−6.15	0.62
Fixed-Income Arbitrage	128	6.69	3.86	−1.3	−6.96	0.77
Global Macro	128	13.85	11.75	20.9	−11.55	1.19
Long/Short Equity	128	11.51	10.72	57.2	−11.43	0.78
Managed Futures	128	6.48	12.21	−22.6	−9.35	0.18
Multistrategy	125	9.10	4.43	5.6	−4.76	0.83
SP500	120	11.90	15.84	100.0	−14.46	1.47
Banks	128	21.19	13.03	55.8	−18.62	1.96
LIBOR	128	−0.14	0.78	3.5	−0.94	−0.01
USD	128	−0.52	7.51	7.3	−5.35	−0.11
Oil	128	15.17	31.69	−1.6	−22.19	1.38
Gold	128	1.21	12.51	−7.2	−9.31	−0.17
Lehman Bond	128	6.64	4.11	0.8	−2.71	0.50
Large Minus Small Cap	128	−1.97	13.77	7.6	−20.82	0.02
Value Minus Growth	128	0.86	18.62	−48.9	−22.78	0.40
Credit Spread (not ann.)	128	4.35	1.36	−30.6	2.68	3.98
Term Spread (not ann.)	128	1.65	1.16	−11.6	−0.07	1.20
VIX (not ann.)	128	0.03	3.98	−67.3	−12.90	0.03

VARIABLE	MAX	SKEW	KURT	ρ_1	ρ_2	ρ_3	p-VALUE OF LB-Q
CSFB/Tremont Indexes:							
Hedge Funds	8.53	0.12	1.95	12.0	4.0	−0.5	54.8
Convertible Arbitrage	3.57	−1.47	3.78	55.8	41.1	14.4	0.0
Dedicated Short Seller	22.71	0.90	2.16	9.2	−3.6	0.9	73.1
Emerging Markets	16.42	-0.58	4.01	30.5	1.6	−1.4	0.7
Equity Market Neutral	3.26	0.25	0.23	29.8	20.2	9.3	0.0
Event Driven	3.68	−3.49	23.95	35.0	15.3	4.0	0.0
Distressed	4.10	−2.79	17.02	29.3	13.4	2.0	0.3
Event-Driven Multistrategy	4.66	−2.70	17.63	35.3	16.7	7.8	0.0
Risk Arbitrage	3.81	−1.27	6.14	27.3	−1.9	−9.7	1.2
Fixed-Income Arbitrage	2.02	−3.27	17.05	39.2	8.2	2.0	0.0
Global Macro	10.60	0.00	2.26	5.5	4.0	8.8	65.0
Long/Short Equity	13.01	0.26	3.61	16.9	6.0	−4.6	21.3
Managed Futures	9.95	0.07	0.49	5.8	−9.6	−0.7	64.5
Multistrategy	3.61	−1.30	3.59	−0.9	7.6	18.0	17.2
SP500	9.78	−0.61	0.30	−1.0	−2.2	7.3	86.4
Banks	11.39	−1.16	5.91	26.8	6.5	5.4	1.6
LIBOR	0.63	−0.61	4.11	50.3	32.9	27.3	0.0
USD	5.58	0.00	0.08	7.2	−3.2	6.4	71.5
Oil	36.59	0.25	1.17	−8.1	−13.6	16.6	7.3
Gold	16.85	0.98	3.07	−13.7	−17.4	8.0	6.2
Lehman Bond	3.50	−0.04	0.05	24.6	−6.3	5.2	3.2
Large Minus Small Cap	12.82	−0.82	5.51	−13.5	4.7	6.1	36.6
Value Minus Growth	15.85	−0.44	3.01	8.6	10.2	0.4	50.3
Credit Spread (not ann.)	8.23	0.82	−0.30	94.1	87.9	83.2	0.0
Term Spread (not ann.)	3.85	0.42	−1.25	97.2	94.0	91.3	0.0
VIX (not ann.)	19.48	0.72	4.81	−8.2	−17.5	−13.9	5.8

Despite their heterogeneity, several indexes do share a common characteristic: negative skewness. Convertible arbitrage, emerging markets, event driven, distressed, event-driven multistrategy, risk arbitrage, fixed-income arbitrage, and fund of funds indexes all have skewness coefficients of less than zero, in some cases substantially so. This property is an indication of tail risk exposure (see Lo 1999 for an explicit example involving short selling out-of-the-money put options on the S&P 500 Index) and is consistent with the nature of the investment strategies employed by funds in those categories. For example, fixed-income arbitrage strategies are known to generate fairly consistent profits, with occasional losses that may be extreme; hence, a skewness coefficient of −3.27 is not surprising. A more direct measure of tail risk, or "fat tails," is kurtosis; the normal distribution has a kurtosis of 3.00, so values greater than this represent fatter tails than the normal. Not surprisingly, the two categories with the most negative skewness—event driven (−3.49) and fixed-income arbitrage (−3.27)—also have the largest kurtosis, 23.95 and 17.05, respectively.

Several indexes also exhibit a high degree of positive serial correlation, as measured by the first three autocorrelation coefficients, ρ_1, ρ_2, and ρ_3, as well as the p-value of the Ljung-Box Q-statistic, which measures the degree of statistical significance of the first three autocorrelations.[9] In comparison to the S&P 500, which has a first-order autocorrelation coefficient of −1.0 percent, the autocorrelations of the hedge fund indexes are very high, with values of 55.8 percent for convertible arbitrage, 39.2 percent for fixed-income arbitrage, and 35.0 percent for event driven, all of which are significant at the 1 percent level according to the corresponding p-values. Serial correlation can be a symptom of illiquidity risk exposure, which is particularly relevant for systemic risk; we shall focus on this issue in more detail in the next section.

TASS Data

TABLE 8.3 contains basic summary statistics for the funds in the TASS live, graveyard, and combined databases (see p. 184–185). Not surprisingly, there is a great deal of variation in mean returns and volatilities both across and within categories and databases. For example, the 127 convertible arbitrage funds in the live database have an average mean return of 9.92 percent and an average standard deviation of 5.51 percent, but in the graveyard database the forty-nine convertible arbitrage funds have an average mean return of 10.02 percent and a much higher average standard deviation of 8.14 percent. Not surprisingly, average volatilities in the graveyard database are uniformly higher than those in the live database because the higher-volatility funds are more likely to be eliminated.[10]

Average serial correlations also vary considerably across categories in the combined database, but six categories stand out: convertible arbitrage (31.4 percent), fund of funds (19.6 percent), event driven (18.4 percent), emerging markets (16.5 percent), fixed-income arbitrage (16.2 percent), and multistrategy (14.7 percent). Given the descriptions of these categories provided by TASS and common wisdom about the nature of the strategies involved—these categories include some of the most illiquid securities traded—serial correlation seems to be a reasonable proxy for illiquidity and smoothed returns (see Lo 2001; Getmansky, Lo, and Makarov 2004; and the following section). Alternatively, equities and futures are among the most liquid securities in which hedge funds invest, and not surprisingly, the average first-order serial correlations for equity market neutral, long/short equity, and managed futures are 5.1 percent, 9.5 percent, and –0.6 percent, respectively. Dedicated short-seller funds also have a low average first-order autocorrelation, 5.9 percent, which is consistent with the high degree of liquidity that often characterizes short sellers (by definition, the ability to short a security implies a certain degree of liquidity).

These summary statistics suggest that illiquidity and smoothed returns may be important attributes of hedge fund returns, which can be captured to some degree by serial correlation and the time-series model of smoothing discussed in the next section.

Measuring Illiquidity Risk

The different categories of hedge funds in the TASS database suggest that these funds are likely to exhibit a heterogeneous array of risk exposures. However, a common theme surrounding systemic risk is credit and liquidity. Although they are separate sources of risk exposures for hedge funds and their investors—one type of risk can exist without the other—liquidity and credit have been inextricably intertwined in the minds of most investors because of the problems encountered by Long-Term Capital Management and many other fixed-income relative-value hedge funds in August and September 1998. Because many hedge funds rely on leverage, the size of the positions is often considerably larger than the amount of collateral supporting those positions. Leverage expands small profit opportunities into larger ones but also expands small losses into larger losses. And when adverse changes in market prices reduce the collateral's market value, credit is withdrawn quickly, and the subsequent forced liquidation of large positions over a short time can lead to widespread financial panic, as occurred after the Russian government defaulted on its debt in August 1998. Along with the many benefits of a truly global financial system is the

TABLE 8.3 *Summary Statistics of TASS Funds*

CATEGORY	SAMPLE SIZE	ANNUALIZED MEAN (%) MEAN	ANNUALIZED MEAN (%) SD	ANNUALIZED SD (%) MEAN	ANNUALIZED SD (%) SD	ρ_1 (%) MEAN	ρ_1 (%) SD
Live Funds							
Convertible Arbitrage	127	9.92	5.89	5.51	4.15	33.6	19.2
Dedicated Short Seller	14	0.33	11.11	25.10	10.92	3.5	10.9
Emerging Markets	130	17.74	13.77	21.69	14.42	18.8	13.8
Equity Market Neutral	173	6.60	5.89	7.25	5.05	4.4	22.7
Event Driven	250	12.52	8.99	8.00	7.15	19.4	20.9
Fixed-Income Arbitrage	104	9.30	5.61	6.27	5.10	16.4	23.6
Global Macro	118	10.51	11.55	13.57	10.41	1.3	17.1
Long/Short Equity	883	13.05	10.56	14.98	9.30	11.3	17.9
Managed Futures	195	8.59	18.55	19.14	12.52	3.4	13.9
Multistrategy	98	12.65	17.93	9.31	10.94	18.5	21.3
Fund of Funds	679	6.89	5.45	6.14	4.87	22.9	18.5
Graveyard Funds							
Convertible Arbitrage	49	10.02	6.61	8.14	6.08	25.5	19.3
Dedicated Short Seller	15	1.77	9.41	27.54	18.79	8.1	13.2
Emerging Markets	133	2.74	27.74	27.18	18.96	14.3	17.9
Equity Market Neutral	87	7.61	26.37	12.35	13.68	6.4	20.4
Event Driven	134	9.07	15.04	12.35	12.10	16.6	21.1
Fixed-Income Arbitrage	71	5.51	12.93	10.78	9.97	15.9	22.0
Global Macro	114	3.74	28.83	21.02	18.94	3.2	21.5
Long/Short Equity	532	9.69	22.75	23.08	16.82	6.4	19.8
Managed Futures	316	4.78	23.17	20.88	19.35	−2.9	18.7
Multistrategy	41	5.32	23.46	17.55	20.90	6.1	17.4
Fund of Funds	273	4.53	10.07	13.56	10.56	11.3	21.2
Combined Funds							
Convertible Arbitrage	176	9.94	6.08	6.24	4.89	31.4	19.5
Dedicated Short Seller	29	1.08	10.11	26.36	15.28	5.9	12.2
Emerging Markets	263	10.16	23.18	24.48	17.07	16.5	16.2
Equity Market Neutral	260	6.94	15.94	8.96	9.21	5.1	21.9
Event Driven	384	11.31	11.57	9.52	9.40	18.4	21.0
Fixed-Income Arbitrage	175	7.76	9.45	8.10	7.76	16.2	22.9
Global Macro	232	7.18	22.04	17.21	15.61	2.3	19.3
Long/Short Equity	1,415	11.79	16.33	18.02	13.25	9.5	18.8
Managed Futures	511	6.23	21.59	20.22	17.07	−0.6	17.4
Multistrategy	139	10.49	19.92	11.74	15.00	14.7	20.9
Fund of Funds	952	6.22	7.17	8.26	7.75	19.6	20.0

CATEGORY	ANNUALIZED SHARPE RATIO		ANNUALIZED ADJUSTED SHARPE RATIO		LJUNG-BOX p-VALUE (%)	
	MEAN	SD	MEAN	SD	MEAN	SD
Live Funds						
Convertible Arbitrage	2.57	4.20	1.95	2.86	19.5	27.1
Dedicated Short Seller	−0.11	0.70	0.12	0.46	48.0	25.7
Emerging Markets	1.36	2.01	1.22	1.40	35.5	31.5
Equity Market Neutral	1.20	1.18	1.30	1.28	41.6	32.6
Event Driven	1.98	1.47	1.68	1.47	31.3	34.1
Fixed-Income Arbitrage	3.61	11.71	3.12	7.27	36.6	35.2
Global Macro	0.86	0.68	0.99	0.79	46.8	30.6
Long/Short Equity	1.03	1.01	1.01	0.95	38.1	31.8
Managed Futures	0.48	1.10	0.73	0.63	52.3	30.8
Multistrategy	1.91	2.34	1.46	2.06	31.1	31.7
Fund of Funds	1.53	1.33	1.48	1.16	33.7	31.6
Graveyard Funds						
Convertible Arbitrage	1.89	1.43	1.58	1.46	27.9	34.2
Dedicated Short Seller	0.20	0.44	0.25	0.48	55.4	25.2
Emerging Markets	0.37	0.91	0.47	1.11	48.5	34.6
Equity Market Neutral	0.52	1.23	0.60	1.85	46.6	31.5
Event Driven	1.22	1.38	1.13	1.43	39.3	34.2
Fixed-Income Arbitrage	1.10	1.77	1.03	1.99	46.0	35.7
Global Macro	0.33	1.05	0.37	0.90	46.2	31.0
Long/Short Equity	0.48	1.06	0.48	1.17	47.8	31.3
Managed Futures	0.26	0.77	0.37	0.97	48.4	30.9
Multistrategy	1.10	1.55	1.58	2.06	49.4	32.2
Fund of Funds	0.62	1.26	0.57	1.11	40.9	31.9
Combined Funds						
Convertible Arbitrage	2.38	3.66	1.85	2.55	21.8	29.3
Dedicated Short Seller	0.05	0.59	0.19	0.46	52.0	25.2
Emerging Markets	0.86	1.63	0.84	1.31	42.2	33.7
Equity Market Neutral	0.97	1.24	1.06	1.53	43.3	32.3
Event Driven	1.71	1.48	1.49	1.48	34.1	34.3
Fixed-Income Arbitrage	2.59	9.16	2.29	5.86	40.4	35.6
Global Macro	0.60	0.92	0.70	0.90	46.5	30.8
Long/Short Equity	0.82	1.06	0.81	1.07	41.7	31.9
Managed Futures	0.34	0.91	0.50	0.88	49.8	30.9
Multistrategy	1.67	2.16	1.49	2.05	36.7	32.9
Fund of Funds	1.27	1.37	1.21	1.22	35.8	31.8

cost that a financial crisis in one country can have dramatic repercussions in several others—that is, contagion.

The basic mechanisms driving liquidity and credit are familiar to most hedge fund managers and investors, and the recent literature has made considerable progress in modeling both credit and illiquidity risk. (See, for example, Bookstaber 1999 and 2000, Kao 2000, and their citations.) However, the complex network of creditor/obligor relationships, revolving credit agreements, and other financial interconnections is largely unmapped. Perhaps some of the newly developed techniques in the mathematical theory of networks will allow us to construct systemic measures for liquidity and credit exposures and the robustness of the global financial system to idiosyncratic shocks. The "small-world" networks considered by Watts and Strogatz (1998) and Watts (1999) seem to be particularly promising starting points.

A more immediate method for gauging the illiquidity risk exposure of a given hedge fund is to examine the autocorrelation coefficients ρ_k of the fund's monthly returns, where $\rho_k \equiv \text{Cov}[R_t, R_{t-k}]/\text{Var}[R_t]$ is the kth-order autocorrelation of $\{R_t\}$,[11] which measures the degree of correlation between month t's return and month $t-k$'s return. To see why autocorrelations may be useful indicators of liquidity exposure, recall that one of the earliest financial asset pricing models is the Martingale model, in which asset returns are serially uncorrelated ($\rho_k = 0$ for all $k \neq 0$). Indeed, the title of Samuelson's (1965) seminal paper—"Proof That Properly Anticipated Prices Fluctuate Randomly"—succinctly summarizes the motivation of the Martingale property: In an informationally efficient market, price changes must be unforecastable if they are properly anticipated, that is, if they fully incorporate the expectations and information of all market participants.

This extreme version of market efficiency is now recognized as an idealization that is unlikely to hold in practice. (See, for example, Farmer and Lo 1999 and Lo 2004.) In particular, market frictions such as transactions costs, borrowing constraints, costs of gathering and processing information, and institutional restrictions on short sales and other trading practices do exist, and they all contribute to the possibility of serial correlation in asset returns that cannot easily be "arbitraged" away precisely because of the presence of these frictions. From this perspective, the degree of serial correlation in an asset's returns can be viewed as a proxy for the magnitude of the frictions, and illiquidity is one of most common forms of such frictions. For example, it is well known that the historical returns of residential real estate investments are considerably more highly autocorrelated than, say, the returns of the S&P 500 indexes during the same sample period. Similarly, the returns of S&P 500 futures contracts exhibit less serial correlation than those of the index itself. In both examples, the more liquid instrument exhibits less serial correlation than the less liquid, and the economic rationale is a modified version of Samuelson's (1965) argument: Predictability in asset returns will be exploited and eliminated only to the extent allowed by market frictions. Despite the fact that the returns to residential real estate are highly predictable, it is impossible to take full advantage of such predictability because of the high transaction costs associated with real estate transactions, the inability to short sell properties, and other frictions.[12]

A closely related phenomenon that buttresses this interpretation of serial correlation in hedge fund returns is the "nonsynchronous trading" effect, in which the autocorrelation is induced in a security's returns because those returns are computed with closing prices that are not necessarily established at the same time each day (see, for example, Campbell, Lo, and MacKinlay 1996, Chap. 3). But in contrast to the studies by Lo and MacKinlay (1988, 1990) and Kadlec and Patterson (1999), in which the authors conclude that it is difficult to generate serial correlations in weekly U.S. equity portfolio returns much greater than 10 percent to 15 percent through nonsynchronous trading effects alone, Getmansky, Lo, and Makarov (2004) argue that in the context of hedge funds, significantly higher levels of serial correlation can be explained by the combination of illiquidity and "performance smoothing" (see below), of which nonsynchronous trading is a special case. To see why, note that the empirical analysis in the nonsynchronous-trading literature is devoted exclusively to exchange-traded equity returns, not hedge fund returns; hence, the corresponding conclusions may not be relevant in this context. For example, Lo and MacKinlay (1990) argue that securities would have to go without trading for several days on average to induce serial correlations of 30 percent, and they dismiss such nontrading intervals as unrealistic for most exchange-traded U.S. equity issues. However, such nontrading intervals are considerably more realistic for the types of securities held by many hedge funds—for example, emerging-market debt, real estate, restricted securities, control positions in publicly traded companies, asset-backed securities, and other exotic over-the-counter derivatives. Therefore, nonsynchronous trading of this magnitude is likely to be an explanation for the serial correlation observed in hedge fund returns.

But even when prices are synchronously measured—as they are for many funds that mark their portfolios to market at the end of the month to strike a net asset value at which investors can buy into or cash out of the fund—there are several other channels by which illiquidity exposure can induce serial correlation in the reported returns of hedge funds. Apart from the nonsynchronous-trading effect, naive methods for determining the fair market value, or "marks," for illiquid securities can yield serially correlated returns. For example, one approach to valuing illiquid securities is to extrapolate linearly from the most recent transaction price (which, in the case of emerging-market debt, might be from several months ago), which yields a price path that is a straight line, or at best a series of straight lines. Returns computed from such marks will be smoother, exhibiting lower volatility and higher serial correlation than true economic returns—that is, returns computed from mark-to-market prices where the market is sufficiently active to allow all available information to be impounded in the price of the security. Of course, for securities that are more easily traded and with deeper markets, mark-to-market prices are more readily available, extrapolated marks are not necessary, and serial correlation is therefore less of an issue. But for securities that are thinly traded, or not traded at all for extended periods of time, marking them to market is often an expensive and time-consuming procedure that cannot easily be performed frequently.[13] Therefore, serial correlation may serve as a proxy for a fund's liquidity exposure.

Even if a hedge fund manager does not make use of any form of linear extrapolation to mark the securities in his portfolio, he may still be subject to smoothed returns if he obtains marks from broker-dealers who engage in such extrapolation. For example, consider the case of a conscientious hedge fund manager attempting to obtain the most accurate mark for his portfolio at month's end by getting bid/offer quotes from three independent broker-dealers for every security in his portfolio and then marking each security at the average of the three quote midpoints. By averaging the quote midpoints, the manager is inadvertently downward-biasing price volatility, and if any of the broker-dealers employ linear extrapolation in formulating their quotes (and many do, through sheer necessity because they have little else to go on for the most illiquid securities), or if they fail to update their quotes because of light volume, serial correlation will also be induced in reported returns.

Finally, a more prosaic channel by which serial correlation may arise in the reported returns of hedge funds is through "performance smoothing," the unsavory practice of reporting only part of the gains in months when a fund has positive returns, to partially offset potential future losses and thereby reduce volatility and improve risk-adjusted performance measures such as the Sharpe ratio. For funds containing liquid securities that can be easily marked to market, performance smoothing is more difficult and, as a result, less of a concern. Indeed, it is only for portfolios of illiquid securities that managers and brokers have any discretion in marking their positions. Such practices are generally prohibited by various securities laws and accounting principles, and great care must be exercised in interpreting smoothed returns as deliberate attempts to manipulate performance statistics. After all, as discussed above, there are many other sources of serial correlation in the presence of illiquidity, none of which are motivated by deceit. Nevertheless, managers do have certain degrees of freedom in valuing illiquid securities—for example, discretionary accruals for unregistered private placements and venture capital investments—and Chandar and Bricker (2002) conclude that managers of certain closed-end mutual funds do use accounting discretion to manage fund returns around a passive benchmark. Therefore, the possibility of deliberate performance smoothing in the less-regulated hedge fund industry must be kept in mind in interpreting any empirical analysis of serial correlation in hedge fund returns.

Getmansky, Lo, and Makarov (2004) address these issues in more detail by first examining other explanations of serial correlation in hedge fund returns that are unrelated to illiquidity and smoothing—in particular, time-varying expected returns, time-varying leverage, and incentive fees with high-water marks—and showing that none of them can account for the magnitudes of serial correlation. They propose a specific econometric model of smoothed returns that is consistent with both illiquidity exposure and performance smoothing, and they estimate it using the historical returns of individual funds in the TASS hedge fund database. They find that funds with the most significant amount of smoothing tend to be the more illiquid—for example, emerging market debt, fixed-income arbitrage, and so on—and after correcting for the effects of smoothed returns, some of the most successful types of funds tend to have considerably less attractive performance characteristics.

However, for the purpose of developing a more highly aggregated measure to address systemic risk exposure, a simpler approach is to use serial correlation coefficients and the Ljung-Box Q-statistic (see chapter note 9). To illustrate this approach, we estimate these quantities using monthly historical total returns of the ten largest mutual funds (as of February 11, 2001), from various start dates through June 2000, and of twelve hedge funds from various inception dates to December 2000. Monthly total returns for the mutual funds were obtained from the University of Chicago's Center for Research in Securities Prices. The twelve hedge funds were selected from the Altvest database to yield a diverse range of annual Sharpe ratios (from 1 to 5) computed in the standard way ($\sqrt{12}\,\widehat{SR}$, where $\widehat{SR}$ is the Sharpe ratio estimator applied to monthly returns), with the additional requirement that the funds have a minimum five-year history of returns.[14] The names of the hedge funds have been omitted to maintain their privacy, and we will refer to them only by their stated investment styles, for example, relative value fund, risk arbitrage fund, and so on.

TABLE 8.4 reports the means, standard deviations, $\hat{\rho}_1$ to $\hat{\rho}_6$, and the p-values of the Q-statistic using the first six autocorrelations for the

TABLE 8.4 *Autocorrelations for Sample Mutual Funds and Hedge Funds*

FUND	START	SAMPLE SIZE	μ (%)	σ (%)	ρ_1 (%)	ρ_2 (%)	ρ_3 (%)	ρ_4 (%)	ρ_5 (%)	ρ_6 (%)	$p(Q_6)$ (%)
Mutual Funds											
Vanguard 500 Index	76.10	286	1.30	4.27	−4.0	−6.6	−4.9	−6.4	10.1	−3.6	31.9
Fidelity Magellan	67.01	402	1.73	6.23	12.4	−2.3	−0.4	0.7	7.1	3.1	17.8
Investment Company of America	63.01	450	1.17	4.01	1.8	−3.2	−4.5	−1.6	6.3	−5.6	55.9
Janus	70.03	364	1.52	4.75	10.5	0.0	−3.7	−8.2	2.1	−0.6	30.3
Fidelity Contrafund	67.05	397	1.29	4.97	7.4	−2.5	−6.8	−3.9	2.7	−4.5	42.3
Washington Mutual Investors	63.01	450	1.13	4.09	−0.1	−7.2	−2.6	0.7	11.6	−2.6	16.7
Janus Worldwide	92.01	102	1.81	4.36	11.4	3.4	−3.8	−15.4	−21.4	−10.3	11.0
Fidelity Growth and Income	86.01	174	1.54	4.13	5.1	−1.6	−8.2	−15.6	2.1	−7.3	30.9
American Century Ultra	81.12	223	1.72	7.11	2.3	3.4	1.4	−3.7	−7.9	−6.0	81.0
Growth Fund of America	64.07	431	1.18	5.35	8.5	−2.7	−4.1	−3.2	3.4	0.3	52.5
Hedge Funds											
Convertible/Option Arbitrage	92.05	104	1.63	0.97	42.6	29.0	21.4	2.9	−5.9	−9.7	0.0
Relative Value	92.12	97	0.66	0.21	25.9	19.2	−2.1	−16.4	−6.2	1.4	3.3
Mortgage-Backed Securities	93.01	96	1.33	0.79	42.0	22.1	16.7	22.6	6.6	−2.0	0.0
High-Yield Debt	94.06	79	1.30	0.87	33.7	21.8	13.1	−0.8	13.8	4.0	1.1
Risk Arbitrage A	93.07	90	1.06	0.69	−4.9	−10.8	6.9	−8.5	9.9	3.1	74.1
Long/Short Equities	89.07	138	1.18	0.83	−20.2	24.6	8.7	11.2	13.5	16.9	0.1
Multistrategy A	95.01	72	1.08	0.75	48.9	23.4	3.4	0.8	−2.3	−12.8	0.1
Risk Arbitrage B	94.11	74	0.90	0.77	−4.9	2.5	−8.3	−5.7	0.6	9.8	93.4
Convertible Arbitrage A	92.09	100	1.38	1.60	33.8	30.8	7.9	−9.4	3.6	−4.4	0.1
Convertible Arbitrage B	94.07	78	0.78	0.62	32.4	9.7	−4.5	6.5	−6.3	−10.6	8.6
Multistrategy B	89.06	139	1.34	1.63	49.0	24.6	10.6	8.9	7.8	7.5	0.0
Fund of Funds	94.10	75	1.68	2.29	29.7	21.2	0.9	−0.9	−12.4	3.0	6.8

sample of mutual and hedge funds. The first subpanel shows that the ten mutual funds have very little serial correlation in returns, with first-order autocorrelations ranging from –3.99 percent to 12.37 percent, and with p-values of the corresponding Q-statistics ranging from 10.95 percent to 80.96 percent, implying that none of the Q-statistics is significant at the 5 percent level. The lack of serial correlation in these ten mutual fund returns is not surprising. Because of their sheer size, these funds consist primarily of highly liquid securities, and, as a result, their managers have very little discretion in marking such portfolios. Moreover, many of the SEC regulations that govern the mutual fund industry—for example, requirements for detailed prospectuses, daily net asset value calculations, and quarterly filings—were enacted specifically to guard against arbitrary marks, price manipulation, and other unsavory investment practices.

The results for the twelve hedge funds vary considerably among themselves. In sharp contrast to the mutual fund sample, the hedge fund sample displays substantial serial correlation, with first-order autocorrelation coefficients that range from –20.17 percent to 49.01 percent, with eight out of twelve funds that have Q-statistics with p-values less than 5 percent and ten out of twelve funds with p-values less than 10 percent. The only two funds with p-values that are not significant at the 5 percent or 10 percent levels are the risk arbitrage A and risk arbitrage B funds, which have p-values of 74.10 percent and 93.42 percent, respectively. These results are consistent with the notion of serial correlation as a proxy for illiquidity risk because among the various types of funds in this sample, the risk-arbitrage type is likely to be among the most liquid, since, by definition, such funds invest in securities that are exchange traded, for which trading volume is typically heavier than usual because of the impending merger events on which risk arbitrage is based.

Having established the relevance of serial correlation as a proxy for illiquidity, we now turn to the measurement of illiquidity in the context of systemic risk. To that end, let $\rho_{1t,i}$ denote the first-order autocorrelation coefficient in month t for fund i using a rolling window of past returns. Then an aggregate measure of illiquidity, ρ_t^*, in the hedge fund sector may be obtained by a cross-sectional weighted average of these rolling autocorrelations, where the weights ω_{it} are simply the proportion of AUM for fund i:

$$\rho_t^* \equiv \sum_{i=1}^{N_t} \omega_{it}\rho_{1t,i} \tag{1}$$

$$\omega_{it} \equiv \frac{\text{AUM}_{it}}{\sum_{j=1}^{N_t} \text{AUM}_{jt}}, \tag{2}$$

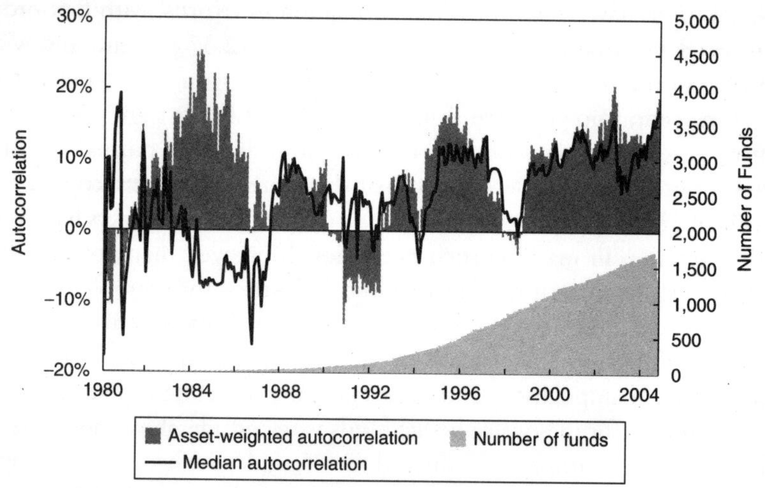

FIGURE 8.2 *TASS Hedge Fund Database Correlations, January 1980 to August 2004*

where N_t is the number of funds in the sample in month t, and AUM_{jt} is the AUM for fund j in month t.

FIGURE 8.2 plots these weighted correlations from January 1980 to August 2004 using all funds in the TASS combined database with at least thirty-six consecutive trailing months of nonmissing returns, along with the number of funds each month (at the bottom, measured by the right vertical axis) and the median correlation in the cross-section.[15] The median correlation is quite different from the asset-weighted correlation in the earlier part of the sample, but as the number of funds increases over time, the behavior of the median becomes closer to that of ρ_t^*.

Figure 8.2 also shows considerable swings in ρ_t^* over time, with dynamics that seem to be related to liquidity events. In particular, consider the following events: Between November 1980 and July 1982 the S&P 500 dropped 23.8 percent. In October 1987 the S&P 500 fell by 21.8 percent. In 1990 the Japanese "bubble economy" burst. In August 1990 the Persian Gulf War began with Iraq's invasion of Kuwait, ending in January 1991 with Kuwait's liberation by coalition forces. In February 1994 the U.S. Federal Reserve started a tightening cycle that caught many hedge funds by surprise, causing significant dislocation in bond markets worldwide.

The end of 1994 witnessed the start of the "Tequila crisis" in Mexico. In August 1998 Russia defaulted on its government debt. And between August 2000 and September 2002 the S&P 500 fell by 46.3 percent. In the aftermath of each of these events, the weighted autocorrelation rose, in most cases abruptly. Of course, the fact that we are using a thirty-six-month rolling window suggests that as outliers drop out of the window, correlations can shift dramatically. However, as a coarse measure of liquidity in the hedge fund sector, the weighted autocorrelation seems to be intuitively appealing and informative. Figure 8.2 shows that over the most recent past, the weighted autocorrelation is on the rise, implying that hedge funds are taking more illiquidity exposure. This is another indirect indicator of a rise in systemic risk in the hedge fund industry.

Hedge Fund Liquidations

Since the collapse of LTCM in 1998, it has become clear that hedge fund liquidations can be a significant source of systemic risk. In this section, we consider several measures of liquidation probabilities for hedge funds in the TASS database, including a review of hedge fund attrition rates documented in Getmansky, Lo, and Mei (2004) and a logit analysis of hedge fund liquidations in the TASS graveyard database. By analyzing the factors driving hedge fund liquidations, we may develop a broader understanding of the likely triggers of systemic risk in this sector.

Because of the voluntary nature of inclusion in the TASS database, graveyard funds do not consist solely of liquidations. TASS gives one of seven distinct reasons for why a given fund is assigned to the graveyard, ranging from "liquidated" (status code 1) to "unknown" (status code 9). It may seem reasonable to confine our attention to those graveyard funds categorized as liquidated or perhaps to drop those funds that are closed to new investment (status code 4) from our sample. However, because our purpose is to develop a broader perspective on the dynamics of the hedge fund industry, we argue that using the entire graveyard database may be more informative. For example, by eliminating graveyard funds that are closed to new investors, we create a downward bias in the performance statistics of the remaining funds. Because we do not have detailed information about each of these funds, we cannot easily determine how any particular selection criterion will affect the statistical properties of the remainder. Therefore, we choose to include the entire set of graveyard funds in our analysis but caution readers to keep in mind the composition of this sample when interpreting our empirical results.

To estimate the influence of various hedge fund characteristics on the likelihood of liquidation, in this section we report the results of a logit analysis of liquidations in the TASS database. "Logit" can be viewed as a generalization of the linear regression model to situations in which the dependent variable takes on only a finite number of discrete values (see, for example, Maddala 1983 for details). To estimate the logit model of liquidation, we use a sample of 4,536 TASS funds from February 1977 to August 2004, of which 1,765 are in the graveyard database and 2,771 are in the live database. As discussed earlier, the graveyard database was initiated only in January 1994; hence, this will be the start date of our sample for purposes of estimating the logit model of liquidation. For tractability, we focus on annual observations only, so the dependent variable Z_{it} indicates whether fund i is live or liquidated in year t.[16] Over the sample period from January 1994 to August 2004, we have 23,925 distinct observations for Z_{it}, and after filtering out funds that do not have at least two years of history, we are left with 12,895 observations.

Associated with each Z_{it} is a set of explanatory variables, listed in **TABLE 8.5**. The motivation for AGE, ASSETS, and RETURN is well

TABLE 8.5 Z_{it} *Variables*

VARIABLE	DEFINITION
AGE	The current age of the fund (in months)
ASSETS	The natural logarithm of current total assets under management
ASSETS_{-1}	The natural logarithm of total assets under management as of December 31 of the previous year
RETURN	Current year-to-date total return
RETURN_{-1}	Total return last year
RETURN_{-2}	Total return two years ago
FLOW	Fund's current year-to-date total dollar inflow divided by previous year's assets under management, where dollar inflow in month t is defined as $\text{FLOW}_\tau = \text{AUM}_\tau - \text{AUM}_{\tau-1}(1 + R_\tau)$ and AUM_τ is the total assets under management at the beginning of month τ, R_τ is the fund's net return for month τ, and year-to-date total dollar inflow is simply the cumulative sum of monthly inflows since January of the current year
FLOW_{-1}	Previous year's total dollar inflow divided by assets under management the year before
FLOW_{-2}	Total dollar inflow two years ago divided by assets under management the year before

known—older funds, funds with greater assets, and funds with better recent performance are all less likely to be liquidated, so we would expect negative coefficients for these explanatory variables (recall that a larger conditional mean for Z^* implies a higher probability that $Z_{it} = 1$, or liquidation). The FLOW variable is motivated by the well-known "return-chasing" phenomenon, in which investors flock to funds that have had good recent performance, and leave funds that have underperformed (see, for example, Chevalier and Ellison 1997; Sirri and Tufano 1998; and Agarwal, Daniel, and Naik 2004). Because AUM is highly persistent—with a correlation of 94.3 percent between its contemporaneous and lagged values—we include only the lagged variable ASSETS_{-1} in our logit analysis, yielding the following specification, which we call model 1:

$$\begin{aligned} Z_{it} = \mathrm{G}(&\beta_0 + \beta_1\text{AGE}_{it} + \beta_2\text{ASSETS}_{it-1} + \beta_3\text{RETURN}_{it} \\ &+ \beta_4\text{RETURN}_{it-1} + \beta_5\text{RETURN}_{it-2} + \beta_6\text{FLOW}_{it} \\ &+ \beta_7\text{FLOW}_{it-1} + \beta_8\text{FLOW}_{it-2} + \varepsilon_{it}). \end{aligned} \tag{3}$$

TABLE 8.6 contains maximum-likelihood estimates of equation (3) in the first three columns. Note that most of the parameter estimates are highly significant. This significance results from the unusually large sample size, which typically yields statistically significant estimates because of the small standard errors implied by large samples (recall that the standard errors of consistent and asymptotically normal estimators converge to 0 at a rate of $1/\sqrt{n}$, where n is the sample size). This result suggests that we may wish to impose a higher threshold of statistical significance in this case, to provide a better balance between type I and type II errors.[17]

The negative signs of all the coefficients other than the constant term confirm our intuition that age, AUM, cumulative return, and fund flows all have a negative impact on the probability of liquidation. The fact that RETURN_{-2} is not statistically significant suggests that the most recent returns have the highest degree of relevance for hedge fund liquidations, a possible indication of the short-term, performance-driven nature of the hedge fund industry. The R^2 of this regression is 29.3 percent, which implies a reasonable level of explanatory power for this simple specification.[18]

To address the fixed effects associated with the calendar year and the hedge-fund-style category, in model 2 we include indicator variables for ten out of eleven calendar years and ten out of eleven hedge fund categories,

TABLE 8.6 *Parameter Estimates of Equation 3*

VARIABLE	MODEL 1 β	MODEL 1 SE(β)	MODEL 1 p-VALUE (%)	MODEL 2 β	MODEL 2 SE(β)	MODEL 2 p-VALUE (%)	MODEL 3 β	MODEL 3 SE(β)	MODEL 3 p-VALUE (%)
Sample Size		12,895			12,895			12,895	
R^2 (%)		29.3			34.2			34.2	
Constant	4.73	0.34	<.01	2.31	0.41	<.01	−5.62	0.18	<.01
AGE	−0.03	0.00	<.01	−0.03	0.00	<.01	−1.62	0.07	<.01
$ASSETS_{-1}$	−0.26	0.02	<.01	−0.19	0.02	<.01	−0.34	0.04	<.01
RETURN	−2.81	0.19	<.01	−2.86	0.20	<.01	−0.67	0.05	<.01
$RETURN_{-1}$	−1.39	0.16	<.01	−1.40	0.17	<.01	−0.36	0.04	<.01
$RETURN_{-2}$	−0.04	0.09	67.5	−0.38	0.14	0.7	−0.12	0.04	0.7
FLOW	−0.63	0.08	<.01	−0.49	0.07	<.01	−32.72	4.91	<.01
$FLOW_{-1}$	−0.13	0.04	0.0	−0.11	0.03	0.1	−7.53	2.33	0.1
$FLOW_{-2}$	−0.09	0.02	<.01	−0.11	0.02	<.01	−1.74	0.36	<.01
I(1994)				0.79	0.38	3.9	0.79	0.38	3.9
I(1995)				1.24	0.27	<.01	1.24	0.27	<.01
I(1996)				1.83	0.20	<.01	1.83	0.20	<.01
I(1997)				1.53	0.21	<.01	1.53	0.21	<.01
I(1998)				1.81	0.18	<.01	1.81	0.18	<.01
I(1999)				2.10	0.18	<.01	2.10	0.18	<.01
I(2000)				2.25	0.17	<.01	2.25	0.17	<.01
I(2001)				1.97	0.17	<.01	1.97	0.17	<.01
I(2002)				1.46	0.16	<.01	1.46	0.16	<.01
I(2003)				1.55	0.16	<.01	1.55	0.16	<.01
I(ConvertArb)				0.44	0.20	2.9	0.44	0.20	2.9
I(DedShort)				0.05	0.37	88.9	0.05	0.37	88.9
I(EmrgMkt)				0.25	0.15	10.2	0.25	0.15	10.2
I(EqMktNeut)				0.12	0.20	54.7	0.12	0.20	54.7
I(EventDr)				0.33	0.15	3.0	0.33	0.15	3.0
I(FixedInc)				0.50	0.19	1.1	0.50	0.19	1.1
I(GlobMac)				0.32	0.18	7.4	0.32	0.18	7.4
I(LongShortEq)				0.18	0.11	10.2	0.18	0.11	10.2
I(MgFut)				0.49	0.12	<.01	0.49	0.12	<.01
I(Multistrat)				0.17	0.25	49.4	0.17	0.25	49.4

VARIABLE	MODEL 4 β	MODEL 4 SE(β)	MODEL 4 p-VALUE (%)	MODEL 5 β	MODEL 5 SE(β)	MODEL 5 p-VALUE (%)
Sample Size		12,846			12,310	
R^2 (%)		34.5			35.4	
Constant	−5.67	0.18	<.01	−7.04	0.26	<.01
AGE	−1.66	0.07	<.01	−2.08	0.10	<.01
$ASSETS_{-1}$	−0.36	0.04	<.01	−0.38	0.06	<.01
RETURN	−0.67	0.05	<.01	−0.61	0.06	<.01
$RETURN_{-1}$	−0.36	0.04	<.01	−0.44	0.06	<.01
$RETURN_{-2}$	−0.12	0.05	1.1	−0.17	0.07	1.3
FLOW	−33.27	5.04	<.01	−32.93	6.74	<.01
$FLOW_{-1}$	−7.60	2.37	0.1	−19.26	4.71	<.01
$FLOW_{-2}$	−1.64	0.36	<.01	−1.83	0.51	0.0
I(1994)	0.82	0.39	3.4	1.01	0.54	5.9
I(1995)	1.18	0.28	<.01	1.37	0.37	0.0
I(1996)	1.83	0.21	<.01	1.92	0.28	<.01
I(1997)	1.52	0.21	<.01	2.03	0.27	<.01
I(1998)	1.80	0.19	<.01	2.29	0.24	<.01
I(1999)	2.05	0.18	<.01	2.25	0.24	<.01
I(2000)	2.19	0.17	<.01	2.08	0.24	<.01
I(2001)	1.96	0.17	<.01	1.80	0.25	<.01
I(2002)	1.41	0.16	<.01	1.50	0.22	<.01
I(2003)	1.53	0.16	<.01	1.71	0.22	<.01
I(ConvertArb)	0.43	0.20	3.4	0.16	0.34	62.5
I(DedShort)	−0.03	0.39	94.3	0.20	0.49	68.0
I(EmrgMkt)	0.24	0.15	11.7	0.54	0.20	0.7
I(EqMktNeut)	0.15	0.20	46.7	0.53	0.25	3.4
I(EventDr)	0.31	0.15	4.7	−0.01	0.24	97.4
I(FixedInc)	0.45	0.20	2.3	0.33	0.30	26.8
I(GlobMac)	0.24	0.18	20.2	0.33	0.25	17.9
I(LongShortEq)	0.15	0.11	16.6	0.14	0.15	36.4
I(MgFut)	0.49	0.13	0.0	0.71	0.16	<.01
I(Multistrat)	0.18	0.25	48.5	0.85	0.29	0.3

yielding the following specification:

$$
\begin{aligned}
Z_{it} = \mathrm{G}[\beta_0 &+ \sum_{k=1}^{10} \zeta_k \, \mathrm{I}(\mathrm{YEAR}_{k,i,t}) + \sum_{k=1}^{10} \xi_k \, \mathrm{I}(\mathrm{CAT}_{k,i,t}) \\
&+ \beta_1 \mathrm{AGE}_{it} + \beta_2 \mathrm{ASSETS}_{it-1} + \beta_3 \mathrm{RETURN}_{it} \\
&+ \beta_4 \mathrm{RETURN}_{it-1} + \beta_5 \mathrm{RETURN}_{it-2} + \beta_6 \mathrm{FLOW}_{it} \\
&+ \beta_7 \mathrm{FLOW}_{it-1} + \beta_8 \mathrm{FLOW}_{it-2} + \varepsilon_{it}],
\end{aligned}
\tag{4}
$$

where

$$
\mathrm{I}(\mathrm{YEAR}_{k,i,t}) \equiv \begin{cases} 1 & \text{if } t=k \\ 0 & \text{otherwise} \end{cases}; \tag{5a}
$$

$$
\mathrm{I}(\mathrm{CAT}_{k,i,t}) \equiv \begin{cases} 1 & \text{if fund } i \text{ is in category } k \\ 0 & \text{otherwise} \end{cases}. \tag{5b}
$$

The columns labeled "model 2" in Table 8.6 contain the maximum-likelihood estimates of (4) for the same sample of funds as in model 1. The coefficients for AGE, ASSETS, and RETURN exhibit the same qualitative properties as they do in model 1, but the fixed-effect variables do provide some additional explanatory power, yielding an R^2 of 34.2 percent. In particular, the coefficients for the 1999 and 2000 indicator variables are higher than those of the indicator variables for other years, a manifestation of the impact of August 1998 and the collapse of LTCM and other fixed-income, relative-value hedge funds. The impact of LTCM can also be seen from the coefficients of the category indicators—at 0.50, the fixed-income relative value has the largest estimate among all ten categories. The managed futures category has a comparable coefficient of 0.49, which is consistent with the higher volatility of such funds and the fact that this category exhibits the highest attrition rate, 14.4 percent, during the 1994–2003 sample period (see Getmansky, Lo, and Mei 2004 for a more detailed discussion of hedge fund attrition rates). However, the fact that the convertible arbitrage and event driven categories are the next largest, with coefficients of 0.44 and 0.33, respectively, is somewhat surprising given their unusually low attrition rates of 5.2 percent and 5.4 percent, respectively (Getmansky, Lo, and Mei 2004). This fact suggests that the conditional probabilities produced by a logit analysis—which controls for AUM, fund flows, and performance—yield information not readily available from the unconditional frequency counts of simple attrition statistics. The remaining category indicators are statistically insignificant at the 5 percent level.

To facilitate comparisons across explanatory variables, we standardize each of the nonindicator explanatory variables by subtracting its mean and dividing by its standard deviation and then re-estimating the parameters of equation (4) via maximum likelihood. This procedure yields estimates that are renormalized to standard deviation units of each explanatory variable and that are contained in the columns labeled "model 3" of Table 8.6. The renormalized estimates show that fund flows are an order of magnitude more important in determining the probability of liquidation than AUM, returns, or age, with normalized coefficients of –32.72 and –7.53 for FLOW and FLOW_{-1}, respectively.

Finally, we re-estimate the logit model in equation (4) for two subsets of funds, using standardized explanatory variables. In model 4, we omit graveyard funds that have either merged with other funds or been closed to new investments (status codes 4 and 5), yielding a subsample of 12,846 observations. And in model 5, we omit all graveyard funds except those that have liquidated (status code 1), yielding a subsample of 12,310 observations. The last two sets of columns in Table 8.6 show that the qualitative features of most of the estimates are unchanged, with the funds in model 5 exhibiting somewhat higher sensitivity to the lagged FLOW variable. However, the fixed-effects category in model 5 does differ in some ways from the comparable category in each of models 2 through 4, with significant coefficients for emerging markets, equity market neutral, and multistrategy, as well as for managed futures, suggesting significant differences between the full graveyard sample and the subsample of funds with status code 1.

Because of the inherent nonlinearity of the logit model, the coefficients of the explanatory variables cannot be as easily interpreted as in the linear regression model. One way to remedy this situation is to compute the estimated probability of liquidation implied by the parameter estimates $\hat{\beta}$ and specific values for the explanatory variables, which is readily accomplished by observing that

$$p_{it} \equiv \text{Prob}(Z_{it} = 1) = \text{Prob}(Z^{*}_{it} > 0) \tag{6a}$$

$$= \text{Prob}(X'_{it}\,\beta + \varepsilon_{it} > 0) = \frac{\exp(X'_{it}\,\beta)}{1+\exp(X'_{it}\,\beta)}; \tag{6b}$$

$$\hat{p}_{it} = \frac{\exp(X'_{it}\,\hat{\beta})}{1 + \exp(X'_{it}\,\hat{\beta})}. \tag{6c}$$

TABLE 8.7 reports year-by-year summary statistics for the estimated liquidation probabilities $\{\hat{p}_{it}\}$ of each fund in our sample, where each $\hat{p}_{it}$ is computed using values of the explanatory variables in year t. The left panel of Table 8.7 contains summary statistics for estimated liquidation probabilities from model 1, and the right panel contains corresponding figures from model 5. We have also stratified the estimated liquidation probabilities by their liquidation status—live funds, graveyard funds, and the combined sample.[19]

TABLE 8.7 *Year-by-Year Summary Statistics for Estimated Liquidation Probabilities*

STATISTIC	1994	1995	1996	1997	1998	1999	2000	2001	2002	2003	2004
						MODEL 1					
						Live Funds					
Mean	4.19	5.47	5.84	5.04	6.32	5.17	5.59	6.84	8.92	7.11	11.04
SD	7.49	9.33	11.15	9.74	9.66	8.61	8.15	9.23	10.15	8.00	10.91
Min	0.01	0.01	0.00	0.00	0.00	0.00	0.00	0.00	0.00	0.00	0.00
10%	0.13	0.19	0.19	0.18	0.31	0.20	0.35	0.44	0.68	0.41	0.89
25%	0.43	0.51	0.52	0.56	0.99	0.79	1.10	1.39	2.05	1.45	2.66
50%	1.16	1.46	1.52	1.59	2.71	2.18	2.80	3.69	5.62	4.49	7.55
75%	4.21	6.03	5.11	4.83	7.20	5.55	6.54	8.39	12.01	10.22	16.31
90%	12.13	16.17	16.85	13.27	16.76	12.80	13.78	16.23	21.61	17.26	26.33
Max	52.49	58.30	72.97	90.06	77.63	87.06	75.83	92.36	79.02	92.44	79.96
Count	357	483	629	773	924	1,083	1,207	1,317	1,480	1,595	1,898
						Graveyard Funds					
Mean	36.59	32.85	31.89	39.75	30.64	27.68	22.78	28.17	25.22	21.55	17.01
SD	24.46	22.77	18.86	22.70	21.67	19.24	17.67	20.03	18.22	15.91	14.30
Min	4.91	2.50	1.05	0.25	0.00	0.53	0.22	0.98	0.13	0.02	0.25
10%	6.08	8.39	10.63	9.29	6.86	4.98	2.41	5.94	5.50	2.64	2.26
25%	22.06	16.28	17.47	21.81	12.13	12.84	9.14	12.07	10.58	8.32	6.43
50%	32.82	28.53	27.44	39.78	25.20	24.03	19.81	23.28	21.50	19.18	13.35
75%	48.40	49.79	43.36	56.94	46.21	39.62	34.92	41.01	37.98	32.28	25.26
90%	71.63	58.62	60.08	71.13	61.74	50.75	45.84	58.90	48.81	45.42	34.67
Max	77.37	97.42	79.51	88.70	85.41	84.87	87.89	78.68	94.65	72.29	67.10
Count	10	27	73	62	104	129	176	175	167	158	68
						Combined Funds					
Mean	5.07	6.92	8.55	7.61	8.78	7.56	7.77	9.35	10.57	8.42	11.24
SD	9.86	12.10	14.53	14.44	13.59	12.39	11.41	13.01	12.26	9.90	11.10
Min	0.01	0.01	0.00	0.00	0.00	0.00	0.00	0.00	0.00	0.00	0.00
10%	0.14	0.20	0.22	0.20	0.38	0.22	0.39	0.53	0.77	0.43	0.93
25%	0.45	0.55	0.62	0.62	1.10	0.91	1.20	1.62	2.28	1.60	2.72
50%	1.23	1.72	1.84	1.88	3.34	2.63	3.35	4.49	6.31	4.97	7.69
75%	4.89	7.67	8.96	6.25	9.81	7.92	9.03	11.28	13.94	11.74	16.46
90%	14.96	20.53	27.36	22.94	25.11	21.39	20.97	24.21	25.98	21.48	26.97
Max	77.37	97.42	79.51	90.06	85.41	87.06	87.89	92.36	94.65	92.44	79.96
Count	367	510	702	835	1,028	1,212	1,383	1,492	1,647	1,753	1,966

MODEL 5											
STATISTIC	1994	1995	1996	1997	1998	1999	2000	2001	2002	2003	2004
Live Funds											
Mean	1.06	2.22	4.30	3.43	4.70	4.05	3.80	3.40	4.07	4.45	1.76
SD	3.28	6.01	10.97	8.70	9.51	8.87	7.72	6.76	6.58	6.33	2.70
Min	0.00	0.00	0.00	0.00	0.00	0.00	0.00	0.00	0.00	0.00	0.00
10%	0.00	0.01	0.02	0.02	0.06	0.04	0.07	0.07	0.09	0.07	0.03
25%	0.02	0.04	0.09	0.10	0.27	0.23	0.33	0.33	0.44	0.43	0.15
50%	0.07	0.16	0.36	0.45	1.03	0.96	1.18	1.26	1.74	2.04	0.72
75%	0.52	1.25	2.61	2.26	4.03	3.22	3.49	3.63	4.75	6.01	2.31
90%	2.61	5.85	11.24	9.12	14.21	10.09	9.88	8.10	10.52	12.03	4.71
Max	35.62	42.56	76.54	86.91	77.72	80.45	75.95	91.82	73.06	81.10	29.28
Count	357	483	629	773	924	1,083	1,207	1,317	1,480	1,595	1,898
Graveyard Funds											
Mean	24.23	23.50	34.07	42.30	36.17	31.46	32.55	22.82	20.68	20.18	4.60
SD	24.12	20.12	25.19	26.95	25.12	21.96	22.47	19.84	18.94	16.27	6.20
Min	1.00	4.92	1.88	1.49	0.00	0.11	0.02	0.51	0.03	0.03	0.04
10%	5.31	5.53	5.25	8.61	4.49	2.12	3.95	2.00	2.61	3.02	0.13
25%	11.79	7.99	11.28	21.29	15.56	12.66	15.91	6.43	5.29	6.42	0.97
50%	18.02	17.66	33.94	37.54	28.92	30.16	27.57	19.11	14.32	14.03	3.16
75%	26.24	32.58	54.36	64.53	60.14	46.31	48.38	33.10	33.19	30.61	5.51
90%	48.95	51.10	68.87	80.97	69.54	64.68	61.91	55.75	46.84	43.06	10.17
Max	64.10	69.64	82.29	93.17	87.67	89.00	90.90	76.34	90.02	67.86	33.31
Count	5	14	41	46	68	64	68	58	76	89	35
Combined Funds											
Mean	1.38	2.82	6.12	5.62	6.85	5.58	5.33	4.22	4.88	5.29	1.81
SD	4.94	7.62	14.21	13.84	13.79	11.85	11.17	8.68	8.44	8.01	2.82
Min	0.00	0.00	0.00	0.00	0.00	0.00	0.00	0.00	0.00	0.00	0.00
10%	0.00	0.01	0.02	0.03	0.06	0.05	0.07	0.07	0.09	0.08	0.03
25%	0.02	0.04	0.10	0.11	0.30	0.24	0.35	0.35	0.48	0.49	0.15
50%	0.08	0.19	0.43	0.54	1.24	1.06	1.32	1.42	1.93	2.28	0.73
75%	0.56	1.38	3.58	3.02	5.57	4.27	4.40	4.15	5.36	6.63	2.36
90%	3.06	7.02	19.05	16.84	22.27	17.07	15.37	9.65	12.50	13.79	4.85
Max	64.10	69.64	82.29	93.17	87.67	89.00	90.90	91.82	90.02	81.10	33.31
Count	362	497	670	819	992	1,147	1,275	1,375	1,556	1,684	1,933

For both models 1 and 5, the mean and median liquidation probabilities are higher for graveyard funds than for live funds, a reassuring sign that the explanatory variables are indeed providing explanatory power for the liquidation process. For model 1, the combined sample shows an increase in the mean and median liquidation probabilities in 1998, as expected, and another increase in 2001, presumably due to the bursting of the technology bubble in U.S. equity markets. Most troubling from the perspective of systemic risk, however, is the fact that the mean and median liquidation probabilities for 2004 (which includes data only up to August) are 11.24 percent and 7.69 percent, respectively, the highest levels in our entire sample. This result may be a symptom of the enormous growth that the hedge fund industry has enjoyed in recent years, which increases both the number of funds entering and exiting the industry, but may also indicate more challenging market conditions for hedge funds in the coming months. Note that the mean and median liquidation probabilities for model 5 do not show the same increase in 2004—another manifestation of the time lag with which the graveyard database is updated. (Recall that model 5 includes only those funds with status code 1, but a large number of funds that eventually receive this classification had not yet reached their eight- to ten-month limit by August 2004.) Therefore, model 1's estimated liquidation probabilities are likely to be more accurate for the current year.[20]

The logit estimates and implied probabilities suggest that a number of factors influence the likelihood of a hedge fund's liquidation, including past performance, AUM, fund flows, and age. Given these factors, our estimates imply that the average liquidation probability for funds in 2004 is over 11 percent, which is higher than the historical unconditional attrition rate of 8.8 percent. To the extent that a series of correlated liquidations stresses the capital reserves of financial counterparties, this is yet another indirect measure of an increase in systemic risk in the hedge fund industry.

Regime-Switching Models

Our final hedge-fund-based measure of systemic risk is motivated by the phase-locking example of Lo (1999), in which the return-generating process exhibits apparent changes in expected returns and volatility that are discrete and sudden—for example, the Mexican peso crisis of 1994–1995, the Asian crisis of 1997, and the global flight to quality precipitated by the default of Russian GKO debt in August 1998. Linear models are generally incapable of capturing such discrete shifts; hence, more sophisticated methods are required. In particular, we propose to model such shifts by a regime-switching process in which two states of the world are hypothesized, and the data are allowed to determine the parameters of these states and the likelihood of transitioning from one to the other. Regime-switching models have been used in a number of contexts, ranging from Hamilton's (1989) model of the business cycle to Ang and Bekaert's (2004) regime-switching asset allocation model, and we propose to apply one to the CSFB/Tremont Indexes to obtain another measure of systemic risk, that is, the possibility of switching from a normal to a distressed regime.

Denote by R_t the return of a hedge fund index in period t and suppose R_t satisfies the following:

$$R_t = I_t \cdot R_{1t} + (1 - I_t) \cdot R_{2t}; \tag{7a}$$

$$R_{it} \sim \mathcal{N}(\mu_i, \sigma_i^2); \tag{7b}$$

$$I_t = \begin{cases} 1 \text{ with probability } p_{11} \text{ if } I_{t-1} = 1 \\ 1 \text{ with probability } p_{21} \text{ if } I_{t-1} = 0 \\ 0 \text{ with probability } p_{12} \text{ if } I_{t-1} = 1 \\ 0 \text{ with probability } p_{22} \text{ if } I_{t-1} = 0 \end{cases}. \tag{7c}$$

This specification is similar to the well-known "mixture of distributions" model. However, unlike standard mixture models, the regime-switching model is not independently distributed over time unless $p_{11} = p_{21}$. Once estimated, forecasts of changes in regime can be readily obtained as well as forecasts of R_t itself. In particular, because the k-step transition matrix of a Markov chain is simply given by $\mathbf{P}^k$, the conditional probability of the regime I_{t+k} given date t data $\mathcal{R}_t \equiv (R_t, R_{t-1}, \ldots, R_1)$ takes on a particularly simple form:

$$\text{Prob}(I_{t+k} = 1 | \mathcal{R}_t) = \pi_1 + (p_{11} - p_{21})^k \, [\text{Prob}(I_t = 1 | \mathcal{R}_t) - \pi_1], \tag{8a}$$

$$\pi_1 \equiv \frac{p_{21}}{p_{12} + p_{21}}, \tag{8b}$$

where $\text{Prob}(I_t = 1|\mathcal{R}_t)$ is the probability that the date t regime is 1 given the historical data up to and including date t (this is a by-product of the maximum-likelihood estimation procedure). Using similar recursions of the Markov chain, the conditional expectation of R_{t+k} can be readily derived as

$$E[R_{t+k}|\mathcal{R}_t] = a_t' \, \mathbf{P}^k \mu; \tag{9a}$$

$$a_t = [\text{Prob}(I_t = 1|\mathcal{R}_t) \ \text{Prob}(I_t = 0|\mathcal{R}_t)]'; \tag{9b}$$

$$\mu \equiv [\mu_1 \ \ \mu_2]'. \tag{9c}$$

TABLE 8.8 reports the maximum-likelihood estimates of the means and standard deviations in each of two states for the fourteen CSFB/Tremont Hedge Fund Indexes, as well as the transition probabilities for the two states. Note that two rows in Table 8.8 are in boldface—dedicated short seller

TABLE 8.8 *Means and Standard Deviations for CSFB/Tremont Hedge Fund Indexes*

INDEX	p_{11}	p_{21}	p_{12}	p_{22}	ANNUALIZED MEAN		ANNUALIZED SD		LOG(L)
					STATE 1	STATE 2	STATE 1	STATE 2	
Hedge Funds	100.0%	1.2%	0.0%	98.8%	6.8%	12.4%	2.9%	9.9%	323.6
Convertible Arbitrage	89.9%	17.9%	10.1%	82.1%	16.1%	−1.6%	1.9%	6.1%	404.0
Dedicated Short Seller	**23.5%**	**12.6%**	**76.5%**	**87.4%**	**−76.2%**	**11.7%**	**2.3%**	**16.5%**	**208.5**
Emerging Markets	100.0%	1.2%	0.0%	98.8%	11.5%	6.6%	8.2%	20.3%	218.0
Equity Market Neutral	95.0%	2.4%	5.0%	97.6%	4.4%	13.8%	2.1%	3.1%	435.1
Event Driven	98.0%	45.0%	2.0%	55.0%	13.3%	−47.0%	3.8%	14.0%	377.0
Distressed	97.9%	58.0%	2.1%	42.0%	15.2%	−57.5%	4.8%	15.6%	349.4
ED Multistrategy	98.7%	38.4%	1.3%	61.6%	12.0%	−55.2%	4.5%	15.0%	363.6
Risk Arbitrage	89.4%	25.6%	10.6%	74.4%	9.6%	3.1%	2.7%	6.9%	391.8
Fixed-Income Arbitrage	95.6%	29.8%	4.4%	70.2%	10.0%	−12.2%	1.9%	6.6%	442.3
Global Macro	100.0%	1.2%	0.0%	98.8%	13.6%	14.0%	3.2%	14.2%	286.3
Long/Short Equity	98.5%	2.5%	1.5%	97.5%	6.1%	21.1%	6.3%	15.3%	285.0
Managed Futures	**32.0%**	**22.2%**	**68.0%**	**77.8%**	**−6.0%**	**10.7%**	**3.8%**	**13.7%**	**252.1**
Multistrategy	98.2%	25.0%	1.8%	75.0%	10.8%	−7.6%	3.2%	9.2%	387.9

and managed futures—because the maximum-likelihood estimation procedure did not converge properly for these two categories, implying that the regime-switching process may not be a good model of their returns. The remaining twelve series yielded well-defined parameter estimates, and, by convention, we denote by "state 1" the lower-volatility state.

Consider the second row, corresponding to the convertible arbitrage index. The parameter estimates indicate that in state 1, this index has an expected return of 16.1 percent with a volatility of 1.9 percent, but in state 2, the expected return is –1.6 percent with a volatility of 6.1 percent. The latter state is clearly a crisis state for convertible arbitrage, while the former is a more normal state. The other hedge fund indexes have similar parameter estimates—the low-volatility state is typically paired with higher means, and the high-volatility state is paired with lower means. While such pairings may seem natural for hedge funds, there are three exceptions to this rule: For equity market neutral, global macro, and long/short equity, the higher volatility state has higher expected returns. This outcome suggests that for these strategies, volatility may be a necessary ingredient for their expected returns.

From these parameter estimates, it is possible to estimate the probability of being in state 1 or 2 at each point in time for each hedge fund index. For example, in **FIGURE 8.3** we plot the estimated probabilities of being in

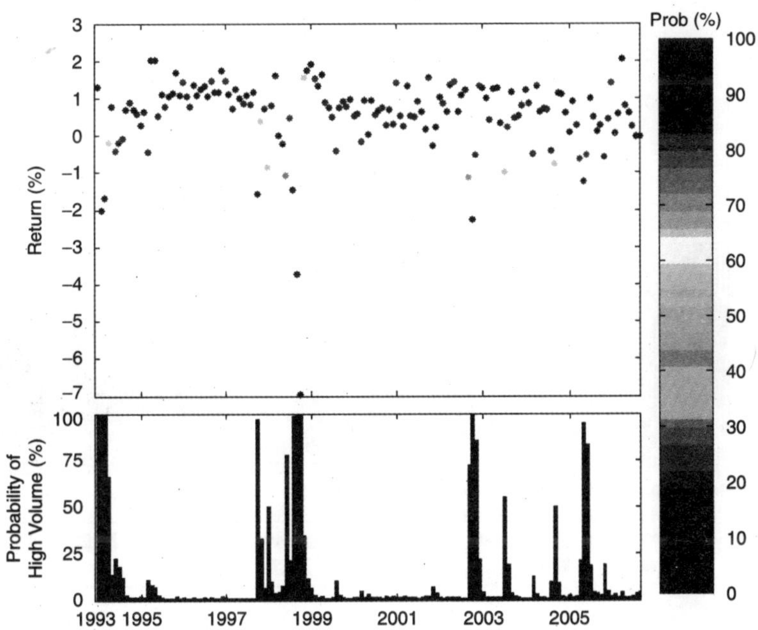

FIGURE 8.3 *CSFB/Tremont Hedge Fund Index Fixed-Income Arbitrage*

state 2, the high-volatility state, for the fixed-income arbitrage index for each month from January 1994 to August 2004. We see that this probability begins to increase in the months leading up to August 1998 and hits 100 percent in August and several months thereafter. However, this is not an isolated event; it occurs on several occasions both before and after August 1998.

To develop an aggregate measure of systemic risk based on this regime-switching model, we propose summing the state-2 probabilities across all hedge fund indexes every month to yield a time series that captures the likelihood of being in low-mean periods. Of course, the summed probabilities—even if renormalized to lie in the unit interval—cannot be interpreted formally as a probability because the regime-switching process was specified individually for each index, not jointly across all indexes. Therefore, the interpretation of the low-mean state for convertible arbitrage may be quite different from the interpretation of the low-mean state for equity market neutral. Nevertheless, as an aggregate measure of the state of the hedge fund industry, the summed probabilities may contain useful information about systemic risk exposures. **FIGURE 8.4** contains this indicator. The low-mean indicator has local maxima in 1994 and 1998 as expected, but there is a stronger peak around 2002, largely due to equity

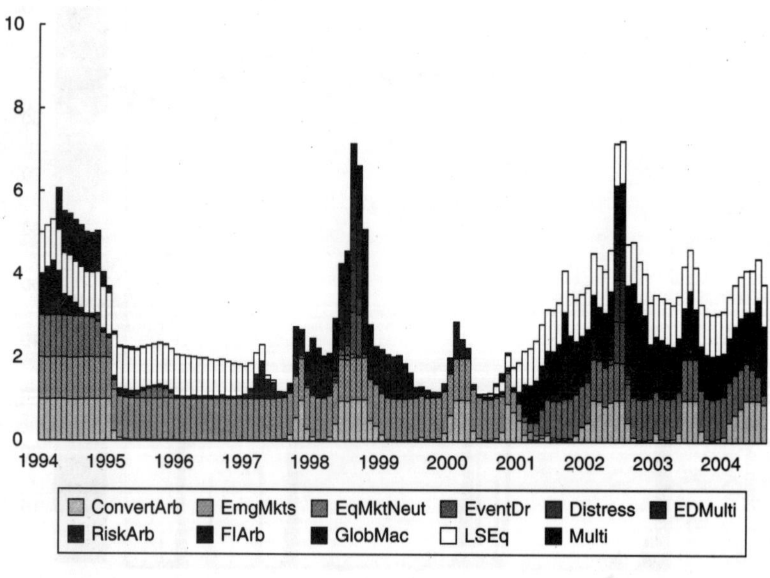

FIGURE 8.4 *Hedge Fund Indexes, January 1994–August 2004*

market neutral, global macro, and long/short equity. This pattern corresponds remarkably well to the common wisdom that over the past two years, these three strategy classes have underperformed for a variety of reasons.[21] The implications of Figure 8.4 for systemic risk are clear: The probabilities of being in low-mean regimes have increased for a number of hedge fund indexes, which may foreshadow increased leverage for funds in these categories as well as fund outflows in the coming months, both of which would place additional stress on the industry, leading to an increase in systemic risk.

The Current Outlook

A definitive assessment of the systemic risks posed by hedge funds requires certain data that are currently unavailable and are unlikely to become available in the near future—for example, counterparty credit exposures, the net degree of leverage of hedge fund managers and investors, the gross amount of structured products involving hedge funds, and so on. Therefore, we cannot determine the magnitude of current systemic risk exposures with any degree of accuracy. However, based on the analytics developed in this study, there are a few tentative conclusions that we can draw:

1. The hedge fund industry has grown tremendously over the last few years, fueled by the demand for higher returns in the face of stock-market declines and mounting pension-fund liabilities. These massive fund inflows have had a material impact on hedge fund returns and risks in recent years, as evidenced by changes in correlations, reduced performance, and increased illiquidity as measured by the weighted autocorrelation ρ_t^*.
2. Mean and median liquidation probabilities for hedge funds have increased in 2004, based on logit estimates that link several factors to the liquidation probability of a given hedge fund, including past performance, AUM, fund flows, and age. In particular, our estimates imply that the average liquidation probability for funds in 2004 is over 11 percent—higher than the historical unconditional attrition rate of 8.8 percent. A higher attrition rate is not surprising for a rapidly growing industry, but it may foreshadow potential instabilities that can be triggered by seemingly innocuous market events.
3. The banking sector is exposed to hedge fund risks, especially smaller institutions, but the largest banks are also exposed through proprietary trading activities, credit arrangements and structured products, and prime brokerage services.

4. The risks facing hedge funds are nonlinear and more complex than those facing traditional asset classes. Because of the dynamic nature of hedge fund investment strategies and the impact of fund flows on leverage and performance, hedge fund risk models require more sophisticated analytics and more sophisticated users.
5. The sum of our regime-switching models' low-mean state probabilities is one proxy for the aggregate level of distress in the hedge fund sector. Recent measurements suggest that we may be entering a challenging period of lower expected returns. This new regime, coupled with the recent uptrend in the weighted autocorrelation ρ_t^* and the increased mean and median liquidation probabilities for hedge funds in 2004, derived from our logit model, implies that systemic risk is increasing.

We hasten to qualify our tentative conclusions by emphasizing their speculative nature, and we hope that our analysis spurs additional research and data collection to refine both the analytics and the empirical measurement of systemic risk in the hedge fund industry. As with all risk management challenges, we should hope for the best and prepare for the worst. The question is, How?

One possibility, put forward by Getmansky, Lo, and Mei (2004), is to create an independent organization along the lines of the NTSB to sift through the wreckage of all major hedge fund collapses, ultimately producing a publicly available report that documents the specific causes of each collapse, along with recommendations on how to avoid similar disasters in the future. Although there may be common themes in the demise of many hedge funds—too much leverage, too concentrated a portfolio, operational failures, securities fraud, or insufficient AUM—each liquidation has its own unique circumstances and is an opportunity for hedge fund managers and investors to learn and improve.

In the event of an airplane crash, the NTSB assembles a team of engineers and flight-safety experts who are immediately dispatched to the crash site to conduct a thorough investigation, including interviewing witnesses, poring over historical flight logs and maintenance records, and sifting through the wreckage to recover the flight recorder, or "black box," and, if necessary, reassembling the aircraft from its parts to determine the ultimate cause of the crash. Once its work is completed, the NTSB publishes a report summarizing the team's investigation, concluding with specific recommendations for avoiding future occurrences of this type of accident. The report is entered into a searchable database that is available to the general public (see www.ntsb.gov/ntsb/query.asp), and this kind of information has been one of the major factors underlying the remarkable safety record of commercial air travel.

For example, it is now current practice to spray airplanes with deicing fluid just prior to takeoff when the temperature is near freezing and it is raining or snowing. This procedure was instituted in the aftermath of USAir Flight 405's crash on March 22, 1992. Flight 405 stalled just after becoming airborne because of ice on its wings, despite the fact that deicing fluid was applied before it left its gate. Apparently, Flight 405's takeoff was delayed because of air traffic, and ice reaccumulated on its wings while it waited for a departure slot on the runway in the freezing rain. The NTSB Aircraft Accident Report—adopted February 17, 1993, and available through several Internet sites—contains a sobering summary of the NTSB's findings (Report AAR-93/02, page vi):

> The National Transportation Safety Board determines that the probable causes of this accident were the failure of the airline industry and the Federal Aviation Administration to provide flightcrews with procedures, requirements, and criteria compatible with departure delays in conditions conducive to airframe icing and the decision by the flightcrew to take off without positive assurance that the airplane's wings were free of ice accumulation after 35 minutes of exposure to precipitation following deicing. The ice contamination on the wings resulted in an aerodynamic stall and loss of control after liftoff. Contributing to the cause of the accident were the inappropriate procedures used by, and inadequate coordination between, the flightcrew that led to a takeoff rotation at a lower than prescribed air speed.

Current deicing procedures have no doubt saved many lives thanks to NTSB Report AAR-93/02, but this particular innovation was paid for by the lives of the twenty-seven individuals who did not survive the crash of Flight 405. Imagine the waste if the NTSB did not investigate this tragedy and produce concrete recommendations to prevent such situations from happening again.

Hedge fund liquidations are, of course, considerably less dire, generally involving no loss of life. However, as more pension funds make allocations to hedge funds, and as the "retailization" of hedge funds continues, losses in the hedge fund industry may have more significant implications for individual investors, in some cases threatening retirement wealth and basic living standards. Moreover, the spillover effects of an industry-wide shock to hedge funds should not be underestimated, as the events surrounding LTCM in the fall of 1998 illustrated. For these reasons, a "Capital Markets Safety Board" (CMSB) dedicated to investigating, reporting, and archiving the "accidents" of the hedge fund industry—and the financial services sector more generally—may yield significant social benefits in much the same way that the NTSB has improved transportation safety enormously for all air travelers. By maintaining teams of experienced professionals—forensic accountants, financial engineers from industry and academia, and securities and tax attorneys—who work together on a regular basis to investigate a number of hedge fund liquidations, this investigative body would be able to determine quickly and accurately how each liquidation came about, and the resulting reports would be an invaluable source of ideas for improving financial markets and avoiding future liquidations of a similar nature.

Of course, formal government investigations of major financial events do occur from time to time, as in the April 1999 report of the President's Working Group on Financial Markets. However, this interagency report was put together on an ad hoc basis with committee members who had not worked together previously and regularly on forensic investigations of this kind. With multiple agencies involved, and none in charge of the investigation, the administrative overhead becomes more significant. Although any thorough investigation of the financial services sector is likely to involve the SEC, the Commodity Futures Trading Commission, the U.S. Treasury, and the Federal Reserve—and interagency cooperation should be promoted—there are important operational advantages in tasking a single independent office with the responsibility for coordinating all such investigations and serving as a repository for the expertise in conducting forensic examinations of financial incidents.

The establishment of the CMSB will not be inexpensive. Currently, regulatory agencies like the SEC are understaffed and overburdened, and this condition is likely to worsen as financial markets grow in size and complexity. In addition, the lure of the private sector makes it challenging for government agencies to attract and retain individuals with expertise in these highly employable fields. Individuals trained in forensic accounting, financial engineering, and securities law now command substantial premiums on Wall Street over government pay scales. Although the typical public-sector employee is likely to be motivated more by civic duty than financial gain, it would be unrealistic to build an organization on altruism alone.

However, the cost of an independent CMSB is more than justified by the valuable lessons that would be garnered from a systematic analysis of financial incidents and the public dissemination of recommendations by seasoned professionals who review multiple cases each year. The benefits would accrue not only to the wealthy—which is currently how the hedge fund industry is tilted—but would also flow to retail investors in the form of more stable financial markets, greater liquidity, reduced borrowing and lending costs as a result of decreased systemic risk exposures, and a wider variety of investment choices available to a larger segment of the population because of increased transparency, oversight, and, ultimately, financial security. It is unrealistic to expect that market crashes, panics, collapses, and fraud will ever be completely eliminated from our capital markets, but we should avoid compounding our mistakes by failing to learn from them.

Appendix

The following is a list of category descriptions, taken directly from TASS documentation, that define the criteria used by TASS in assigning funds in their database to one of eleven possible categories:

Convertible arbitrage. This strategy is identified by hedge investing in the convertible securities of a company. A typical investment is to be long the convertible bond and short the common stock of the same company. Positions are designed to generate profits from the fixed-income security as well as the short sale of stock while protecting principal from market moves.

Dedicated short seller. Dedicated short seller was once a robust category of hedge funds before the long bull market rendered the strategy difficult to implement. A new category, short biased, has emerged. The strategy is to maintain net short as opposed to pure short exposure. Short biased managers take short positions in mostly equities and derivatives. The short bias of a manager's portfolio must be constantly greater than zero to be classified in this category.

Emerging markets. This strategy involves equity or fixed-income investing in emerging markets around the world. Because many emerging markets do not allow short selling or offer viable futures or other derivative products with which to hedge, emerging markets investing often employs a long-only strategy.

Equity market neutral. This investment strategy is designed to exploit equity market inefficiencies and usually involves being simultaneously long and short matched equity portfolios of the same size within a country. Market neutral portfolios are designed to be either beta or currency neutral or both. Well-designed portfolios typically control for industry, sector, market capitalization, and other exposures. Leverage is often applied to enhance returns.

Event driven. This strategy is defined as "special situations" investing designed to capture price movement generated by a significant pending corporate event such as a merger, corporate restructuring, liquidation, bankruptcy, or reorganization. There are three popular subcategories in event-driven strategies: risk (merger) arbitrage, distressed/high yield securities, and Regulation D.

Fixed-income arbitrage. The fixed-income arbitrageur aims to profit from anomalies in the prices of related interest rate securities. Most managers trade globally with a goal of generating steady returns with low volatility. This category includes interest rate swap arbitrage, U.S. and non-U.S. government bond arbitrage, forward yield curve arbitrage, and mortgage-backed-securities arbitrage. The mortgage-backed market is primarily U.S.-based and over-the-counter, and is particularly complex.

Global macro. Global macro managers carry long and short positions in any of the world's major capital or derivative markets. These positions reflect their views on overall market direction as influenced by major economic trends and/or events. The portfolios of these funds can include stocks, bonds, currencies, and commodities in the form of cash or derivative instruments. Most funds invest globally in both developed and emerging markets.

Long/short equity. This directional strategy involves equity-oriented investing on both the long and short sides of the market. The objective is to not be market neutral. Managers have the ability to shift from value to growth, from small to medium to large capitalization stocks, and from a net long position to a net short position. Managers may use futures and options to hedge. The focus may be regional, such as long/short U.S. or European equity, or sector specific, such as long and short technology or health care stocks. Long/short equity funds tend to build and hold portfolios that are substantially more concentrated than those of traditional stock funds.

Managed futures. This strategy invests in listed financial and commodity futures markets and currency markets around the world. The managers are usually referred to as commodity trading advisers, or CTAs. Trading disciplines are generally systematic or discretionary. Systematic traders tend to use price and market-specific information (often technical) to make trading decisions, while discretionary managers use a judgmental approach.

Multistrategy. The funds in this category are characterized by their ability to dynamically allocate capital among strategies falling within several traditional hedge fund disciplines. The use of many strategies, and the ability to reallocate capital between them in response to market opportunities, means that such funds are not easily assigned to any traditional category. The multistrategy category also includes funds employing unique strategies that do not fall under any of the other descriptions.

Fund of funds. A "multimanager" fund employs the services of two or more trading advisers or hedge fund managers who are allocated cash by the trading manager to trade on behalf of the fund.

References

Agarwal, Vikas, Naveen D. Daniel, and Narayan Naik. 2004. "Flows, Performance and Managerial Incentives in Hedge Funds." EFA 2003 Annual Conference Paper No. 501 (July 22).

Ang, Andrew, and Geert Bekaert. 2004. "How Do Regimes Affect Asset Allocation?" *Financial Analysts Journal* 60 (March/April): 86–99.

Baquero, Guillermo, Jenke ter Horst, and Marno Verbeek. 2005. "Survival, Look-Ahead Bias and Persistence in Hedge Fund Performance." *Journal of Financial and Quantitative Analysis* 40: 493–517.

Bookstaber, Richard. 1999. "A Framework for Understanding Market Crisis." In *Risk Management: Principles and Practices, AIMR Conference Proceedings*. Charlottesville, VA: Association for Investment Management and Research.

———. 2000. "Understanding and Monitoring the Liquidity Crisis Cycle." *Financial Analysts Journal* 56 (September/October): 17–22.

Brown, Stephen J., William N. Goetzmann, and Robert G. Ibbotson. 1999. "Offshore Hedge Funds: Survival and Performance, 1989–95." *Journal of Business* 72 (January): 91–118.

Brown, Stephen J., William N. Goetzmann, Robert G. Ibbotson, and Stephen A. Ross. 1992. "Survivorship Bias in Performance Studies." *Review of Financial Studies* 5: 553–80.

Brown, Stephen J., William N. Goetzmann, and James M. Park. 2001. "Careers and Survival: Competition and Risk in the Hedge Fund and CTA Industry." *Journal of Finance* 56 (October): 1869–86.

Campbell, John Y., Andrew W. Lo, and A. Craig MacKinlay. 1996. *The Econometrics of Financial Markets*. Princeton, NJ: Princeton University Press.

Carpenter, Jennifer N., and Anthony W. Lynch. 1999. "Survivorship Bias and Attrition Effects in Measures of Performance Persistence." *Journal of Financial Economics* 54 (December): 337–74.

Chan, Nicholas, Mila Getmansky, Shane M. Haas, and Andrew Lo. 2007. "Systemic risk and hedge funds." In *The Risks of Financial Institutions,* edited by Mark Carey and René M. Stulz. Chicago: University of Chicago Press.

Chandar, Nandini, and Robert Bricker. 2002. "Incentives, Discretion, and Asset Valuation in Closed-End Mutual Funds." *Journal of Accounting Research* 40 (September): 1037–70.

Chevalier, Judith, and Glenn Ellison. 1997. "Risk Taking by Mutual Funds as a Response to Incentives." *Journal of Political Economy* 105 (December): 1167–1200.

Cox, David R., and E. Joyce Snell. 1989. *The Analysis of Binary Data*, 2nd ed. London: Chapman and Hall.

Farmer, J. Doyne, and Andrew W. Lo. 1999. "Frontiers of Finance: Evolution and Efficient Markets." *Proceedings of the National Academy of Sciences* 96 (August 31): 9991–92.

Fung, William, and David Hsieh. 1997. "Survivorship Bias and Investment Style in the Returns of CTAs." *Journal of Portfolio Management* 24 (Fall): 30–41.

———. 2000. "Performance Characteristics of Hedge Funds and Commodity Funds: Natural vs. Spurious Biases." *Journal of Financial and Quantitative Analysis* 35 (September): 291–307.

Getmansky, Mila, Andrew Lo, and Igor Makarov. 2004. "An Econometric Model of Serial Correlation and Illiquidity in Hedge Fund Returns." *Journal of Financial Economics* 74 (December): 529–609.

Getmansky, Mila, Andrew Lo, and Shauna X. Mei. 2004. "Sifting Through the Wreckage: Lessons from Recent Hedge-Fund Liquidations." *Journal of Investment Management* 2: 6–38.

Hamilton, James D. 1989. "A New Approach to the Economic Analysis of Nonstationary Time Series and the Business Cycle." *Econometrica* 57 (March): 357–84.

Hendricks, Darryll, Jayendu Patel, and Richard Zeckhauser. 1997. "The J-Shape of Performance Persistence Given Survivorship Bias." *Review of Economics and Statistics* 79 (May): 161–66.

Kadlec, Gregory B., and Douglas M. Patterson. 1999. "A Transactions Data Analysis of Nonsynchronous Trading." *Review of Financial Studies* 12: 609–30.

Kao, Duen-Li. 2000. "Estimating and Pricing Credit Risk: An Overview." *Financial Analysts Journal* 56 (July/August): 50–66.

Kendall, Maurice, Alan Stuart, and J. Keith Ord. 1983. *The Advanced Theory of Statistics. Volume 3: Design and Analysis, and Time-Series*. 4th ed. New York: Macmillan.

Leamer, Edward E. 1978. *Specification Searches*. New York: John Wiley and Sons.

Liang, Bing. 2003. "The Accuracy of Hedge Fund Returns." *Journal of Portfolio Management* 29 (Spring): 111–22.

Ljung, G. M., and G. E. P. Box. 1978. "On a Measure of Lack of Fit in Time Series Models." *Biometrika* 65: 297–303.

Lo, Andrew W. 1999. "The Three P's of Total Risk Management." *Financial Analysts Journal* 55 (January/February): 13–27.

———. 2001. "Risk Management for Hedge Funds: Introduction and Overview." *Financial Analysts Journal* 57 (November/December): 16–33.

———. 2002. "The Statistics of Sharpe Ratios." *Financial Analysts Journal* 58, no. 4: 36–52.

———. 2004. "The Adaptive Markets Hypothesis: Market Efficiency from an Evolutionary Perspective." *Journal of Portfolio Management* 30 (30th anniversary issue): 15–29.

Lo, Andrew W., and A. Craig MacKinlay. 1988. "Stock Market Prices Do Not Follow Random Walks: Evidence From a Simple Specification Test." *Review of Financial Studies* 1 (Spring): 41–66.

———. 1990. "An Econometric Analysis of Nonsynchronous Trading." *Journal of Econometrics* 45: 181–211.

Maddala, G.S. 1983. *Limited-Dependent and Qualitative Variables in Econometrics.* Cambridge: Cambridge University Press.

Mishkin, Frederic S. 1997. *The Economics of Money, Banking, and Financial Markets*, 5th ed. Reading, MA: Addison Wesley.

Nagelkerke, N. J. D. 1991. "A Note on a General Definition of the Coefficient of Determination." *Biometrika* 78: 691–92.

President's Working Group on Financial Markets. 1999. *Hedge Funds, Leverage, and the Lessons of Long-Term Capital Management, Report of the President's Working Group on Financial Markets.*

Samuelson, Paul A. 1965. "Proof That Properly Anticipated Prices Fluctuate Randomly." *Industrial Management Review* 6 (Spring): 41–49.

Schneeweis, Thomas, Richard Spurgin, and David McCarthy. 1996. "Survivor Bias in Commodity Trading Advisor Performance." *Journal of Futures Markets* 16 (October): 757–72.

Sirri, Erik R., and Peter Tufano. 1998. "Costly Search and Mutual Fund Flows." *Journal of Finance* 53 (October): 1589–1622.

ter Horst, Jenke R., Theo E. Nijman, and Marno Verbeek. 2001. "Eliminating Look-Ahead Bias in Evaluating Persistence in Mutual Fund Performance." *Journal of Empirical Finance* 8 (September): 345–73.

Watts, Duncan J. 1999. *Small Worlds: The Dynamics of Networks Between Order and Randomness.* Princeton, NJ: Princeton University Press.

Watts, Duncan J., and Steven H. Strogatz. 1998. "Collective Dynamics of 'Small-World' Networks." *Nature* 393 (June 4): 440–42.

Chapter Notes

1. Accordingly, hedge fund track records are often summarized with multiple statistics, for example, mean, standard deviation, Sharpe ratio, market beta, Sortino ratio, maximum drawdown, worst month, and so on.

2. For further information about these data see www.hedgeindex.com (CSFB/Tremont Indexes) and www.tremont.com (TASS). We also use data from Altvest, the University of Chicago's Center for Research in Security Prices, and Yahoo!Finance.

3. Once a hedge fund decides not to report its performance or is liquidated, closed to new investment, restructured, or merged with other hedge funds, the fund is transferred into the graveyard database. A hedge fund can only be listed in the graveyard database after being listed in the live database. Because the TASS database fully represents returns and asset information for live and dead funds, the effects of survivorship bias are minimized. However, the database is subject to *backfill bias*; when a fund decides to be included in the database, TASS adds the fund to the live database and includes all available prior performance of the fund. Hedge funds do not need to meet any specific requirements to be included in the TASS database. Because of reporting delays and time lags in contacting hedge funds, some graveyard funds can be incorrectly listed in the live database for a period of time. However, TASS has adopted a policy of transferring funds from the live to the graveyard database if they do not report over an eight- to ten-month period.

4. For studies attempting to quantify the degree and impact of survivorship bias, see Baquero, Horst, and Verbeek (2005), Brown et al. (1992), Brown, Goetzmann, and Ibbotson (1999), Brown, Goetzmann, and Park (2001), Carpenter and Lynch (1999), Fung and Hsieh (1997, 2000), Hendricks, Patel, and Zeckhauser (1997), Horst, Nijman, and Verbeek (2001), and Schneeweis, Spurgin, and McCarthy (1996).

5. TASS defines returns as the change in net asset value during the month (assuming the reinvestment of any distributions on the reinvestment date used by the fund) divided by the net asset value at the beginning of the month, the net of management fees, incentive fees, and other fund expenses. Therefore, these reported returns should approximate the returns realized by investors. TASS also converts all foreign-currency-denominated returns to U.S.-dollar returns using the appropriate exchange rates.

6. See the references in chapter note 4.

7. This correspondence is no coincidence—TASS is owned by Tremont Capital Management (acquired by Lipper in March 2005), which created the CSFB/Tremont Indexes in partnership with Credit Suisse First Boston.

8. Under the null hypothesis of no correlation, the approximate standard error of the correlation coefficient is $1/\sqrt{60} = 13\%$.

9. Ljung and Box (1978) propose the following statistic to measure the overall significance of the first k autocorrelation coefficients: $Q = T(T+2)\sum_{j=1}^{k}\hat{\rho}_j^2/(T-j)$, which is asymptotically χ_k^2 under the null hypothesis of no autocorrelation. By forming the sum of squared autocorrelations, the statistic Q reflects the absolute

magnitudes of the $\hat{\rho}_j$'s irrespective of their signs; hence, funds with large positive or negative autocorrelation coefficients will exhibit large Q-statistics. See Kendall, Stuart, and Ord (1983, chap. 50.13) for further details.

10. This effect works at both ends of the return distribution—funds that are wildly successful are also more likely to leave the database since they have less of a need to advertise their performance. That the graveyard database also contains successful funds is supported by the fact that in some categories—for example, convertible arbitrage, equity market neutral, and dedicated short seller—the average mean return in the graveyard database is the same as or higher than in the live database.

11. The kth-order autocorrelation of a time series, $\{R_t\}$, is defined as the correlation coefficient between R_t and R_{t-k}, which is simply the covariance between R_t and R_{t-k} divided by the square root of the product of the variances of R_t and R_{t-k}. But since the variances of R_t and R_{t-k} are the same under the assumption of stationarity, the denominator of the autocorrelation is simply the variance of R_t.

12. These frictions have led to the creation of real-estate investment trusts (REITs), and the returns to these securities—which are considerably more liquid than the underlying assets on which they are based—exhibit much less serial correlation.

13. Liang (2003) presents a sobering analysis of the accuracy of hedge fund returns that underscores the challenges of marking a portfolio to market.

14. See www.investorforce.com for further information about the Altvest database.

15. The number of funds in the early years is relatively low, reaching a level of fifty or more only in late 1988; therefore, the weighted correlations before then may be somewhat less informative than those after that date.

16. Note that a fund cannot "die" more than once, so liquidation occurs exactly once for each fund i in the graveyard database. In particular, the time series observations of funds in this database will always be $\{0, 0, \ldots, 0, 1\}$. This fact suggests that a more appropriate statistical technique for modeling hedge fund liquidations is survival analysis, which we plan to pursue in a future study. However, for purposes of summarizing the impact of certain explanatory variables on the probability of hedge fund liquidations, logit analysis is a reasonable choice.

17. See Leamer (1978) for further discussion of this phenomenon, known as "Lindley's paradox."

18. This R^2 is the adjusted generalized coefficient of determination proposed by Nagelkerke (1991), which renormalizes Cox and Snell's (1989) R^2 measure by its maximum (which is less than unity) so that it spans the entire unit interval. See Nagelkerke (1991) for further discussion.

19. Note that the usage of "graveyard funds" in this context is somewhat different, involving a time dimension as well as liquidation status. For example, in this context the set of graveyard funds in 1999 refers to only those funds that liquidated in 1999 and does not include liquidations before or after 1999.

20. The TASS reporting delay also affects model 1, suggesting that its estimated liquidation probabilities for 2004 are biased downward as well.

21. Large fund flows into these strategies, and changes in equity markets such as decimalization, the rise of electronic communication networks (ECNs), automated trading, and Regulation FD, are often cited as reasons for the decreased profitability of these strategies.

INDEX

ABOUT THE EDITOR

H. Gifford Fong is president of Gifford Fong Associates, a firm specializing in the analysis of fixed-income markets, derivative products, and asset allocation. The company's areas of emphasis include independent valuation, model validation, and portfolio strategy analysis.

Fong is a graduate of the University of California, where he earned his BS, MBA, and JD degrees. He is the editor of the *Journal Of Investment Management* (JOIM) and founder of the JOIM Conference Series. He is a member of the following: the advisory group to the Regents of the University of California Committee on Investments; the Dean's Advisory Council of the Massachusetts Institute of Technology (MIT) Sloan School of Management; the Haas Hall of Fame, Haas School of Business, University of California, Berkeley; and the Board of Trustees, University of California, Berkeley Foundation.

In addition, Fong coauthored several books, including *Fixed-Income Portfolio Management* and *Advanced Fixed Income Portfolio Management: The State of the Art.* He is also the author of numerous professional-journal publications. Fong has received a number of honors, including the Institute for Quantitative Research in Finance Award and the *Financial Analysts Journal* Graham and Dodd Award of Excellence.

